# A FUNNY WAY TO MAKE A LIVING!

## AN AUTOBIOGRAPHY

# A FUNNY WAY TO MAKE A LIVING!

AN AUTOBIOGRAPHY OF DAD'S ARMY'S
CHIEF WARDEN HODGES

## BILL PERTWEE

SUNBURST BOOKS

This edition published 1996 by
Sunburst Books
Kiln House, 210 New Kings Road
London SW6 4NZ

Copyright
Text © Bill Pertwee 1996
Layout and Design © Sunburst Books 1996

ISBN 1 85778 268 2

Printed and bound in The United Kingdom

# CONTENTS

# DEDICATION

*To my family past and present*

# FOREWORD

## By Jimmy Perry OBE

I first met Bill at the read through of the pilot episode of *Dad's Army* in March 1968. The atmosphere was very tense as we sat round the table in a back room of the 'Feathers' public house by the Hogarth Roundabout in Chiswick, which at the time was a BBC rehearsal room. The cast was uncertain and apprehensive as to what they had let themselves in for. None of us had the faintest idea of the huge success that the series would eventually have. Being one of the co-writers, I was probably the most nervous one of the lot and when it came to the coffee break I was delighted when Bill said to me, 'I think this series is going to be a winner.'

I shall always be grateful to Bill for all his efforts to keep us cheerful in the early days of the show. As *Dad's Army* went from strength to strength, so Bill seemed to spend an awful lot of his time being thrown into rivers, the sea, muddy ponds and on one occasion, having a dustbin full of custard poured over him. He was subjected to every humiliation but always came up smiling.

In his long career Billl has experienced playing variety theatres, the golden days of television and, of course, radio, the medium in which he excels.

His story tells it all. From the Tropics of exotic Brazil to becoming, in the words of General Norman Schwarzkopf, *the world's most famous air raid warden*.

*Jimmy Perry*

# 1 COVER IT UP WITH A COUGH

It was a gloriously sunny day in Norfolk, almost too warm to be wearing a battledress uniform. I was sitting in a canvas chair enjoying a cuppa in the tea break before filming another scene for *Dad's Army* on the Stamford military training area, a place we came to know pretty well over a period of nine years. The make-up girls were bustling about trying to down cups of tea and at the same time touching up actors' faces slightly tanned and perspiring from the warm day and their previous scenes. The queue for the tea and cakes was diminishing. The caterers were starting to clear up the debris of empty cups and plates and getting their van cleaned up ready for the next day's filming. Writers David Croft and Jimmy Perry were in earnest conversation with the filming scripts, making sure that they were up to schedule with all the shots they needed for the episodes of the programme we were filming on that particular annual trip to Thetford in lovely East Anglia.

As I sat there, just breathing in the air and listening to the occasional bird calling to its mate, not really thinking too hard about the contribution I would be making to the proceedings later on that day, Arthur Lowe walked over to me. 'Warden,' he said (he called me Warden on and off the set generally), 'the viewing figures have just arrived from the JICTA (don't ask me what it means) ratings system and last week *Dad's Army* was watched by 18 million people.' I think that was the first time I realised the enormity of the impact the programme was making on television audiences. I don't know why, but I have always felt that television programmes involving me were being watched by one person – 'the camera' being that one person. So the information Arthur Lowe had just imparted really hit home.

I had never previously grasped the same sort of information when I was involved in the radio series *Beyond our Ken* and *Round the Horne*. When I was told, 'We had 15 million listeners last week, you know,' it didn't sink in. That was in the heyday of radio, or latter days of it, in the 1960s. Figures like this for several radio programmes were bandied about at that time. Justifiably so, for BBC radio was producing so many popular shows and the listening public was ready to enjoy its favourites on the same day each week and the same spot on the dial. But to realise that *Dad's Army* was actually being seen by 18 million people was quite another kettle of fish. I don't think it quite dawned on me even when I was being recognised in the odd pub or two, or if I was out shopping. To me my private life was not connected to what I did on television. A little later one incident really made me realise that, as far as the viewing audiences were concerned, the cast of a popular TV programme are a bit special, something I have always found pretty weird.

The incident happened when my son Jonathan and I went to our local swimming pool. It happened to be in the school holidays, and as soon as we got in the pool I was surrounded by several children who started singing the *Dad's Army* signature tune and repeating various phrases from the show: 'Put that light out', 'They don't like it up 'em', 'You stupid boy', and so on. I tried to enjoy the swim with Jonathan but he became more and more isolated from me as the children followed me about the pool. One of the lady attendants came along and said, 'I'm sorry Mr Pertwee, if you'd like to come back another day we'll give you and your son a free pass.' We took her advice and went off and had a snack in a cafe somewhere. I don't expect any apologies on those occasional situations; we have to realise the public think of us as their personal friends, and we ought to appreciate that. There are, however, examples of events which can get out of hand unless you are careful.

I was having dinner with Arthur Lowe once when a drunken diner came over to us. He stood with his hand planted in Arthur's dinner plate trying incoherently to make conversation, his hand dripping with some of Arthur's boeuf bourguignonne.

It was not a happy sight. Arthur was very good about it and was rescued by the restaurant manager who, of course, brought him a fresh plate of food. Another night the whole cast of *Dad's Army* was eating out in a restaurant in Manchester and about 50 people gathered outside gaping through the window. The manager thought he was in for a financial bonanza. Arthur Lowe's comment was, 'Now I know how the monkeys must feel when they're having their customary tea party at the zoo.'

As for thinking at the time we made the series that the programmes would be even more popular 25 years later with the showing of repeats: it would have seemed incomprehensible. The same thing applies to the popularity of the early radio programmes I took part in 35 years ago, now available again on BBC recordings. The humour doesn't appear to have dated, and the programmes are also being enjoyed all over again by those who heard it first time around.

These few thoughts seem even more extraordinary in retrospect as I put pen to paper. Anyone who writes an autobiography must remember a certain moment or event that really sets them thinking. I remember one such year in particular – 1955. This was the year of the very first summer show of my theatrical career, in fact my first introduction to show business proper. It was quite a small show – just eight of us and a pianist at the Gorleston Pavilion near Great Yarmouth. The experience was completely new to me; I had had a succession of jobs before this but nothing on the stage. The show had to have five changes of programme so that people on holiday could see all five shows during their two weeks' stay. We would rotate them every three days. If the audience enjoyed the shows they would send up little presents to the cast, or at least something for their favourite artiste, on the last Friday evening, before their holiday finished and they left the resort on Saturday.

At first my despair at having to learn all the routines, some of which – certainly the solo spots of eight to ten minutes each – I was supposed to write as well, stopped me from getting a proper night's sleep. However, once I settled down, it was one of the most enjoyable times of my life.

The experienced principal comedian of the show to whom, amongst other things, I had to feed lines in sketches, would sometimes give me a piece of paper not much bigger than a postage stamp and say, 'This is one of the sketches we're doing in next week's programme.' He had obviously done the sketch many times before in other shows and knew it off by heart. In one particular sketch he said to me, 'All you've got to do is walk out to the audience and say, "Cliff (that was his name) is getting ready to meet the Mayor in his parlour, over there (pointing off-stage – there was no money for scenery in a small seaside show) up the alabaster balustrade." I will keep coming on in a state of undress saying, "I won't be a minute".' Each of his appearances was met with peals of laughter and he played it for all he was worth, using his comedic experience. I had to ad lib in between his appearances, mostly saying, 'Up the alabaster balustrade,' until he was ready. I said to him, 'What happens if I dry up?' – the theatrical term for forgetting your lines – and he said, 'Oh just cover it up with a cough.' It wasn't perhaps the best boost to my lack of confidence then, but I was to learn many more things to do or not to do over the next 40 years and more in the crazy business of entertainment.

I will come back to that period in my life in due course. The mid-1950s for me was a time for trying my best to get by, and I certainly didn't have time to think or dream that I would eventually meet and work with artistes from all spheres of the entertainment business – like Charlie Chester, Jack Warner, Beryl Reid, Ted Ray, Kenneth Horne, Kenneth Williams, Gracie Fields, Roy Hudd, Max Miller, Marty Feldman, Norman Wisdom, Morecombe and Wise and also Syd James, Barbara Windsor, Michael Denison, Derek Nimmo, the cast of *Dad's Army*, Bernard Cribbins, Peggy Mount, Tom Jones and Frankie Vaughan. Plus such Americans as Georgie Burns, Jack Benny, Bob Hope, Phil Harris, Alice Faye, Dick Haymes, Danny Kaye and Sammy Davis Junior. And not forgetting all the wonderful writers who give us the words to say: Eric Merriman, Vince Powell, Ray Cooney, Eddie Braben, Galton and Simpson, Muir and Norden, Jimmy Perry and David Croft, etc. Then what about some of the cricketing personalities with whom I've actually played cricket – Bill Edrich, Peter May, Colin Cowdrey, Fred Trueman – and those I've had fun with: Denis Compton, David Gower, Brian Statham, John Arlott and Brian Johnston.

But I think we'd better start way back in 1926, 70 years ago.

$\star$   $\star$   $\star$   $\star$   $\star$   $\star$   $\star$   $\star$   $\star$   $\star$   $\star$   $\star$   $\star$

It started out as just another year, but certain events are, perhaps, worth remembering: A. P. F. (Percy) Chapman captained the England cricket team which, in the final Test Match at the Oval, won back the Ashes from Australia after 14 years. Our present Queen was born. Pilot Sir Alan Cobham made two record-breaking flights from London to Cape Town and London to Australia. There was also a General Strike – happily an event that has never occurred since.

Also in 1926, on 21 July at a house called St Helen's, in Amersham, Buckinghamshire, a son was born (the third of three) to Frank and Dulce Pertwee. Dulce wanted to call their son Bill after her brother-in-law, Bill Tobin, of whom we will hear plenty more later, together with his crazy and wonderful family. The priest told her at the baptism that he would have to be named William as Bill wasn't a proper name and was just a diminutive. The son was, however, always to be known as Bill or Billy to family and friends. His second name was Desmond, and Anthony was added later when he was confirmed by Cardinal Griffin in the 1930s.

I was born with a flat nose, very different from other members of my immediate family. The shape of it was apparently caused by my rather difficult birth; this was not enhanced when my brother dropped me down a stairway when I was very young. The only reaction to this was a grin and sicking up my recently taken meal! Much later, in my early teens, the nose collided with the back of a bus: there was obviously no chance of covering that up with a cough! In subsequent years I was known to my young friends as 'Flat Nose'.

I was also born with slightly slanting eyes, perhaps a characteristic of my South American ancestry (my mother was Brazilian but without a trace of slanting eyes; she was a very pretty woman). I was nicknamed 'Chung Lung Soo' by my father, after a famous illusionist of that name. I wonder what the priest would have thought of that! So with a flat nose and slanting eyes I was already given up as a lost cause by some of my relations, but my mother loved me as only a mother can.

My mother, Dulce Adelina (née Thompson) was born in Brazil, exactly where I'm not sure. Two places were mentioned, São Paulo and Niterói, but her family must have eventually settled in or near Rio before she was very old. My brother John (not actor Jon, he was a second cousin) had a fantastic memory and this, together with his research, has been a tremendous help with the early history of our families. In fact I couldn't have given the forthcoming details without it.

My mother's father, Henry James Thompson, was an Irish Catholic, although his father was an Orangeman who married a Catholic girl, Catharina. Henry J. was always known as 'Tiny', although he was a robust looking man in his pictures. Tiny left his birthplace in Cork and travelled to Brazil; why Brazil I don't know, but he must have had some knowledge of engineering because once in South America he, along with another gentleman called Murley Gotto, founded the Rio City Improvements Co, whose chief aims were to improve Rio's railways, roads, sewage and drainage. They were in a terrible state and had been for some time under the reign of Dom Pedro II. Pedro abdicated in 1889 when the slave trade was abolished and 700,000 were freed. He left the country and returned to his roots in Portugal.

To get back to Tiny Thompson; he married Anna Silva Pinto, a Brazilian girl born and bred. She was, my mother told me, very beautiful and a loving mother. She and Henry eventually had five children: three girls, Georgina (known as Gigi), Dulce and Amy, and two boys, Tommy and Johnnie. My father went out to Rio around the turn of the century to work for the City Improvements Co. He returned to England before World War 1 and eventually married Tiny's daughter Dulce. Tiny had a great sense of fun. My father told me that Tiny would ride on the open top-deck of a tram and, as another passed in the opposite direction, he would gently tip the hats from the passing passengers with his walking stick, much to their annoyance. My father and Uncle Bill Tobin, who also had a good sense of humour, invariably accompanied Tiny on these trips, and they told me that sometimes you could see four or five hats sailing away in the breeze.

Tiny also opened a toy shop but I don't think it lasted too long because, as my mother told me, he was in the habit of giving the toys away to the poorer children of the neighbourhood. He would also at times give away cash to the street beggars on the way home on a Friday. When his wife asked what they were going to do for money over the weekend, Tiny would say, 'Don't worry, we've got a roof over our heads and plenty of love in the house.' This was his Irish temperament coming out, coupled with a little South American 'mañana'. I think a certain amount of this was passed down to his children and grandchildren – what a lovely mixture: Irish and Brazilian.

My brothers and I had an even greater mix, as our father came from French Huguenot stock. Unfortunately my maternal grandmother died at the very early age of 35, from what illness I know not, leaving Tiny to bring up the children, all of whom were sent to England for their schooling.

My mother, Dulce, was sent to a convent in Norwood at the age of 12. Now comes a family mystery: Dulce, still very young, married a gentleman called Mackie and they had a daughter probably about 1908-9, but sadly both father and baby daughter died within a short time of one another. My mother was naturally heartbroken by these events, and was sent away to Wales to recuperate. Why Wales was chosen, we shall never know. My two brothers were told about that period in my mother's life by accident when they were quite young, but were asked not to mention it again, which they never did. I certainly did not know any details, although she did mention to me once that she had been married before; I didn't pursue the matter, more's the pity.

Her grief was only a foretaste of other heartbreaks during her lifetime, although her marriage to my father was a real love match. If she ever talked about baby girls she would always say, 'If it were me, I would call her Cherry'; so perhaps that was the name of the baby that died. I hope that by the end of this book I will have solved the mystery concerning my mother's first marriage.

As I have said, my father was of Huguenot descent and a direct descendant of Georges Pertwee (then spelt Pertuis and in various other ways). I myself have been known as Tiptree, Peewit and Twerptree on various occasions! Georges escaped from France in 1685, anticipating the revocation of the Edict of Nantes in October of that year, and the subsequent persecution of those who weren't Catholic. He settled in Essex, and that's where the majority of the Pertwees have been ever since. My grandfather James owned Boreham Old Hall near Chelmsford where my father was born. When I visited the hall about 15 years ago I expected something rather grand but it was a moderate-sized building in the heart of the village.

Grandad was a farmer and had seven daughters and two sons, one of whom, from his first marriage to Elizabeth Cooper, was killed in a riding accident when he was 11. His second marriage, to Harriet Carter, produced one child, my father. He was then 54 and his wife 48. My father was called James after his father, but in view of the lad who had died, the family always knew him by his second name, Frank (Francis). James is a family name anyway. My father had the same initials as the dead boy, J. F. C. P., which could not have been a coincidence.

My Dad did not follow his father into farming but eventually took up engineering as a living, as did his half brother Herbert, who was a marine engineer and invented various mechanisms for submarine warfare. He gave the patents away to the country; had he sold them, he would probably have finished up quite wealthy. Herbert's real mission in life seems to have been setting up the Sailors' Home on the Marine Parade at Great Yarmouth. This was destined to comfort many sailors shipwrecked along the East Coast. The home became his life's work and after he died it was carried on by his daughter, Nesta, whom I got to know quite well before she died a few years ago. The building is now a Maritime Museum.

However back to my father: he was rather a weakling as a lad, suffering from asthma which was to dog him for most of his life. At the age of five he was sent as a boarder to Felstead School in Essex. This must have been an horrendous experience at such a young age, even for a very fit child. In keeping with other public schools of the period, the regime at Felstead was tough and the punishments often sadistic. My brother told me that the school had had a clergyman as headmaster from its foundation. Father was thrashed on several occasions with branches from a gooseberry bush: the thorns had to be picked out of his battered and bleeding body by the matron. One boy was smacked round the ears so hard in one assault that he collapsed unconscious on the ground and was left deaf for the rest of his life. My father felt that he got some of his own back on the school when in the 1930s he backed a Derby winner called 'Felstead'.

By the turn of the century my father had graduated as an engineer, although I'm not sure where he gained his degree. After his mother Harriet died he travelled to Rio and gained employment with the City Improvements Co. One of the things that persuaded him to go to South America was a suggestion by his doctor that the climate might help his asthmatic condition. He returned to this country before World War 1 to enlist in the army.

There are no known facts as to how my mother and father met in England, or even Brazil, as the period from 1910 until they married is, as I have already mentioned, a bit of a mystery. It is pretty obvious that my father would have known that Tiny Thompson's daughter was in England following her schooling as he had worked for him in Rio. What I do know is that my parents' wedding was at Our Lady of Loreto, near Kew Gardens, in Richmond, Surrey, on 8 May 1915.

My father joined the Border Regiment soon after the outbreak of war in 1914, the year his father died at the age of 91. He and his two wives were buried in adjoining graves at

Boreham Church. Dad had several postings in the services, although he was not fit enough to go abroad. These included the War Office, Seaford in Sussex and Caversham near Reading in Berkshire. He and my mother, now married, loved Caversham. By 1917 they were living in Luton in Bedfordshire, where their first son, James Raymond, was born in 1917. I believe this was also the year that my father was discharged from the army on medical grounds. Their firstborn was badly affected by eczema and had to be bathed in olive oil. With a lot of care his condition improved, but I remember him suffering minor outbreaks later in life.

After Luton my parents moved to Twyford Avenue in Ealing, West London, where their second son, John Douglas, was born in 1919. Soon after this the family upped sticks and went back to Rio, presumably to enable my father to look for work which was scarce then in Britain. They left on the *Olympic*, the remaining liner of the White Star Line; her sister ships, the *Titanic* and the *Britannic*, had both been sunk, the latter when returning with wounded servicemen from the Dardanelles. There is now a theory that the *Titanic* was originally going to be called the *Olympic* and vice versa. Interesting isn't it!

By this time my mother's father – Tiny – had died, and the Rio City Improvements Co was being run by Murley Gotto and, for a short time, Tiny's sons Johnnie and Tommy, both of whom had returned from war service. Johnnie had been severely injured in the Dardanelles fiasco against the Turks and his wounds were to be of concern for the rest of his life.

Within 18 months of returning to Rio my mother was told that if she stayed in that climate she would, without a serious operation, endanger her life. This was the second time her life had been threatened by illness; when she was a tiny girl she was so ill that she was given the last rites by a priest. It is quite amazing to realise now that with all her problems – mental and physical – she would live to the age of 89. Apparently my two brothers had a nanny each during their short stay in Brazil and they all became so fond of one another that when the family returned to the UK in 1922, one of the girls, Ludi, threw herself under a tram and was crippled for life. My brother was heartbroken on learning this several years later.

So back my parents came to England with their two young sons, and by 1922 they had rented a bungalow in Amersham near where my mother's two sisters, Gigi and Amy, were living with their families.

By 1926 my father had finally found employment with Bristows Tarvia, a tar macadam firm. Despite his qualifications, his job for Bristows involved selling road-making products to various county councils. To do this he travelled all over the south of England in a car supplied by the firm. The family had moved into another house in Amersham – St Helen's – where I first saw the light of day. During the whole of my mother's and father's lives they never owned a house, always renting them. I believe this was the situation with most people in those days. It was certainly convenient as far as Dad was concerned: we had to move house frequently because his job took him to different areas of England and Wales.

The landlord of St Helen's was Bertram Chevalier, brother of the famous Albert Chevalier who wrote *My Old Dutch* ('we've been together now for 40 years' etc). My mother remarked to Bertram one day that his brother must have had a wonderful wife to write such a lovely song. 'On the contrary,' Bertram said, 'he had had a most unhappy marriage and was separated from his wife.'

My brothers meanwhile had already started their schooling in the Amersham area. In 1927 we apparently moved to nearby Rickmansworth, to a house owned by a French gentleman called Pavlow, whose baby daughter Muriel was later to become a well known stage and screen actress.

In 1929 we moved again, this time to Hereford as my father's territory now covered Herefordshire, Monmouthshire and most of Wales. After a short stay in an insalubrious area, we moved to Oakdene in Church Road, Tupsley. I am told that the long drive from Rickmansworth to Hereford was quite a business with the whole family, including Bimbo the dog and all our luggage, in Dad's Morris Cowley car! However my father soon adjusted to his new patch, and my brothers settled in to their new school, Hereford High. This was a great relief as John had had an unhappy time at his school in Amersham.

My first concrete memories date from our stay at Hereford; I am sure some children can remember from an even earlier age. I remember always playing with a ball – in fact in most of my young days I seem to remember having a ball to play with, and can even remember my father saying on one occasion, 'Why does that child keep bouncing a ball about?' I think it was a sort of comforter. I believe now that I always had to be doing something, and playing with a ball is a physical thing.

My mother had engaged a home help to live in – Florrie Ainge who came from an orphanage at Stoke Newington in north London. She was a friendly girl and she and my mother got on well. I also remember Dad was a great one for having a drink in a pub or hotel. He just liked to have a chat over a drink, a habit I also enjoy: it's something about the atmosphere that appeals to me. Dad would generally go for his whisky and soda to the 'Green Dragon' Hotel near Hereford Cathedral.

We had quite a large greenhouse on the side of the house at Tupsley. In it was a grapevine and a lovely and quite special smell. If I go into a greenhouse now I am instantly transported back to Hereford and that unique aroma. About 15 years ago I went down to Hereford for a week to appear with Clive Dunn (Corporal Jones of *Dad's Army*) in a variety show. The theatre venue was a converted swimming pool, the stage area was the deep end and the audience sat in the shallow end. The rake from shallow to deep gave the audience a sort of back stalls to front effect. (I hasten to add there was no water in the baths!) While I was there I searched out Oakdene and, believe it or not, the greenhouse was still there! I didn't knock on the door and say, 'I used to live here 50 years ago'; perhaps my instinct was to leave the childhood memories where they were. If the greenhouse was the original structure, it had done well for 45 years or more. I did have a whisky and soda (although I never normally take soda with it!) in the 'Green Dragon', thinking of my father doing the same all those years ago.

# 2 BAD TIMES ARE JUST AROUND THE CORNER

(With acknowledgements to Noel Coward)

When I was about six years old we travelled to our next house at Glasbury-on-Wye in Radnorshire, 25 miles from Hereford and just a few miles from Hay-on-Wye. Notorious because of a murder trial when we arrived, Hay is best-known today for its book shops. There is a disused cinema which has been turned into a gigantic book shop; you can browse there not just for a few hours but fordays. All the shops in the town appear to be owned by a gentleman who styles himself the 'King of the Principality of Hay' – a bit eccentric but it's good to know there are still some eccentrics in today's sombre world.

Our new abode at Glasbury was The Old Vicarage – 600 years old and quite lovely, right on the banks of the River Wye. It had originally been built as a home for monks who served the abbey, just across the river at Aberlynfi (pronounced Aber-lunvi). There was a big stone near the staircase in the Vicarage which we were told was the start of a tunnel under the river to the abbey. The noise of the water lapping under the floor when the river flooded was evident to my family, but I can't remember it and would have been frightened to death if I had. The tunnel had obviously collapsed over the years, otherwise one wouldn't have heard the water. In the sitting room there were window seats with hinged lids that revealed deep coffers. We were told by the villagers that the monks used them as hiding places when they were being persecuted.

Our maid Florrie had to leave while we were there, I think to have an operation, and she arranged for her sister Elsie to replace her. Elsie was always talking about mysterious things and told me there were probably a lot of ghosts at the Vicarage. I was really perturbed about this and from then on I wouldn't go to sleep without a light. We had a lovely old barn next to the house and the upper part was all furnished. It made a marvellous play-room for me, but after the ghost stories I wouldn't go in there unless someone was with me. My parents were pretty cross with Elsie for putting all those thoughts into my head.

The Vicarage was in a beautiful setting in the summer, but sometimes in the winter, when the river was in flood, it was quite frightening. The water sometimes reached the top of the garden wall, and you could see trees and the odd sheep or cow floating past. In fine weather my father used to sit on the steps and do a bit of fishing; he might spend all day there, many times without catching anything, or if he did it would just be an eel or two. I think he found it relaxing, and perhaps it took his mind off the bad times which were looming up in his business life. I knew nothing of this and was busy just enjoying myself. I was to experience the soporific effect of being by a river dangling a line into the water when I was evacuated to Sussex during the last war when I spent many a happy day with friends on the banks of the River Arun at Pulborough.

Some of my memories of life at The Old Vicarage are still quite vivid. My father was travelling for his firm and when he came home at weekends he invariably brought me an addition to my Hornby train set, perhaps a pair of points, a signal, a tunnel, another carriage or a guard's van. I have always been fascinated with the old fashioned guard's van which had an open look-out point at either end surrounded by a rail which the guard used to lean over, generally waving to a porter or two, as the train left the station. I rather think I would still like to own a real one; there are several about on the many preserved railways in this country.

I frequently spend a day or two enjoying the atmosphere of these thriving little railways dotted around the country. Only a couple of years ago I had my first ride in a guard's van on Sir William McAlpine's personal railway line which runs alongside his house in the grounds of his private estate. There is a story about his line concerning some Japanese businessmen who were entertained by Sir Bill at his home. On the way back to London the driver of their car overheard one of them say, 'Fancy building a house so close to a railway line!'

I should mention here that for some reason my mother had given my two brothers nicknames: John had become 'Fedge' and James had become 'Jiggy'. The latter is perhaps not so far from Jimmy, but how John became Fedge is slightly more mysterious. For as long as I can remember I have, and will continue for the sake of this book, refer to them as Fedge and Jiggy.

Brother Jiggy had been given a working model yacht which he duly presented to me, and it was decided to launch it on a fairly calm day on the River Wye. However currents and winds started up, and off went my yacht out of sight down the river, leaving me in floods of tears. Jiggy rushed to the nearby road bridge joining Glasbury to Aberlynfi and there was my yacht, caught up against one of the concrete piers of the bridge from which he was able to rescue it. All was calm again in the household, but that awful moment, when it was lost to sight in what looked to me like a raging torrent, is still with me.

The local grocer was a Mr Jenkin Morgan who died quite suddenly while we were there. My mother was most upset as she had become friendly with him, and when she went in to order anything she would always be offered a chair, and no matter how small the order, such as a quarter of cheese, it could be delivered, 'If Madam so wishes.' Those were the days! My mother always said she liked the Welsh people very much: perhaps there was some connection with this and the time she was sent to Wales to recuperate after her first husband and child died. She was always fond of a friend of mine with whom I worked in the theatre during the 1960s and 70s, Ronald Evans. In common with most Welsh folk, Ron used to burst into song at the drop of a hat and always treated my mother to an aria or three when he visited us, particularly after he'd had a glass or more of White

Shield Worthington. We had many laughs with Ron and his late wife Joan over the years.

My brother remembered we had a gardener at the Vicarage called Percy, and a young lad, Jack Philips, who used to take me for walks. In the late 1970s I was recording some radio programmes in Cardiff and I had a day or two off so I went up to Glasbury via the Brecon Beacons, and after having a look at The Old Vicarage (which seemed smaller than I'd remembered it!), I took myself over to the nearby 'Maesllwch (pronounced Mushloo) Arms' where my father used to pop in for his lunchtime drink when he was at home. I ordered a pint and was just about to pay when the landlord said, 'It has been paid for.' I thanked him, imagining my kind benefactor was a *Dad's Army* fan, as this sort of thing does sometimes happen.

Later I went to the bar once more and asked for a fill-up. The same thing happened. I asked who was making this generous gesture and I was told it was a Mr Jack Philips in the public bar. You can imagine what an evening of memories we exchanged; well, a lot of water had gone under the bridge since the early 1930s! It seemed that it was drinks all round from everybody to everybody. Jack recalled those days for me and most of the villagers, who appeared to be filling up the bars. Even if I'd been sober it was far too late to drive back to Cardiff, so it was a night's sleep at the Maesllwch and an early morning drive back to the more disciplined events in the recording studios.

My brothers were at a local private school run by the Lloyd family who were qualified teachers, but it seems from what I gleaned later on that Fedge was a bit brighter than their teaching. I was now nearly seven, but there was no money left for my private education and my father wasn't going to have me mixing with children from the local state school (known as 'board' schools in those days). I believe now that my father felt guilty that he wasn't earning enough to give me a private education as he had for my two brothers. My own son, after a brief time at a private school, went to two state schools, which didn't harm him, but I can understand my father's feelings when he was presented with the problem. I suspect schools then were not up to the standard they are now. I'm sure it didn't bother me, I was just having a good time. I was oblivious of the financial disasters that had crept up on the family; they had apparently manifested themselves even before I was born.

The aftermath of the Great War had brought about an enormous unemployment problem in the country. The hope that things would get better never materialised. My father's orders were obviously getting scarcer but my mother appeared to me to be just the same, keeping the home together and always giving us enough food. My staple diet through choice was dry bread with salt on it or dipped in the blood of the joint when it was being cooked. I was also mad about bananas, which from an early age I had called 'beetards'. I do remember my mother's brother Tommy paying us a visit on a trip from Rio, and shortly afterwards my mother benefited from her godfather's will to the tune of £1,000. This was a terrific lot of money in the 1930s, but when my brothers asked what she would do with it, she confessed that it was all spoken for – so my parents must have had a large number of bills to pay and were obviously in hock with the bank as well. Anyway that £1,000 must have been a godsend.

A lasting and quite moving memory from my time at Glasbury was brought about by a piece of music. My brothers were both Boy Scouts and a huge jamboree was held in a large field in the village. I was taken along to watch what I suspect was the closing ceremony. The field sloped upwards and I could see my brother Jiggy holding one of the scout banners as all the groups of scouts from the adjoining districts – it seemed like hundreds to me – started singing *Land of Hope and Glory*. Whenever I hear that wonderful piece of music now, whether it be on the last night of the Proms or at other times, I am transported back to that field in Glasbury.

I'm not sure how much effect it has on the young when families are moving around from house to house, but it didn't seem to bother me, or I don't remember it doing so. We were once again on the move in 1933 from Glasbury to Colnbrook, near Windsor. All the chores a move entails for grown-ups – filling up packing cases, seeing the telephone, gas and electricity people, arranging the removal company, and leaving the place tidy and clean (something about which my mother was meticulous) – wouldn't have crossed the mind of a seven-year old. I just piled in to the car with the family and Bimbo the dog and all the last-minute chattels. I would probably have made sure I had my Hornby train set with me, and then just sat back in anticipation of another adventure, this time a very long drive from Radnorshire.

The reason for the move to Colnbrook was that my parents' financial position had worsened. Luckily, however, Teddy Heilbron – the husband of my mother's sister Amy – had been left a cottage in an aunt's will and suggested that, as money was a problem, we could have the cottage rent-free until it was sold. A little later Uncle Teddy gave my parents a monthly allowance: much to their shame, they had to accept it gratefully.

Living near to London gave my father a chance to get to his firm's head office to see what the future held for the company. He was told that orders for rebuilding roads had virtually reached a standstill, so along with some other travellers he was made redundant. He was allowed to keep his Morris Cowley car but there was no other payment of any kind. Worry always brought on one of his asthma attacks, and this combined with his bronchitis was starting to be a big problem; all this caused more expense what with having to buy the few drugs that were available for his illness, plus, of course, doctors' fees. There was no NHS, family allowances or housing benefit available in those days, but still my mother coped with everything; it must have been a terrible strain.

Colnbrook was a lovely spot; the cottage had a big garden with a dovecote, and there were plenty of fields around. There was a large stream, the River Colne, a tributary of the Thames, near our house. I used to love going there in the summer, watching its clear water washing over the pebbles. I learnt to swim in that large stream, and there was always someone fishing there, but I was most fascinated with the kingfishers that swooped about, dipping very quickly into the water and out again in the same movement, showing off the beautiful blues and golds of their plumage. I have a lovely print and a hand-painted plate of a kingfisher on my wall at home, and they just have to be my favourite birds, probably all because of that stream at Colnbrook.

There was a small branch line near us running from Uxbridge to Staines; sadly, it no longer exists. The station closest to us was called Poyle Halt, and it really was a halt, just a platform with an old-fashioned bus-type shelter. I think I was only taken there once, but Fedge was a regular visitor when he was travelling on the line. At that time he was a real railway enthusiast and had thoughts of making a career in the administrative department of the railways. His bible was the *Bradshaw Time Table*, a big thick book covering the whole country. However he abandoned the idea of a railway career on the advice of Uncle Teddy. If he had gone in that direction, who knows what might have happened: the future of our railway system could have been quite different! Some of the clowns who have been in charge for the past 30 years haven't done it a lot of good, except perhaps Chris Green, who left fairly recently after a successful period in its management, because of frustration at some of the decisions being taken.

I also remember a pub nearby which always seemed to be inhabited on Saturday evenings by groups of gypsies. Almost always there were fights with fists flying in all directions. It's amazing to realise now that the nearby Hounslow Heath Aerodrome, almost adjacent to Colnbrook, would eventually become London Airport, perhaps the biggest in the world. The actual village of Heathrow is under Number One Runway. There was also another small aerodrome at nearby Heston; a few years later Prime Minister Neville Chamberlain would land there with that notorious piece of paper, signed by himself and Herr Hitler, which came to be known as the Munich Agreement! In 1975 I was involved in the national tour of the *Dad's Army* stage musical and, when playing Bath, I was privileged to see some of the informal letters that Chamberlain had sent home to his son from Germany while on that trip to meet

Hitler. I will expand on that particular and very wonderful occasion at Bath later.

By 1935 my eldest brother Jiggy had become besotted with aeroplanes and would spend his weekends at air displays like those at Hendon, Croydon and Heston. This obsession was already pointing him towards his sad death during the early part of World War 2, but he just loved aeroplanes. I remember he had a wind-up flying model manufactured by Frog Penguin. It had a silver body and you laid it on top of its box and put the propeller into a winder, turned a little handle and the elastic motor was all ready to launch, by hand. You had to be careful to hold the propeller to stop it unwinding before flight. The models were very popular at that time and Jiggy would let me have a go with his sometimes. It would bank and dip and looked just like a real monoplane; I think Jiggy could also make it loop-the-loop by altering slightly the angle of the wings and tail.

Jiggy also spent time travelling to Brooklands race track at Weybridge to watch the well-known drivers of the day showing off their expertise. I suppose speed and a certain amount of danger was another liking of his. I'm a member of the Brooklands Club now and I get pleasure from seeing the remaining banking, now preserved forever, I hope. Most of the huge area of the once proud racing circuit has been built on but there are quite a few original buildings still intact, such as the Sir Malcolm Campbell garage, now a museum. There's also a super shop where you can buy anything connected with racing and also flying – Brooklands was also an important flying centre. Vickers, the British Aircraft Corporation and British Aerospace had a factory there and used the centre of the racing circuit for aircraft testing; there was enough room for quite large aircraft to take-off and land. Barnes Wallis, inventor of the bouncing bomb of No 617 'Dambusters' Squadron fame and the 'Tallboy' 12,000lb bomb used to sink the German battleship *Tirpitz*, lived close by and worked at Brooklands. He also designed the geodetic-framed Wellington bomber and recently the museum has funded the rebuilding of one salvaged from Loch Ness after lying in its waters for some 40 years.

In 1935 the cottage in Colnbrook had to be sold, so it was goodbye to all the good things we had enjoyed there as youngsters: swimming, kingfishers and the lovely garden. However my parents' financial position hadn't improved and my two elder brothers were now increasingly aware of the situation. For me, well, we would soon be off again on another adventure.

Before leaving Colnbrook, however, there is one incident that my family and aunt remembered quite well. I had to have six teeth removed because they were growing the wrong way or some such thing. I was taken to a dentist, Mr Vegar, whom the family had known when we lived at Amersham. Apparently it took the efforts of most of the family to get me to the dentist in the first place, but once in the surgery the fun really began. I still remember the layout of that room. Anyway, the screams and shouts and noise were so horrendous that everyone thought I was being murdered, and when the door was opened they found the nurse lying on the floor half gassed. In those days they just shoved a horrid rubber piece over your mouth and nose, and I had managed to transfer it to the nurse! The dentist was sweating and lying across the chair shouting, 'Get him out of here and take him home and lose him.' (I must have been strong for a eight-year old!) I was eventually taken to Guy's Hospital where a Mr Kelsey Fry had the six teeth out in no time. Kelsey Fry later began a partnership with the great plastic surgeon Archibald Mackindoe at his hospital in East Grinstead where he earned a fine reputation rebuilding the faces of aircrew who had been badly burnt during the last war.

Many years later I had another mishap at the dentist's when an injection needle broke in the roof of my mouth. To this day I avoid having injections if I can, as the sight of a needle going into my mouth causes me to faint within about 10 seconds. I have landed up on several surgery floors, much to the surprise and fright of the dentist!

So off we went again, this time down the A4 to Newbury, also in Berkshire. This turned out to be a very short stay. The reason for this move was that my father had heard there might be some work for him there but, alas, this didn't materialise, and my father's health deteriorated even further. The address, just out-side Newbury, was Battlefield, Wash Common. It was on the site of a bloody battle in the 17th century when the Royalists and Roundheads cut each other to pieces.

I remember very little about that period in my life. I know that Fedge hadn't got a job, so he volunteered to teach me the three 'Rs'. I was a terrible pupil, not taking anything in and screaming and crying and being chased all over the place by my exhausted and frustrated brother. I had some little books with printed lines of writing and, underneath, blank space so that I could copy the words. If I did two before my concentration left me it was a lot; I would look out of the window and start a sort of twitch – something I do to this day when I'm not careful. My friend actress Su Pollard does a very good impression of me when she catches me at it. Poor Fedge, as if it wasn't bad enough not having a job, having to try and teach a horrible little broth-er, who was stupid, idle and twitching all over the place, must have been a nightmare for him.

Jiggy was probably the only member of the family who got any enjoyment from the stay in Newbury – he landed a job in Stradlings Garage. Mucking about with engines was right up his street and set him off on his engineering career. He and Fedge were quite different in temperament; Jiggy loved sport, some-thing Fedge was never keen on as he was much more academ-ic. This is not to say that Jiggy was a dunce: he most certainly wasn't. Not many years ago, when I was driving through Newbury, I saw a large garage with the name Stradlings above it. It's always strange on occasions like that: you try to recollect the past but, as I've said, there is little I remember of Newbury. During our time there, however, I did become aware of some international news, simply because everyone was talking about it. It was the trouble brewing in Abyssinia (today's Ethiopia), and its impending invasion by Mussolini's Italy.

After messages backwards and forwards between my mother and her sister Gigi, who was by then living in Erith in Kent, it was suggested my family should move there. Gigi knew of a large house that had been divided into two flats and had the ground floor vacant. My parents liked the idea of a move to this Thameside town and the proximity to my mother's sister's family. So off we went in the car again.

The large house was called Riversfield and our portion of it was quite wonderful. It was mostly furnished – the landlord, Hedley Mitchell, had a big furniture store in the town – although there was room for what furniture we had; what else was needed we obtained on HP. The house was surrounded by lawns with wide steps leading down from the building. Inside the rooms were very large and, although I can't remember feeling cold, it must have been very costly to heat. One of the rooms held a full-sized billiard table and, when my father was well enough, he and I would have a game: I really got to enjoy it. I still don't know how we existed financially because we just had my father's pension, not from his most recent job at Bristows, but from the Rio City Improvements Co. I am sure this must have been arranged for my father by my mother's brothers, because of course he hadn't worked for the company to any degree since before World War 1. I know how much the pension was, because I used to pay the cheque into the bank for him. It was just over £7 a month!

The linking up with my mother's sister Gigi and her large family at Erith must have brought relief to my parents. Gigi and Bill Tobin had a large family and at least Mum and Dad had their own flesh and blood with whom they could discuss their difficulties. Gigi and Bill had three girls, June (almost the same age as me), Rosemary and Daphne, and three boys, Gayne, Peter and Pat. There was also a beautiful little baby called Michael who, unfortunately, died at about 18 months from meningitis. I remember him being rushed up to Great Ormond Street hospital in London by ambulance, but I understood he died soon afterwards. Gigi so loved children it must have been awful for her. They were a jolly family and quite eccentric in many ways. My mother and Gigi would talk in Portuguese when they were together and then burst into uncontrollable laughter. Bill Tobin was a huge Irishman, very musical and a lovely artist.

Once we were settled at Erith, Fedge got a job at Uncle Bill's firm, the Atlas Preservative Co of which he was the Export Manager. The Managing Director was a 20-year old, Denis Thatcher, later to marry Britain's first lady prime minister, Margaret. Denis's father owned the firm. Fedge's wage was 15s (75p) a week. However, at the end of 1936 Uncle Teddy told him there was a vacancy with a raw paper supplier in the city; Fedge applied for it and was successful. His wage there was £1 5s (£1.25) a week. He borrowed the money for a quarterly season, and in the first three months he had paid that back and also had enough left over to buy his next quarterly season. Goodness knows what he did for meals in London, but he was very well organised. Apart from his war years in the services, Fedge stayed with the Norwegian-based Kellner Partington Paper Pulp Co until 1967, by which time he had become Governing Director – not bad for someone who started as an office boy.

Jiggy got a job with Vickers Armstrong at Rochester and used to travel there on a motorbike. My father's car had to be sold, much to Jiggy's sorrow as he had by then learned to drive it. At Vickers he met up with a Frank Cobbett and his wife Florence, and this association turned into a very close relationship for the three of them. At the time of writing Frank still lives in the area near Swanley where he and Florence had always been.

As far as I was concerned, my schooling started in Erith, at a convent attended by my cousins. I was rather frightened by the nuns – their large black flowing gowns inhibited me. Although my form teacher, Madam Claire, was a very nice and patient person, I think I spent most of the time back in the old routine of gazing out of the window and twitching. The one nun who did put some fear in me was the music and elocution teacher, Madam Bridget. When it was time for us to go to her class she would stand at the top of a long sloping corridor with her hands open wide, giving her black cloak a sort of vampire effect. When I used to turn the corner of the corridor and saw this, I would immediately have diarrhoea. As I was wearing shorts the result was disastrous and Madam Bridget would cry out, 'Oh dear God, Billy's filled his trousers again!'

I had my first outing to the seaside while I was at the convent. The nuns took us to Herne Bay in Kent. We all had packed lunches: mine would have had my favourite bread and salt sandwiches and a large bunch of 'beetards'. Another very notable day out was a trip to Southampton to go aboard a huge ocean liner, the *Majestic*, then one of the world's greatest liners owned by the ill-fated White Star Line. While the White Star *Olympic* had had a charmed life, her two sister ships, the *Titanic* and the *Britannic*, were already at the bottom of the sea.

I must have learned something at the convent, but the only thing I remember was being able to recite 'I must go down to the sea again, to the lonely sea and the sky', although I'm not sure if I knew any more of the Masefield poem.

Isn't it funny how little things stick in your mind! For instance, Fedge had gone to London to witness George V and Queen Mary's Silver Jubilee and had taken a photo of them in their carriage with his Kodak Box Brownie camera, and this photo was passed round the family and talked about for ages. The other silly thing I remember vividly was some minor building going on near the driveway of our house. The foreman was a Mister Sullivan, and I would spend ages talking to him and watching him lay bricks. I was fascinated by this and in fact I still take an interest in building works. Mr Sullivan encouraged me to help him sweep up and carry the odd brick or two which I was delighted to do.

1936 was a year of some momentous events. George V died, there was the Spanish Civil War with its emotional involvement of many nations, and the Berlin Olympic Games when the black American Jessie Owens won gold, much to Hitler's anger. Apart from the death of George V the other events didn't raise any interest as far as I was concerned, they were too far away to concern a child. I do remember the launching of the fastest ship so far, the *Queen Mary*, and being given a Dinky Toy model of it. However the main events in 1936, which also had the effect of making everyone realise the power of radio, were the burning down of the famous Crystal Palace in south-east London and the abdication of Edward VIII. The news of Edward's friendship with Wallis Simpson and the subsequent events was on the wireless the whole time. I remember my mother crying a lot during the abdication crisis, which with all the family problems she was coping with seemed rather strange, but of course Edward had been a bit of a glamour boy as far as the public was concerned.

Before we left Erith (oh yes, we would soon be on the move again) we had a knock on the door one evening and a policeman told us that Jiggy had had an accident on his motorbike in Dartford on his way back from Vickers in Rochester. He had been taken to hospital with a broken nose. He had, though obviously in pain and with some dizziness, got up and turned off the engine of the motorcycle which had crashed into him, the driver of which was in a worse way than Jiggy.

By 1937 Gigi and Bill Tobin had moved to nearby Belvedere, to a large house in Picardy Road. As things had obviously got even more difficult regarding my father's health and ever worsening financial problems, we then also moved to Belvedere to a flat in Upper Brook Street, quite near the Tobins. This move gave me the opportunity to spend much more time with my cousins and I got to know the family much better, spending whole days with them. This was a jolly period for me and gave my mother a break, freeing her to look after my father, whom I seem to remember spending even more time in bed. Bill Tobin used to sit in a cupboard under the stairs practising the trumpet, while at least once a week the local Catholic priest would sit in his study drinking the Tobin's whisky. The family were very enthusiastic Catholics, and I do remember that if I went to church with them, they wouldn't let me have even a drink of water until after we had received communion. The smell of the incense in church and my rumbling tummy used to make me feel very faint. I think I eventually won the day and had a drink before going, but often was told by my cousins that the Devil had got behind me. This caused me to look back a lot on the way to church in case he was there!

I remember seeing the Tobin children leaving the house on weekdays, the girls to school and the boys to work. Gigi would stand at the front door with a pile of hats and as they all passed her, she would slap a hat on their heads – not always the right one. Sometimes one of the girls would leave wearing a trilby with a boy sporting a panama. Nobody seemed to mind and Gigi would end up laughing at all of them. Her son Gayne was always full of mischief and once he hollowed out the centres of some bread rolls his mum had put in the oven to warm and put tame mice inside them. When Gigi came to take the rolls out the mice jumped out at her, followed by screams from my aunt, and the usual admonishing, 'You little swine Gayne, wait until I tell your father!' but she never did.

On another occasion Gayne had forgotten to light the fire before his father came home. He was told to get it going as quickly as possible, so he threw some petrol on the coals and lit it. There was a huge bang and the chimney disintegrated just as his father came through the gate. He took his belt off, which he did on occasions when it was called for, and he gave Gayne a strapping. Bill Tobin was a lovely man, but he took no nonsense from the family; they had to be polite and thoughtful, and if they weren't he would pull them up about it straight away. He would also do some eccentric things. Once while we were playing in the garden at the house (hopscotch was very popular then), I looked up to see furniture flying out of the bedroom window. He had bought some new furniture and the obvious and easiest way as far as he was concerned was to throw the old stuff out of the window instead of going up and down the stairs. Beds, chests of drawers, chairs, etc, came flying through the air, but my cousins took no notice except to say, 'Daddy's bought some new furniture for us.'

Belvedere itself was a large village and the shopkeepers were friendly, particularly the couple which ran the haberdashers, Mr and Mrs Ranby. It was the sort of shop where the windows displayed vast ladies corsets, bodices, large hats, huge bloomers, lyle stockings and voluminous flannel night-dresses, the latter folded discreetly at the back. Mr Ranby also sold elastic, ribbons, buttons and most other accessories. My mother and her sister Gigi would pay the shop a visit for some small thing or other and the fuss that was made of them when they bought half a yard of elastic was amazing. Mr Ranby had a slight lisp, spoke very quietly and slowly, and had the most charming manner. My mother used to say it was most relaxing to go to the Ranby's shop, a chair was always offered and a good chat ensued. I'm sure a pleasant chat was the real reason for a visit in most cases.

I was appearing in a summer show at Eastbourne in 1958 and one night there was a knock on my dressing room door. When I opened it, there stood Mr and Mrs Ranby. They had retired many years before and were living at the Chatsworth Hotel on the sea front. Several teas and lunches together followed this meeting and I also took my mother to see them; as you can imagine they had the longest chat they'd ever had.

Although my brothers were helping financially at home from their meagre wages, it seemed as if another move was imminent. Mum's brother Johnny came to England and I'm sure would have tried to help the situation. I do remember he ordered a bicycle for me from Gamages store in London and it was to be delivered by van. On the day in question I perched myself on a little raised wall near the gate to watch out for it. The hours passed, and I even missed lunch not giving up my vantage point, but still no sign of the Gamages van. At long last I realised it wasn't coming. Oh the disappointment! I'll bet I was in a terrible mood that evening, and I'm sure Mum would have tried to console me by telling me it would be along the next day. And so it was, early in the morning, a beautiful BSA bicycle; oh joy!

I also used the little perch near the gate to talk to a night-watchman who was guarding a hole in the road. He had a brazier to keep himself warm and to toast his bread. What a funny and futile act for me, a 10-year old, talking to a man guarding a hole. Actually, I think I was quite fascinated with the brazier.

My father listened to the radio a lot and I used to sit beside his bed and listen with him. He loved the comedy programmes, in particular artistes like Billy Bennett who did ridiculous rhyming parodies of well-known monologues. He would appear in an outsized tail suit with brown boots and a ridiculously large, false, walrus moustache, or in some other garb which gave a flavour to the particular monologue he was doing. (I learned these facts in later years.) His bill matter for the music halls and radio was 'Almost a Gentleman'. A sample of Bennett's parody of *The Road to Mandalay* went as follows:

*There were no maps for soldiers in this land of Gunga-Din,*
*So they picked the toughest warrior out and tattooed on his skin.*
*On his back he's got Calcutta, lower down he's got Bombay,*
*And you'll find him sitting peacefully on the road to Mandalay.*

There was Gillie Potter, with his greeting, 'Good evening England, this is Gillie Potter here speaking to you in basic English.' Elsie and Doris Waters, the sisters of Jack Warner (much later TV's *Dixon of Dock Green*) created the characters Gert and Daisy, always gossiping about their husbands. Then there was Ronald Frankau, a raconteur and one half of the Murgatroyd and Winterbottom double act with Tommy Handley, and Norman Long with his songs at the piano was another of Dad's favourite entertainers.

Max Miller 'the cheeky chappie' was another slightly saucy comedian. He was once banned from the BBC, but by today's standards the reason for his ban was like Noddy in Toyland! Miller was one of the greatest stand-up comedians of them all. I had the privilege and joy of doing an impression of him at both the Shaftesbury and London Palladium theatres in the 1970s and 1980s. What a thrill to walk out on to that famous Palladium stage, wow!

Another artiste my father loved was Robb Wilton. He was slightly different from the others being a humorist not a gag man; how wonderful he was. He had a series running on radio in the late 1930s called *Mr Muddlecombe JP*, in which the eponymous hero sat on a bench sorting out various problems. He had a fairly slow delivery and was always trying to give the impression that he was in charge and all problems were surmountable. Over the years he must have been one of the most impersonated entertainers ever. Thank goodness some radio and film recordings of him still survive today.

Muddlecombe's problem of a bypass was a real gem, and my father continually chuckled at the situations he tried to untangle. A Muddlecombe routine would go something like this:

*A debate in the Council Chamber of his home town of Nether Backwash when a bypass was being opposed by the townspeople.*

**Muddlecombe:** We must keep up to date. Every decent town nowadays has its bypass.
**Shopkeeper:** But we don't have enough passers-by to want a bypass.
**Muddlecombe:** No, but the passers-by who do pass by if they had a bypass to pass by would be able to pass by the bypass.

When it was disclosed that his own house would be pulled down as well as the whole High Street to build the bypass he says:

**Muddlecombe:** But that's all there is of Nether Backwash. If there's no Nether Backwash there's no need for a bypass.

This is only a short version of the banter in the Council Chamber, but conveyed by Wilton in his unique style it sounded hilarious. Robb Wilton was also a very good situation storyteller and World War 2 gave him two wonderful catch phrases 'The day war broke out', describing what had happened, and 'The day I joined the Home Guard', such as:

My Missus said to me, 'What are you?'
I said, 'I'm one of the Home Guard.'
She said, 'What do you do?'
I said, 'I've got to stop Hitler's Army from landing.'
She said, 'What, just you?'
I said, 'Oh no, there's Charlie Evans and Harry . . .
Well there's seven or eight of us altogether.'
She said, 'Do you know this fellow Hitler?'
I said, 'Of course not.'

She said, 'How will you know if it's him if he lands?'
I said, 'Well I've got a tongue in me head haven't I?' . . . etc.

They always met in a hut behind the 'Dog and Pullet'!
Wonderful stuff!

There was a lot of Wilton's attitude in Captain Mainwaring in
*Dad's Army*, combined with another great radio artiste, Sandy
Powell – 'Can you hear me Mother?' We'll talk more about
Sandy later on.

*Band Wagon* was a slightly new departure for the medium. It
starred Arthur Askey and Richard Murdoch. This was the first
situation-style comedy on radio. Askey and Murdoch had this
imaginary flat at the top of Broadcasting House with inhabi-
tants Lewis the Goat and charlady Nausia Bagwash. It really
depended on the stars' wonderful timing and rapport with one
another and was great entertainment. There was Harry Hemsley
and his imaginary family of children, one of whom talked complete gobbledygook. Hemsley would then ask one of the other
children to interpret with a 'What does Horace say Winnie?'
and Winnie would say 'Horace says yes' or some other short
word. The audience would always wait for Winnie's answer
because they knew what was coming – a lesson in letting the
audience in on the joke.

A magazine programme every week called *Monday Night at
Seven,* and later *Monday Night at Eight,* was compulsive listening
as was the ever present *Henry Hall and his Orchestra* which had
been popular for some time. Later Henry introduced an even
more popular show, *Henry Hall's Guest Night* in which, apart
from his marvellous orchestra, he introduced all the top entertainers of the day. People waited for that hesitant announcement
by Hall himself, 'This is Henry Hall speaking, and tonight is my
guest night.' Considering the way his voice delivered that line,
it is amazing that it become impersonated not only by people
in the profession, but also the general public.

Henry Hall was a nice man, and came across as a gentleman.
I met him when he retired to Eastbourne. His son Mike became
an impresario, putting on theatrical productions; and who

would have thought in those halcyon days of radio that a quietly spoken man introducing *Records of your Choice* would become the first disc jockey to have a following comparable with those of today. His name was Christopher Stone. What a wonderful communicator radio is. Even with the advent of television the importance of radio is obvious, with many local stations around the country giving up-to-date weather forecasts and indicating traffic delays, as well as keeping local people in touch with one another on phone-ins. Radio has certainly come along since the 1920s.

I have often wondered whether listening to those radio programmes with my father sowed some sort of seed in me for doing various voices and impersonations – how I actually started my career in entertainment. But as a boy of 10 or 11 I was very shy – I still am in some ways – and the idea of ever performing in public would have frightened me to death. As far as radio was concerned, the biggest listening audience ever in 1937 was surely the coronation of King George VI and Queen Elizabeth. I do remember Gracie Fields singing *Sing As We Go* from her successful film at that time, and I was taken to my first film, *Treasure Island* with Wallace Beery as Long John Silver. I was frightened to death. The cinema was the Regal in Bexleyheath. First there was one of the 'shorts' that in those days used to precede the main picture; it was hilarious, the main comedy actor in it was Guy Kibbee.

Later in 1937 we moved just a short way away to an old house called The Rookery and this, although we didn't know it at the time, was to be our last move as a complete family. The Rookery was a dark house on a hill surrounded by trees and to me was a little forbidding. By 1938 Hitler had marched into Austria without a shot being fired and had his beady eyes on Czechoslovakia. Most people in this country were beginning to think we could sooner or later be engulfed in a war. I know my parents were worried about this possibility, and the probability that my two brothers would be called up for war service as they would both be eligible: Jiggy was then 21 and Fedge 19. These worries didn't help my father's health, and even I started to think about war, as you couldn't miss all the talk of bombing by air. Then came the various meetings between Prime Minister Neville Chamberlain and Adolf Hitler, the German Chancellor, culminating in the Munich Agreement, and the piece of paper bringing forth the message from Chamberlain, 'Peace in our time.' My parents were overjoyed by the news, as I suspect were most people in the country, and even I felt relief as in simple terms I was asking, 'Will there not be any bombing now?'

Naturally there was a backlash from some politicians, particularly Winston Churchill, saying that Chamberlain had sold Czechoslovakia down the river for the sake of what they claimed was only a respite before Hitler made further demands. They said that appeasement wouldn't work with someone like Adolf. Chamberlain did sacrifice the Czechs, but he knew he had to buy time for this country. We were under-armed and our air force was almost non-existent. From the private letters I have seen sent to his son from Germany during the crisis meetings, the Prime Minister was in no doubt that Hitler would break his word, but in 1938 we would have had no chance to defend ourselves had we pledged to defend Czechoslovakia. Poor Chamberlain, he had only been Prime Minister for a year or so and the responsibility of trying to do the right thing must have been a terrible weight on his shoulders. He was not physically the strongest of men, either.

Although peace had been temporarily bought for the country, peace in our house was not improving. My father was now pretty ill, and my mother was in a lot of pain from a prolapse condition brought on by my birth when she really was not fit enough to have me. The doctor insisted she go into hospital for an operation.

I have many memories of Christmas in 1936 and 1937. As a family, Christmas night was generally shared with the Tobins at their house. My father was not able to join in and was happier in bed at home with some peace and quiet. The atmosphere with the Tobins was wonderful, plenty to eat and lots of decorations, with Uncle Bill playing his trumpet and my mother playing the piano and singing, and then finishing up with charades. Uncle Teddy would always appear just before the festivities with a bottle of whisky for Dad and some goodies for the table, and some money for us lads. We would line up and he would give us a £1 to be split between us, 6s 8d each (34p today). You could buy quite a lot for that. I used to go down to Woolworth's and buy the odd thing for Mum and Dad. I still have one of the presents I bought for Mum: it was a small pot with dried flowers in it giving off a perfume. That probably cost 6d as Woolworth's was the 3d and 6d store then.

August 1938 was a milestone in sport for one person: Len Hutton beat Don Bradman's 334, up to then the record Test Match cricket score. In the last Test Match at the Oval, Hutton scored 364. I listened to the wireless commentary with my father and it made such an impression on me that I can recite almost word for word the momentous moment when Hutton beat the record. The commentator was Howard Marshall. He had a wonderfully controlled radio voice, but even he got excited when Hutton hit the ball for four through the covers off the bowling of Fleetwood-Smith. Ben Barnett was the Australian wicket keeper. What a thrill it was for me when in the 1970s I was playing for the Lord's Taveners at Hambledon in Hampshire (the birthplace of cricket) and found myself fielding in the slips alongside Ben Barnett.

I have to jump forward for a moment to 1988 when I went up to Sheffield to be one of the speakers at a tribute to Len Hutton. Excitement grew in me all the way to Sheffield as I was about to meet the great Len, and the hero of that August Test Match in 1938. We were lined up in the Grand Hall at Sheffield for pre-dinner cocktails before the great man arrived. The other speakers were to be the author Jeffrey Archer, and ex-England and Yorkshire captain Norman Yardley. The time arrived and Sir Len and his wife, Lady Dorothy, arrived. My excitement had reached fever pitch, would he perhaps say hello to me?

To my amazement and utter astonishment he came straight over to me and said, 'I must shake your hand, you're my favourite television character from the wonderful *Dad's Army*, this is a real privilege.' I don't remember what I said, I think I just mumbled, 'Thank you.' During the course of the evening he said he had been told I did not live far from him and said, 'Why not come over one morning and have a cup of coffee with us.' I didn't need a second invitation. I had a lovely morning with Len and Dorothy. We talked about cricket, and his sons' involvement in the game – the eldest Richard had played for Yorkshire and England. Len signed my copy of a book about his life that I had had for some time, and I also have a super signed photograph and letter from him.

What a gentleman he was. I realised after our meeting why the team he captained (the first professional to do so) liked him so much; he obviously cared about the players' welfare, particularly on tour. It must also be remembered that not only did he have the responsibility of captaincy on his shoulders, but also he was one of the greatest opening batsmen of all time. A little while later I was playing in a charity match organised by radio's *Test Match Special* scorer Bill Frindall (the Bearded Wonder!), and Richard Hutton and I happened to be batting together. After I had hit a couple of fours Richard said to me, 'The ball seems to go off that bat pretty well.' I showed him the bat, it was a 'Len Hutton Autograph' I had bought in 1948!

But back to The Rookery at Belvedere in 1938. My mother's operation could not be put off any longer as she was now continuously in great pain, and it was decided she should go into hospital in December. The doctor also arranged that my father should go into the same hospital and stay there until my mother had recuperated and was ready to look after him again. Meantime my father had fallen behind with the HP payment on our furniture; I think he was £5 in arrears. The bailiffs came in, in the shape of a little man in a bowler hat called Mr Bonnet; apart from a chair and my father and mother's bed, everything went, even most of the pieces actually belonging to my parents. I was sent down to Aunt Amy in Sussex and Jiggy stayed with his friends the Cobbetts in Dartford. Fedge got digs nearby with the Tobins and had his evening meals with them. After Dad died Fedge and Jiggy spent the last night at The Rookery sleeping on the bare boards, frozen stiff.

Before finally leaving, Fedge had to take Bimbo to the vet to be put down, in those days with one shot from a gun. Fedge was given his collar and lead to take home. He was always a sensitive lad, although he didn't often show it, but that day must have been almost the worst of his life.

Mum had her operation a little while after arriving in hospital, the Bolingbroke at Wandsworth, having given Dad her love and seen him into a sort of geriatric ward. When my mother came round from her operation she was told that he had died that morning, 20 December. My brothers were summoned to the hospital, not only to comfort my mother because of Dad's death, but also for her post-operative condition. It must have been a dreadful nightmare for all concerned. My brother told me that the hospital rang with Christmas carols everywhere you went when he went to visit Mum on the days leading up to Christmas: he hated carols ever after. 1938 was the year of Walt Disney's great animated film *Snow White and the Seven Dwarfs* and everyone was singing the dwarfs' theme song *Whistle While You Work*. There hadn't been much whistling in the Pertwee household in 1938.

By some miracle Mum's brother Johnnie had just arrived in England and he took charge of all the funeral arrangements. I was told about my father quite discreetly by Aunt Amy down in Sussex, but I don't think it really sank in. My brothers arrived at Amy's house, See-Saw, at Roundabouts, near Storrington in Sussex, for Christmas along with a lot of other friends, and as far as I was concerned everything seemed quite jolly on the surface. It was a very cold Christmas, with thick snow on the ground, so we were able to make snowmen and have snowball fights. People skated on a local lake called Monkmead, which I think belonged to a big house there; it was just like a scene from a Christmas card.

The days before Christmas were quite hectic as far as I was concerned. My aunt wanted to keep me occupied and, for instance, arranged for a lady friend of hers called Mops Ascoli to take me round London on a toy-buying spree. I was in a daze most of the time because I'd never actually been in the centre of London before. It was so busy with shoppers crowding in and out of the stores looking for Christmas gifts; we were piling in and out of taxis and seemed to be chasing our own tails. I remember going into Barkers, and Derry and Toms in Kensington High Street. In the latter I met Father Christmas, and as soon as I'd got a present from him Mops was rushing me off somewhere else, always laughing and saying, 'Hurry up.'

I bought a shiny cinematograph gun. You put a strip of film into it, pulled the trigger and film cartoon images appeared on the wall. I also had a small car; it was called a Shuco and was made in Germany. There was a long wire lead coming out of the top of it with a small steering wheel at the end so you could stand up and steer the car round the floor. We finished up with a cream tea somewhere, and then went back to my Aunty Amy's flat which was in West Kensington Court. This was where she stayed when she came to London. It was a smart place with a lift and a restaurant underneath. The flats are still there, but I think the restaurant is now a club. It is situated at the beginning of the Cromwell Road extension, just before you get to the Hammersmith flyover.

Before explaining why I was staying at the London flat, I must mention that Amy herself had to come to London for a few days during which she asked her cook and gardener, Mrs and Mr Clark respectively, to let me stay with them. Mrs Clark was a very nice lady but her husband was a bit grumpy, and if I touched anything in my aunt's garden that he had had anything to do with, he would tell me off and say, 'You touch that again and I'll twist your bloody little ear off.'

So after one night staying in the Clarks' rather dreary and cold cottage, perhaps with the prospect of having my ear twisted off, I got up quite early, packed my case and waited in the road for Amy and her husband, Uncle Teddy, to drive past on their way to spend a few days in London. I knew what route they would be taking, and was determined not to be left with the Clarks. The car did come, and as poor Teddy could not wait to try and sort out what should happen to me, he said, 'Jump in, you'd better come with us.' When we finally got back to Storrington, after a short stay in London, Mrs Clark was at the house to greet us, and she understood everything, never mentioning my sudden departure to anyone.

There was one other time when I was asked to stay with another acquaintance for a couple of nights and I wasn't very delighted with that either. So I climbed out of the bedroom window and with the help of a drainpipe reached the ground, pinched a bike from the garden and made hell-for-leather for Pulborough railway station, which I suppose was about five miles away. I don't know how I got on a London train without a ticket, but there was a policeman waiting to greet me at Victoria station in London to send me back. I'm still not sure how anyone knew I'd gone to Pulborough station.

My mother's brother, Uncle John, took me to lunch in London. Now that was something special, the sort of thing that had not happened to me before. A man at the door in a uniform and a tall hat called me 'Sir'. I was 12 years old and I was told to order whatever I wanted from the menu. Well, with my rather simple tastes in food, I was a bit overwhelmed. There I was, surrounded by all sorts of glasses and plates and heavy silver-plated knives and forks and spoons, and there was some music playing and waiters and waitresses rushing about in all directions. I didn't know where to start, so I ordered a glass of water, and I remember having a large ice-cream in a tall glass flower vase (well it looked like a flower vase!), but what I ate in between the glass of water and the ice-cream I can't remember. Sometimes now when I'm in the Strand I pop into the hotel for a cup of coffee and a sticky bun, and not a great deal has changed in the intervening years; the entrance is still the same, but there's no man there with the tall hat to say 'Sir' to you.

I know I had a great liking for the comedy singer George Formby, and I bought a whole set of his records on the Red Regal Zonophone label. I think they were about 6d (2.5p) each, maybe 1s (5p). I used to play them continuously on my Aunt Amy's large radiogram. *When I'm Cleaning Windows*, *Leaning on a Lamp Post*, *Mr Wu's a Laundry Man*, *Hold Tight* and *Keep Your Seats Please* etc, etc. Amy used to go crazy hearing these songs over and over again, but eventually she got to quite like Formby's infectious laugh in his voice when he sang, and said, 'He's a cheery soul isn't he.' I thought he was marvellous!

I also remember buying a record of Bud Flanagan singing *Music Maestro Please*, a really haunting melody. Even now when I hear that song I'm transported back to the flat in West Kensington Court because that's where I remember playing it a lot. I think Bud Flanagan had a unique style, very simple and with the great warmth so typical of Jewish singers. Little did I know that one day I would be connected with Bud when he sang the signature tune to *Dad's Army* – *Who Do You Think You Are Kidding Mr Hitler?* A lot of people think that it is a wartime song: actually, it was written by Jimmy Perry and Derek Taverner especially for the series, and it was a stroke of genius to get Bud Flanagan to record it – the last engagement he undertook before he died.

While my mother was in hospital I used to receive small parcels of Nestle's Crackermilk chocolate bars. These were very rich with small pieces of nuts in them, very fat making and not good for an already slightly fat boy. As my aunt said, 'He's the only one I know who wears out his trousers from the inside!'

Before the year was out I was taken to a pantomime at the Connaught Theatre in Worthing and apparently disgraced myself by demanding to be taken out after 10 minutes because I didn't like the ugly sisters. They were grotesque, but then of course the 'uglies' in panto are supposed to be.

I don't remember anything about seeing 1938 out and the New Year in. My mother came out of hospital early in 1939 and was brought straight down to my aunt's at Roundabouts to recuperate, so at least she and I were reunited, the first time we'd met since my father had died. We stayed at Roundabouts for a while and it was decided while we were there that I should go to a private school a few miles away, just outside Storrington. The lady who ran the school was rather eccentric with a loud voice, and there only seemed to be a few pupils. I think I spent most of the time as I had in the past, looking out of the window and twitching.

When my mother was feeling strong enough, my brothers went house-hunting and eventually found a flat at Blackheath in south-east London. It was, in fact, right on the heath and was excellently situated for both my brothers work-wise. Fedge had a good train service into London and Jiggy was able to get to Vickers at Rochester by motorbike. On the boys' first visit to Blackheath, Fedge forgetfully left his briefcase on the train. In it was £25 – his year's savings. It doesn't sound much today, but in 1939 it was. After making phone calls to stations down the line and the London termini, nothing was seen of the briefcase again. Poor Fedge, he didn't deserve that stroke of misfortune after his careful savings' plans from very small earnings and the family problems of the previous year.

There were plenty of good shops in nearby Lewisham, especially the main department store Chiesmans, owned incidentally by the Cowdrey family. Son Colin was to become one of England's great cricketers. It was arranged that I should go to St Joseph's College on the heath, run by a Catholic order of brothers. I really don't remember anything about that period, but I bet there was some more twitching on my part. At least I don't remember any more diarrhoea incidents, so the teachers could not have been that intimidating.

I do remember my mother having to have all her teeth out one day, with gas, and she came home in the afternoon and immediately set about preparing my brothers' evening meal. She really had enormous resilience and courage.

The weather was pleasant that summer, and the heath was a lovely spot where cricket matches were played on Saturdays and Sundays. I think this was the summer that I went on my own to see my first professional cricket match, Kent versus Surrey in 1938. I remember waiting for a bus to go home outside the ground and I saw Laurie Fishlock, the Surrey and England opening batsman get on in front of me. I quickly followed him upstairs and asked for his autograph. I also got B.H. Valentine, the Kent player, to sign my book. Those were the days when players travelled by bus and train; a lot of them did this until the 1960s, when the motorcar really took over.

In the 1980s I went to speak at a dinner at the Oval, Surrey's headquarters, and who should be sitting next to me but Laurie Fishlock. I told him how I got his autograph on the bus all those years back; of course, he didn't remember, but said he was glad I thought he had been polite after a long day's cricket.

I woke up one morning in early August at Blackheath, pulled the curtains back in my bedroom, and oh my Lord! Outside my window moving about in the breeze was a gigantic grey and silver balloon. To see that for the first time, close up and still with sleep in my eyes, really was a shock. There were several that morning over the heath, practising manoeuvres in case of war. They were manned by groups of, I think, RAF personnel on the ground. When everyone got over the shock, they naturally provoked a lot of interest.

I am pretty sure my mother and brother had feelings of foreboding – and they were not unfounded; in the very next few weeks the preparations for war gained momentum. Come 1 September and there appeared to be no doubt that a conflict would come. It had been arranged that Gigi's family and ours would be descending on Aunt Amy and Uncle Teddy in Sussex. I seem to remember that we joined my cousins for the journey south, so perhaps we had left Blackheath before 1 September and spent a night or two with them at Erith. Anyway See-Saw at Roundabouts had been prepared for this influx of families, seven or eight in all. What fun it was going to be!

I remember vividly the hours before the Prime Minister's speech at 11 o'clock on 3 September. We had been to church and came back to find most people in a quiet mood, wondering what we were going to hear. There were a lot of people in the house: Amy, Teddy, their son and daughter, my mother and we three brothers and three cousins and their mother Gigi. We younger ones were strolling in the garden and just before 11 o'clock my uncle opened the white French windows and turned the radio up. Big Ben chimed and Neville Chamberlain spoke those never to be forgotten words, 'Unless we heard from Herr Hitler by 11 o'clock this morning that he was prepared to withdraw his troops from Poland, this country would have no option but to consider ourselves at war with Germany. We have received no such undertaking, therefore this country is at war with Germany.'

You could have heard a pin drop. There was silence except for my uncle who said to my aunt, 'Have you put the potatoes on for lunch?' As the ice was broken we were about to go indoors when the air raid siren sounded. Someone said, 'My God they've started.' However, the all clear went very soon afterwards and everyone heaved a sigh of relief. In fact the radar had picked up an unidentified aircraft coming over the coast that turned out to be French. Most people settled down to discuss the momentous news, except, I think, we kids who were chattering about exploring the lovely countryside round about, of which I knew a little having stayed at See-Saw before. Someone said, 'It will all be over by Christmas', but they didn't say which one. I'm sure my mother and her sister Gigi were very apprehensive at the thought of their sons having to go to war. Pat Tobin had already volunteered for the army in 1937 and been drafted to Shanghai. He was in the Royal West Kent Regiment and sub-sequently was sent to Singapore where he was captured by the Japanese, and his terrible nightmare, along with so many others, started. Peter and Gayne, who had been left back in Erith with their father, were of the right age, so too were my brothers Jiggy and Fedge. Little did we know that three out of five of those boys would not see the war out or their families again once it was over. Yes, things would never be quite the same. 3 September 1939 had a lot to answer for.

# 3 SHRAPNEL AND CARROT CAKE

The period from September 1939 until May 1940, when the invasion of Belgium started, became known as the Phoney War as there was no land action involving British forces. But the war at sea certainly wasn't phoney; the German U–Boats were plundering our merchant shipping with great loss of life. Things at home didn't seem to be too bad – there was rationing, but those living in the country weren't badly affected. Of course there were grumblings about shortages of specific foods, but nobody was actually starving.

The wireless kept spirits up with broadcasts from factories 'somewhere in England', such as *Music While You Work* and *Workers' Playtime* where various established performers of the day would, for half an hour at lunch time, regale the listeners with songs and impressions, and comedians with topical jokes about Adolf and his henchmen. A typical song of the day was *We're Going to Hang Out the Washing on the Siegfried Line*, a parody about the German defences. The joke was not to last long but the song has, as has also Flanagan and Allen's rendering of *Run Rabbit Run*, which was written by Noel Gay following a German bomber's lone flight over the Shetland Islands when a few rabbits were killed by a stray bomb.

The one radio programme into which everybody tuned once a week was *ITMA (It's That Man Again),* starring Tommy Handley. Written by Ted Kavanagh and produced by Francis Worsley, it became cult listening with Tommy surrounded by actors and actresses portraying some wonderful topical characters. Maurice Denham played Mrs Fickle and Vodka (who got people's names mixed up), a pig and a hen. Sydney Keith was

American Sam-Scram and his henchman Ali Ooop was played by Horace Percival. Dorothy Summers was Mrs Mopp with the catch-phrase as she burst through the office door, 'Can I do you now, Sir?' Jack Train was Colonel Chinstrap, who had celebrated every event since Mafeking and was always slightly inebriated; he answered, 'I don't mind if I do, Sir,' to almost any question he was asked. Train was also 'Funf', a character based on Lord Haw-Haw who broadcast propaganda messages regularly from Germany. (Actually Haw-Haw's real name was William Joyce. He was a British subject who had joined Moseley's British Union of Fascists and moved to Germany in 1939. He was hanged after the war in 1946.) Clarence Wright and Paula Green were a couple of commercial travellers.

**Commercial Traveller:** Good morning.
**Tommy Handley:** Good gracious.
**Commercial Traveller:** Nice day.
**Tommy Handley:** Delightful.
**Commercial Traveller:** Any tonics, tinctures or pick-me-ups?
**Tommy Handley:** No.
**Commercial Traveller:** I'll call again.
**Tommy Handley:** Good morning.
**Commercial Traveller:** Nice day.

Everything was very fast and the programme was the forerunner of many other radio shows to come. There were more crazy characters and their catch-phrases in *ITMA* than in practically any other radio show since.

I had been placed at a small private school near Roundabouts, run by a Felix Eames, whose wife was the local doctor. This was the first of several major turning points in my life, as my education up to then had been at best sketchy and at worst non-existent. Felix was rather eccentric, and if the pupils seemed a bit bored with the subject he was trying to put across he would say, 'It's a lovely day, why don't we all go for a bike ride and study the countryside.' So off we would all go, sometimes up Bury Hill towards Arundel, and when we were all puffed out he would say, 'Now this lovely plant on the bank here is sometimes called a weed, but in France, which I visit regularly, it is a precious flower.' We would all agree it was a very fine plant and continue on our way.

Felix laughed a lot and schooling became fun, and we did actually try to learn something in between those cycle rides. He was a very arty character: woodwork lessons were a joy and he taught me how to do lino cuts. This proved quite intricate but fascinating to learn and was a crafty way to teach me to write properly. He suggested that I do a lino cut Christmas card as he had a very simple printing press which would turn out 50 or 60 of my cards at a time. He suggested I should sell them to relations and friends, but said I would have to sign each one. The thought of making money spurred me on to practise my signature, which all along had been Felix's idea so that I would get some order into my writing. I went on to sell them at a penny a time, I think – I'm surprised he didn't ask for 10 per cent of my takings, but that would never have occurred to him; the word commission hadn't reached the public at that time.

By the end of 1939 my cousins, the Tobins, had returned to their home in Erith to be reunited with the rest of the family, convinced by the Phoney War and lack of enemy activity that all was safe back in the suburbs of London. My mother and I made the occasional trip into Worthing, which had had its peacetime picture of tranquillity spoilt by rolls and rolls of barbed wire all along the promenade and pier, and the kiosks and little cafes had been closed. One little thing that used to catch my eye on the way to Worthing and back was a house with green tiles at Broadwater; believe it or not the house is still there, I passed it quite recently and remembered it vividly.

Early in 1940 Mum and I moved from Sussex to stay with her cousin Cis at Westcliff-on-Sea in Essex. She had a flat in the Hamlet Court Road next to the Queen's Hotel and the railway station. The hotel used to have dances every Saturday night and some of the big bands of the day played there. It was well attended by servicemen, particularly sailors who were setting up headquarters in requisitioned hotels on the sea front.

Cissy O'Reilly was a widow and very good company. She looked after her daughter, a very pretty girl called Pat, and her mother. Cissy's husband, Bill, had been a great character and a bit of a madman, in the nicest possible way. When he was driving his car one day he came across a hole in the road and decided he could drive his car over it, not realising there were men working in it. Luckily he missed them but I'll bet the workmen were surprised! Bill O'Reilly used to like a drink or two, and one night he came home a little worse for wear and decided to boil himself a cup of milk. He fell asleep near the stove and the milk boiled over, putting the flame out, but the gas stayed on and he died of gas inhalation. Cissy found him in the kitchen the next morning. It must have been a terrible shock for her. She, like most of my mother's side of the family, had a good sense of humour and she needed it.

The general public was cut off from the sea along the promenade at Westcliff and other stretches of the coastline by rolls of barbed wire, except the open air swimming pool between Westcliff and Southend. This seemed strange but once the late spring was with us, and people started using the pool, it really was super. Behind the barbed wire the old fashioned bathing machines, so popular before the war started, were still standing; my mother, who had visited Westcliff many years before, spoke very fondly of them. I remember her saying, 'When they go,' which they would once the elements got hold of them, if not Hitler, 'It will be the end of a gentle age as we knew it.'

We stayed at Westcliff in a flat of our own until after the fall of France, which certainly made things look pretty bad for this country as Hitler had over-run practically the whole of Europe. The one bright bit of news, if you can call evacuation and surrender bright, was Dunkirk, when 330,000 Allied service personnel were picked off the beaches in northern France, to fight again another day. It was a triumph for all concerned, particularly for those people from all over the UK who took little boats across the Channel to help pick up the troops.

My brother Jiggy was about to enlist from his reserved occupation at Vickers Armstrong so he suggested we came up to

Wilmington, near Dartford in Kent, to be near his friends, the Cobbetts. He had found us a small bungalow in the area, so off my mother and I went to be part of one of the most amazing periods of the war. Fedge had been in the Royal Army Medical Corps since 1939, and I vividly remember Jiggy – before we left Sussex for Westcliff – driving my mother and me to Crookham in Hampshire to visit Fedge just after he joined up. We parked on the edge of the parade ground waiting for him to appear, and as he emerged and began marching very smartly towards us, my mother started to cry. She was obviously very moved to see her young son approaching in his uniform. What a time it was for mums all over the country and for sensitive lads like Fedge, thrown into a situation so different to their cosy family existence. Fedge, of course, had already been through a baptism of fire with all the problems when my father died.

However, let's get back to our move to Kent. Our new abode was a bungalow in Birchwood Road, Wilmington (on Dartford Heath), with a pleasant outlook onto fields. I was sent to Dartford Technical College, but all I remember doing there was making a few metal objects; it was, however, a bit more exciting than trying to take in the ordinary lessons. I used to travel into Dartford by bus, and as air activity increased over the south of England, the journey was sometimes accompanied by dogfights in the sky between Spitfires, Hurricanes and Messerschmitts, but it was nothing compared to what was to come. At the time it was a pleasant life with people cooking experimental dishes of all descriptions because of rationing: fish dishes with hard dried lumps of fish that came from Norway, omelettes with dried egg-powder, beetroot jam and carrot cake.

Anthony Eden, the Foreign Secretary, broadcast a message to ask all young men under call-up age and all those over 60 to join the new Local Defence Volunteer Force. There would be area and small group commanders who, it was hoped, would have had some experience of war in World War 1. Before Eden's broadcast had finished, police stations all over the country were inundated with potential recruits. My uncle Bill Tobin was one of them and, having been through a previous war finishing as a captain, with several single-handed escapades against the Germans, he was a valuable recruit. He carried a legacy of the war in the form of pieces of shrapnel still in his body; these used to surface every now and again, and he would remove them with a small knife.

Captain Bill Tobin marched into his local police station and told the sergeant at the desk that he was taking over command of the LDV in his district, 'As from now.' Apparently, according to my Uncle Bill, the sergeant was a bit of a Robb Wilton character, and started shuffling papers around saying he'd take down his particulars. My uncle wasn't having that, and said he would inform the Chief Constable. That seemed to settle it. He went straight home, and although he and his family lived in quite a small road, immediately started single-handedly to remove some of the large furniture from the house and make a barrier of it across the road. His wife, Aunt Gigi, asked him what he was doing and he said, 'Well they won't get through if they come tonight.' I believe Gigi just laughed as she normally did when the 'Captain' did anything eccentric. This incident reminds me of a similar situation that was portrayed in the full length film we made of *Dad's Army* with Warden Hodges remonstrating with Mainwaring when he blocked a road in a similar fashion.

Back at home in Wilmington we had news that my brother Jiggy had been released from Vickers and had enlisted in the RAF as aircrew. Now mother had two of her sons in the services – which, of course, worried her sick. The daylight raids by German bombers escorted by fighters were now increasing and dogfights took place overhead almost every day. These were riveting to watch, and when a plane was hit, you could see the pilot baling out and floating down by parachute. One day a German pilot came down in the field just near our bungalow: as he was gathering up his parachute and sorting himself out a couple of Local Defence volunteers, armed with sticks (their only weapons at that time were pitchforks and broomsticks), went rushing into the field and started doing a sort of war dance around the German pilot with unintelligible cries. The poor pilot fainted and was only revived when a policemen arrived on the scene to make an arrest. I remember my mother saying, 'That man [the pilot] is so young, he's some mother's son. I hope he'll be all right!'

The month of August was crucial in the battle of the skies: the Luftwaffe started attacks in earnest on the 13th. Royal Air Force fighters replied with a skill and ferocity the Germans had not experienced in their conquests hitherto. The raids culminated in the major attack of 15 September (my brother Fedge's birthday incidentally) when the Luftwaffe made one last attempt to smash the RAF by daylight. The battle lasted all day and at the time it was estimated that the Spitfires and Hurricanes had shot down some 185 German aircraft – although this was something of an over-estimate and the true figure was nearer 60. There had, of course, been heavy RAF losses, but Goering would have to try a new tack and it wasn't long before he did so. However, the Battle of Britain, as it was to become known, had effectively been won, bringing those wonderful words from Prime Minister Churchill to our fighter pilots, 'Never in the field of human conflict, was so much owed, by so many, to so few.'

My mother and I had been shopping in Dartford one Saturday and while we were waiting at the bus stop to go home, heavy formations of German bombers started flying towards London using the River Thames as their guide. Before we got on the bus you could see the glow from the fires that the first wave of bombers had created around south-east London. By the time we got home we could hear more waves of aircraft coming in. This was the start of the night-time attacks on London.

Dartford Heath, which was about half a mile from our bungalow, was completely covered with anti-aircraft guns and they were banging away into the early hours of the morning. Shrapnel from their shells fell everywhere, some of the pieces were still red-hot when they landed. We lads had a great time next day picking up these shards as souvenirs. I think the firing of the anti-aircraft guns was mainly for morale purposes – to let people know we were fighting back – because they seemed only to bring down the occasional bomber: it was a comfort at

the time to think we were having a go. The night raids continued, devastating not only whole areas of London, but also
Coventry, Plymouth and other centres. It really was remarkable
how people coped with the air raids: the domestic services did
such a wonderful job, the police, the firemen, the air raid war-
dens, fire watchers, and the nurses and doctors, all of them carrying on day after day, night after night, without sleep or respite.

Late in 1940 Amy and Teddy thought it was time we left the
Dartford area and went back to the country. They knew of a
bungalow that was to let at Findon on the outskirts of
Worthing, some 10 miles away from Roundabouts. We moved
in there and soon settled down; I went back to Mr Eames's
school, which meant a daily bus ride from Findon. Life was fairly uneventful, my brothers were writing home regularly and
Fedge sent the odd bit of money he managed to save from his
meagre army pay.

Jiggy had progressed with his flying training, first with Tiger
Moths, then with Avro Ansons and Airspeed Oxfords. He finished his final course towards the end of May and was posted to
an operational squadron at Dishforth in Yorkshire flying Whitley
bombers. Before that he was sent on leave. He spent the first
few days with his friends Florence and Frank Cobbett at
Wilmington before coming on to stay with us at Findon for the
rest. My mother really made a fuss of him and was extremely
proud to see him in his Pilot Officer's uniform. I remember taking him in tea each morning before going to school. When he
had finished his leave, my mother and I went to Worthing station to see him off on his journey to Yorkshire. He told us he
wouldn't be operational for a while as he would be a newcom-
er to the squadron. This was confirmed in a letter he wrote to
my mother after he arrived. He said everything was fine, his fellows were a nice lot, and he was looking forward to flying again,
something he had always thought about as a young lad.

The letter arrived on the Monday morning, which pleased
my Mum. A few hours later there was a knock on the door. It
was a policeman who said he regretted to have to tell her that
her son had been killed flying back from Germany on the

Sunday night. I wasn't there, as I had already left for school. God knows what must have gone through her head, particularly as she had just read his letter – all the memories that must have flashed through her mind: when she'd nursed him through his terrible excema problems as a baby, the pride of seeing him grow into a most handsome young man, enjoying his engineering career at Vickers and his final ambitions in the RAF finally realised. What else could happen to Mum's already tragic life – it all seemed unbelievable.

Apparently Jiggy had been on a leaflet-dropping mission to Dortmund in the Ruhr on the Sunday night and, coming back over the coast at Middlesbrough, his co-pilot and captain of the aircraft had been informed that Dishforth, the home aerodrome, was shrouded in fog and they were redirected to Driffield. It was believed their altimeter had been shot up and there was a wrong reading regarding their height. Anyway, they crashed into the Pennines and there were no survivors. The irony of that night was that the fog over Dishforth had quickly cleared and it wouldn't have been a problem landing there after all. Amy quickly made arrangements for my mother and myself to come back to See-Saw for the time being. I had been met at school on the Monday afternoon and was told the news. I can't remember what my reaction was except that I spent a long time in the garden during the evening just walking about.

Fedge, and Jiggy's great friend Frank Cobbett, attended the funeral in Dishforth's small cemetery on the edge of the aerodrome. One of Jiggy's crew was also buried there, Flt Sgt Cousins. My mother later reported to me that Fedge was told by one of the airmen at the funeral that the Whitleys were called coffin ships, because of their construction and slow speed. I have visited the cemetery many times when I've been working in Yorkshire and Teesside and it is in a very quiet and peaceful location. The local pub in the village, where the airmen from the aerodrome used to have their pints, is a charming place, and has been a welcome stop-off for me when I've been in the area. The last time I was there I had been to nearby Thirsk racecourse with some folk from a play I was in at the time. I remember that day's racing well, as a horse I had backed actually 'walked' home last; as it passed it turned its head to me and sighed as if to say, 'Well you do better!' I also remember one of the course bookies coming up to me and saying, 'I hear your old mate Kenneth Williams has just died.' It was a bit of a shock, but nothing about Kenneth surprised me too much.

I think during this period in the 1940s my mother drew tremendous strength from her religion. She was a very good Roman Catholic but was also mindful of other religions, after all my father was Church of England and a good man. I remember he always drove my mother to her church at Hay-on-Wye when we lived in Glasbury.

Amy's house did not have enough room to let us sleep there: her son Bobby was at home because his asthma was playing up badly and her daughter 'Mutt' (Evelyn) was living there as well. At first a caravan was organised for Mum and me to sleep in, parked in the woods surrounding the house; later we found a bungalow on the road between Roundabouts and Storrington, rather nearer the latter. This was around the time when I really got into village life: I had made friends in Roundabouts on my various stays there. Richard Barnes and his sister Penelope, who was mad on horses, came from a nice family. Their mother, who had been a teacher, and her husband, who owned an electrical shop in Worthing, were always pleased to see me. It was there that I had my first experience of watching television, on a very small set Mr Barnes had brought back from the shop. The poor man died quite young, after a very simple operation. His son Richard became a very good accountant and is now retired and living near Bognor Regis in Sussex.

A small shy lad whose surname was Robb lived in a nearby house. His father was Air Vice Marshal Robb, who later had a lot to do with the Second Front operations. Peter Cellier, the son of a famous actor, was another boy I knew. Peter has also made his way in the theatre with starring parts in London, films and a TV series. He doesn't live far from me now in Surrey. Another family we got to know were the Levesons. Mother was a real extrovert and was always having parties, even with rationing as it was. Her husband owned and ran a dry cleaning firm in Baker Street in London and was only at home at weekends. He was very charming and both parents were reflected in their sons: John the eldest, Peter and Tony. I have met John several times since those days and I think all the boys are now retired after following in their father's type of business.

In spite of the friendships at Roundabouts, as I've said, I met a different sort of folk in Storrington. I joined the scouts and did a bit of boxing, though without much success, and played some football. I was mixing with a lot of the young people who had been evacuated from their city homes. Living with strange families, there was a certain camaraderie amongst them and all of them, it seemed, went to the same local school. Storrington people took these children to their hearts, and I think the children actually enjoyed their new country surroundings. The shopkeepers got to know the kids and the 'Home Made Bakers' used to give some of them a sticky bun or two.

In the house opposite us there was a tall girl with a jolly laugh. Many years later I went to see a production of *The Mousetrap* at the Ambassadors Theatre and who should be playing one of the leading parts but the girl from across the road in Storrington, Mary Law. We had a great reunion that night. I met her again one day as I was boarding a plane for Canada; she hadn't changed, the jolly laugh was still there.

There was also a coincidence regarding our nextdoor neighbours, the Smiths. I saw Mrs Smith walking up the garden one day to the shed which, amongst other things, was used as a clothes washing house. After a while she walked back and said to me over the fence, 'I've had a baby daughter.' In my immaturity I thought to myself, 'Fancy having a baby in the shed when they live in a bungalow.' Actually she had had a baby girl that morning, and I'm sure indoors. Many, many, years later when I was performing in Sunday concerts at Butlin's Holiday Camps, a tall, strikingly beautiful girl came up to me and said, 'I was born in the next bungalow to you when my parents lived in Storrington.' It was Mr and Mrs Smith's daughter – now that was a coincidence.

I had a serious swimming accident during the summer of 1941 at Eames School, which I was once again attending. I was going through an undisciplined period, doing crazy things, taking chances and generally being stupid. One afternoon while swimming I decided to experiment with some acrobatic diving: I tried a somersault, couldn't pull out in time and banged my head on the bottom of the pool, knocking myself unconscious. There was only one person about, a boy we called Flugey (for what reason I can't remember). He was rather tubby and couldn't swim, but he jumped in and pulled me to the side until help arrived. I was unconscious off and on for a few days and it was arranged that I should see a specialist Aunt Amy knew, a German who had got out of Germany in the mid-1930s. His name was Rau and he gave me a good going over. He said I must have a lot of rest and put me on a course of tablets called Routinal, I think, which would make me sleep. As if my mother hadn't had enough to put up with, here was I giving her more grief. I could never remember Flugey's real name, and it was only just a few years ago that I found out it was Ernie Wallace. I would love to see him again.

At this time I started to have fainting spells: they didn't last long and my mother was told I was just rushing about too much, too soon after the accident. Shortly afterwards I was out on my bike trying to keep up with a bus when it suddenly pulled up as a dog dashed out into the road. I was too near the back of the bus and hit it. Luckily my head was spared another bang but I did come off my bike and my nose took a glancing blow which probably didn't help its already rather flat shape!

I remember one night I heard an aeroplane flying pretty low – quite rare deep in the heart of the country – and the noise was followed by several dull thuds. It wasn't until the next morning that we learned a German bomber had flown off course and had decided to drop its load of bombs to lighten itself, thus extending its flying time. About five bombs had been dropped in a field not far away and none of them had gone off, which was surprising. The army bomb disposal unit was quickly on the job of digging them out and making them safe. I knew the families whose houses backed on to the field; one of them had come down from London and the other from the Southend area. The husbands used to come down at weekends from their businesses and a close friendship developed between us all – later this was to play an important part in my working life and sporting activities. The two families were related by marriage, one being the Goodliffes, the other the Wauds.

I was making myself a nuisance at home by getting very intense; when, for instance, I was making model aircraft from plastic kits, if I couldn't get things quite right at first I would throw a tantrum, even occasionally refusing to go to bed until I had tried to put the mistakes right. My poor mother must have gone through several traumas with me, and she had no man in the house to give me a good clip round the ear. Mr Eames at school also used to get cross with me, and although he was a generous teacher and I really liked him, he could be quite stern. I remember once when I was paying no attention to a French lesson (heavens, I could hardly read English, never mind a foreign language) Felix Eames told me to go to his study. I picked him up, carried him out to the swimming pool and threw him in. I did get the stick for that, but the incident passed off and we continued being the best of friends.

In 1941 Canadian troops started arriving in large numbers in the area. A huge park surrounding a beautiful house quite near us at Storrington became the headquarters of one division. Once they had settled in, the other ranks started making friends with the young girls in the village. The young officers were rather shy, so some of us lads started a sort of dating agency with the slightly posher girls. We would arrange meeting places where they could chat one another up and after initial introductions it was up to them. In return for our services the Canadians would supply us with cigarettes – Sweet Caporal and Camels – tins of ham and other delicacies which they seemed to have in abundance. These we would distribute in the village for payment, at least for the cigarettes.

Some of the soldiers coming back from the village late at night used to knock on our bungalow door and ask if they could come in for a while. My mother used to let them in and make them tea because she didn't want them waking me up with their continual knocking. When she told someone about this they said, 'You shouldn't do it, if you don't know them,' and my mother said, 'Oh they're nice lads, just homesick and they're some mother's sons.' Mum certainly was an extraordinary woman. I suppose she was thinking about Jiggy after his recent death, and would have hoped he would have found some refuge if he had needed it when he was a serviceman.

Meantime it had been decided that I should leave school and get a job, outdoors if possible, which would be good for me after my swimming accident problems. I was engaged by a Mr Gatley who was a well-known farmer in the area. I did all sorts of jobs around the place, and at one point was put in charge of looking after some young calves. Unfortunately they had ring-worm which transferred itself to me. My legs and ankles became badly affected, large white raised circles all over the place. Dr Eames, the wife of my teacher, was called in and painted my legs with iodine and then wrapped them up in plaster from toe to knee. Within 24 hours I had become a raging inferno with a blistering temperature. The doctor was called and she decided to rip all the plaster off to give my legs some air – the agony of this was dreadful, and it left scars visible to this day.

However another trauma was duly over, my mother breathed another sigh of relief and I went back to the farm – but only for a short time. One day I was driving a tractor back into the yard from an outside job when I drove straight into the sur-rounding brick wall. Mr Gatley said, 'I think he'll have to go, he's a disaster area.' So my farming days were numbered.

With Jiggy's death and Fedge by December on his way to the Middle Eastern theatre of war, 1941 was a dreadful year for the Pertwee family, as it was for so many others. It was also the year that the bombing of Pearl Harbor by the Japanese brought America into the war. During the year it was suggested that Mum and I should move back to Westcliff-on-Sea. My mother's cousin, Cis O'Reilly, was now in a bigger flat in Valkyrie Road, only a stone's throw from her previous one.

*Grandfather Henry James (Tiny) Thompson, Grandmother Anna (née Da Silva Pinto, standing) and Great Grandmother Joanna Da Silva Pinto photographed in Rio in 1886.*

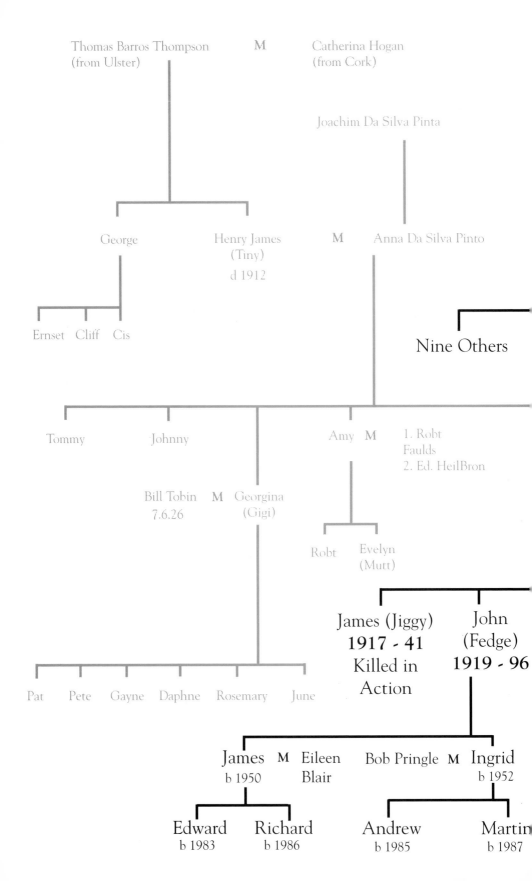

George Pertuis          Exile from France
1634 - 1689

Geogre died at Fingeringhoe
1711

George   M   Jane De Brise
                at St Giles, Colchester 1702

John          M          Mary
b 1714

James         M          Martha Rowley
b 1756

James         M          Mary Vaines
1798 - 1861

James   M   1. Eliza  Cooper          Emma Bickstone   M   Charles
1823 - 1914    2. Harriet Carter

Dulce Adelina   M   1. Fred. Mackie
1890 -1979              2. James Francis Carter          Ernest
                            1879 - 1938

Roland                          Guy

Bill   M   Marion Macleod
b 1926

Michael                          Jon
                                    1919 - 96

Jonathan          Carolyn   Tim      Tara
b 1966            b 1941    b 1962   b 1965

Dariell                          Sean
b 1961                          b 1964

*Far left: My jolly Grandfather Henry James Thompson in 1902.*

*Left: Grandmother Anna c. 1894.*

*Left: My Mother Dulce Adelina Thompson, photographed in Rio sometime in the early 1900s.*

*Right: Marion's Mum, Maudie, in* Der Rosen Cavalier *at Covent Garden in 1913.*

*Above: My Father James Francis Carter Pertwee in Bournemouth in 1918. 'Is it time for my whisky?'*

*Right: 'I've arrived and to prove it I'm here.' In 1927 with Mum and Dad.*

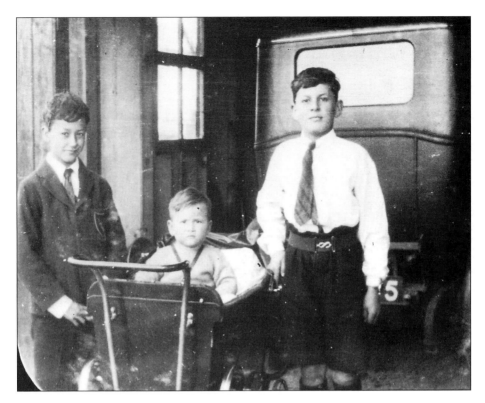

*Above: 'I'd rather go in the car.' Fedge, me and Jiggy in 1928.*

*Left: 'That ball was not out Umpire!' Myself aged about four in 1930 – how do you like my modern tennis gear?*

GOW.85 GENERAL VIEW, GLASBURY ON WYE

*Above: A 1930s postcard featurng our lovely vicarage, right on the bend of the river.*

*Right: Marion, a confident seven-year old, on the front at Broadstairs in 1935.*

*Far right: My brother Jiggy in his RAF uniform in 1941. No wonder Mum was proud of him.*

*Above: Jiggy's career as a pilot lasted for but a few days.*

*Right: In 1943 Fedge was in the Middle East trying to fool Rommel's Afrika Korps.*

*Mushtaq Ali: unfortunately he never did play for Marine.*

*Left: Vijay Merchant – the brilliant Indian opening batsman.*

*Below: The England and Indian teams in 1946: Len Hutton is sitting second from left with Dennis Compton standing just behind him.*

*Left: Len Hutton (left) and the Revd David Sheppard (later Bishop of Liverpool) walking out to the wicket for the Duke of Norfolk's XI against the 1956 Australians. Sheppard was called up for the fourth test at Manchester and scored a brilliant century, helping England to win the series. But everyone will remember it as 'Laker's Match'.*

*Far left: The incomparable Edrich and Compton on their way to more records in 1947.*

*Below: Yours Truly showing how it should be done at Hastings in the 1970s!*

*My early cabaret act in 1956 – pulling faces.*

*Left: Top of the bill in the 1950s, Marion's brothers, right top and bottom.*

*Below: 'Comedy Cocktail' – Marion and me on the variety circuit in 1956. Was the country ready for us?*

*The Watergate Revue in 1954. Pulling faces again; with Beryl Reid, Douglas Argent (centre) and Barry Barton.*

*Above: 'You're a professional now Son'. 'Summertime' Gorleston, Norfolk in 1955. Left to right standing: Cliff Hensley, Flo Lutman, Alice Dells, Henry Lutman, Mary Gale, Pam Lutman, me. Kneeling: Marion, Pam Leithay and Dinah Kaye.*

*Right: 1958-9. Huntley and Palmer's Workers' Playtime, Reading. In the background, Bert Weedon, one of the most influential British guitarists of the 1950s and 1960s.*

*Marion in the title role in* Aladdin *at Torquay in* 1957. *Ooh, she was good!*

*My first real taste of the cameras in 1961.*

*Above: Jonathan in 1966, only six months old and already a new member of Sussex County Cricket Club.*

*Right: My dear old Mum in Bognor Regis in 1968.*

*Right: Jonathan in full uniform aged four, ready to go to his first school in 1970.*

*Far right, top: What a wonderful picture of the young Pertwees in Canterbury in 1988! The four grandchildren: from left to right, Andrew, Edward, Richard and Martin.*

*Far right, bottom: A very proud Grandfather Fedge with Edward and Richard. (All clap hands.)*

*Below: A happy family: from left to right, James and Ingrid with their mum and dad.*

*Michael Pertwee — a really jolly fellow.*

*Dear Bunty and Norman in 1990.*

*Above: Biffa, our last dog.*

*Above right: The Swinging Seventies: at home at the Old Rectory.*

*Below right: A night out with the Water Rats: from left, a friend
– Deborah Snelling – Jonathan and Marion.*

*Above: Another evening with the Water Rats: Marion and me with Michael Robbins and his actress wife Hal Dyer.*

*Above left: Son Jonathan (James) filming in Russia with Oliver Reed in 1995 – 'What do you mean the bar's closed?'*

*Left: Jonathan's pen and ink drawing of actor Clint Eastwood. Not bad, is it? I think so, but I'm his Dad.*

# C|OUPLE|S

What makes a partnership work?
In this series YOU follows the course of true love . . . for better or for worse

# Marion and her Warden

You *magazine: 'She's stubborn,' says Bill.*
*'He's bossy,' says Marion.*

I am not quite sure whether we made this move at the end of that year or early in 1942, probably the latter. I'm also not sure why we did move. Certainly we were less likely to be in danger of air raids in the Sussex countryside than being in the area of the Thames Estuary which was used to guide German bombers into London. Perhaps Storrington had decided they'd had enough of me! I know we left Gyp, our dog, in Storrington, or rather he left us for the Canadian brigade which was camped nearby. I expect the food was more plentiful and he always did make friends with anyone who gave him the odd tit-bit of posh grub. I know we later heard that it was thought he'd gone on the Dieppe raid with the Canadians; I know we never heard anything more of him. Perhaps he was taken prisoner by the Germans after the Dieppe raid – he wouldn't have minded at all had they fed him well. If we'd known where he was we could have sent him a Red Cross doggy parcel!

On arrival in Westcliff I was found a place at Southend College, which is, I think, the headquarters of the Access credit card company now. After a few months there I got a job at the Southend Motor and Aero Club (SMAC). In peacetime the club had some sort of tie-up with the big Kursaal Funfair just past the famous Southend Pier. The SMAC used to do all the repairs to the funfair rides and other vehicles such as the bumper cars. Now it was engaged on war business, and one of the jobs was making parts for the Spitfire's cannons. We had to do night-shift work at times, and during the food breaks we used to make simple petrol cigarette lighters out of brass off-cuts. You could generally get a couple of shillings (10p) for these from your friends.

SMAC was next door to the Regal Theatre and we were often given complimentary tickets to see the variety shows, but I can't remember ever taking advantage of the offer: I wasn't really interested. I joined the Air Training Corps in the area which gave me a chance to play some cricket at the weekends. We had big club rooms in the town where you could play table tennis and snooker; there were also the usual parades, and we took part in special occasion marches through the town.

In spite of the wartime atmosphere Southend was a busy place, with some eating places 'open as usual' and cinemas still presenting twice daily performances. Near where we were living at Westcliff there was the Mascot Cinema and the Metropole. The former showed anything they could get hold of and was a bit primitive, but the Metropole was quite big and comfortable showing more up-to-date movies. Cissy and her daughter and Mum and I used to go to one or the other place at least once a week. One super American musical we saw at the Metropole was *Words and Music*, the story of the writing partnership of Richard Rogers and Lorenz Hart. It was chock full of wonderful melodies sung by all the popular Broadway and Hollywood stars of the day. Every now and again a notice would go up on the screen saying 'the air raid siren has sounded', but no one seemed to take any notice as far as I remember. When the 'all clear' sign was flashed up there was always a big cheer.

Every Friday night there was a 45-minute talent show before the big picture started, this was always very popular and some of it was really good entertainment. There was a resident compère who presented the whole thing very well and even made the losers feel good. When we came out cousin Cis would always get two bottles of stout to take home from the nearby pub's off sales department, and no matter whether the air raid warning was still on or not, the only thing that worried her was getting the stout home safely!

I was also taken to the theatre for the first time, at least to see a play right through after the abortive attempt to see the pantomime a few years before at Worthing. The play at the Palace Theatre, Westcliff, was *Journey's End*, a famous play about life in the trenches in World War 1. Otherwise sport was taking up a lot of my leisure time and I started playing squash with Cissy's daughter, my third cousin Pat, at Southend. Pat was very good and generally beat me. One very hot evening the manager of the hotel, whom we had got to know pretty well, bought us a couple of drinks and on the way home along the lovely Marine Gardens we sat down for a rest and in no time we found ourselves getting rather amorous with one another. I think it was an experimental time for both of us, but we had the common-sense (or at least Pat did) to forget about the incident. We were both about 16 going on 17 so by today's standards I suppose we were quite old to be experimenting.

Pat went on to become a top model even having her picture on the front cover of one issue of *Vogue* magazine, which made her mother very proud. Pat eventually married a very nice chap called Laurie who had a family furriers business in London. He died a few years later which was a shock to everyone. I met Pat in London once in the 1950s when I was trying to make a living early in my career and when she heard that things weren't going too well for me she gave me some money. She had always been a generous lass. We met again very briefly in the 1960s in an antique shop at Arundel in Sussex. She was then living in nearby Angmering but we lost contact after that and I have not seen her since, even though I have tried to trace her address there.

Cissy had two brothers, Ernie and Cliff. Ernie was a little eccentric and was a great coin collector and used to come in to see us and very proudly say, 'Look at this, I purchased it an auction the other day,' and produce some obscure coin wrapped in tissue paper. When Ernie died many years later his coin collection was valued and was worth a great deal of money. The other brother, Cliff, worked at the Aircraft Establishment at Farnborough. He decided quite late in life to marry and for a while he was obviously very happy, but while he and his wife were returning home after a visit to London there was an air raid near Clapham Junction and his wife was actually blown out of the railway carriage door and killed. Cliff was devastated, and almost became a recluse. He spent his last years living in a room above the 'Bird in Hand' pub near Farnborough.

There were a few special occasions in the Air Training Corps (ATC) when we were given the chance to fly in the aircraft based at Rochford Aerodrome just outside Southend. This had been in the front line during the Battle of Britain but was now a sort of auxiliary airport. They had a few Airspeed Oxfords there, the type brother Jiggy had finished his flying training with. It was a great thrill going up and seeing all the surrounding countryside from the skies – sometimes the pilot would venture out over the coast a little and then come in over the pier, all very exciting for us young lads.

I remember one flight in particular: there were about four of us in the aircraft, when one of the hefty lads sat on one of the parachutes lying in the back of the plane and his seat made contact with the parachute buckle and suddenly there was piles of silk billowing around him as the chute started to open. We told the pilot and he just said 'Gather it together and stop it spreading' which we managed to do until we landed.

My mother had been getting letters from my brother Fedge on his progress in the Middle East, although details of places and times were not included for security reasons. He had gone via South Africa with a short stay in Durban before continuing to Egypt. From then on he was in and out of ambulance trains into and out of Syria while General Montgomery who had been given command in the desert, started to plan the amazing Alamein offensive. Fedge was posted now to be part of this, and in October 1942 it all came to fruition and he was heavily involved in collecting the wounded and dead on both sides and assisting in primitive operations. This was the battle which, when won, Winston Churchill called 'the end of the beginning.' If mother had known what Fedge was actually experiencing at the time she would naturally have been very upset. She did of course hear about it after the war when Fedge meticulously wrote it all down almost word for word as it happened.

My mother's sister Gigi had received news that her eldest son Pat had been captured at Singapore and subsequently was posted dead working on the Burma/Siam Railway. Pat was a large lad, about 6ft 3in and weighed about 16 stone when he left England. Through a piece I wrote about him in a recent book of mine – *Stars in Battledress* – a reader wrote to me and told me he was with Pat near the famous River Kwai just before he died when his weight was about 5½ stone. I don't think anyone will ever forgive the Japanese for their cruelty to prisoners, particularly those working on that infamous railway. A little later Gigi was to hear that one of her other sons, Gayne, had been killed in action in Italy during the Allied advance; his adventures in the army had been quite amazing as he revealed to Fedge when they met by chance in Cairo. I wish I had time to recount them here. What a time it was for mothers and wives of servicemen whose men-folk had been slaughtered just because two or three fanatical lunatics wanted to rule the world.

At Westcliff we were still experiencing air raids but somehow it didn't upset the daily routine too much, or if it did I wasn't aware of it. There was an occasion or two when I did feel frightened huddled in an air raid shelter, but my mother always appeared calm. I remember her always having her rosary so her faith in her religion must have played a part in that. If anyone has faith through their religious beliefs, in the way my mother did, then there is nothing wrong with whatever faith you belong to as long as it is not fanatical in an aggressive way as it sometimes is nowadays. I think in my mother's case it was amazing considering the cruel blows she had received in her life.

All through 1943 there was an optimistic feeling that the war was going the Allied army's way, although there were some mighty battles still to come. Personally I was still enjoying myself at SMAC and enjoying my cricket with the ATC.

One incident which was to have far reaching effects for me was a chance meeting in Southend – I can't recall how it happened. I met up again with Norman Waud: I had known him and his family in Sussex. They had lived in the house just in front of the field where the bombs landed but didn't explode. Norman and his family were now back in the area living at Leigh-on-Sea and he was General Manager of the Liverpool Victoria Insurance Society in Southend. He and I had the mutual interest of cricket and I now got to know the family very well, his wife Queenie, son Gilbert and daughter Jean. Queenie was the sister of George Goodliffe who I had also met when we were in Storrington. The Goodliffe brothers, George, Tom and Gilbert Snr had inherited a window cleaning business started by their father which they were trying to keep going.

They were a Streatham and Norwood based family although they ran the business operation from High Holborn. I also met up again with George Goodliffe. I didn't know him too well when the family were in Sussex because he was only there for short times at weekends but I did know his wife Gladys and the three children, Derek, Brian and Cynthia, quite well. Cynthia was just a baby then and apparently I used to dangle her on my knee. The boys were somewhere near my own age, so of course we played together. In 1943 George suggested I might be a help to Hamley's toy shop in London, he apparently knew the manager there. He told me that toys were very hard to come by because of the war and wondered whether I could make some wooden toys for them, (knowing of my interest in woodwork), which in fact was the only thing I had learnt from Felix Eames' school, but it's been very useful to me ever since.

However George said he could show me a fairly simple wooden truck that Hamleys sold, but the supplier couldn't provide any more, so did I think I could copy it? I started up a little 'factory' in cousin Cis's flat, cutting out sides, fronts, bottoms etc with a fretsaw, and then assembling them all together. Wheels were difficult things to find but I got some fairly primitive ones turned for me and then everything was laid out on two ironing boards. Before the parts were assembled I got my mother, Cis, and Cis's aged mother, Aunt Grace, to paint the parts. They all had particular parts in certain colours to do, one using green, the other red, and so forth. We completed a dozen and a half and Goodliffe collected them and took them to Hamleys. They were delighted and I got £2 each. They wanted some more but the household said they'd had enough of being kept up until nearly midnight, standing at the ironing board. So the 'factory' had to close, it had been fun, but hard work.

The news from Fedge in the Middle East was that he had contracted jaundice and had been withdrawn from Montgomery's pursuit of Rommel's Afrika Korps. Apparently he was moved backwards and forwards from hospital to base, and it sounded like all over Egypt and Palestine getting to know it even better than the Arab population. Once the jaundice had been sorted out he went down with diphtheria. The RAMC (Army Medical Corps) had to sort out some horrific situations as a result of men being burned and very seriously wounded. Doctors and staff, of which Fedge was one, just had to decide which cases had a chance of being saved and leaving those too far gone to die peacefully. Terrible decisions to have to make.

I remember exactly the moment we heard that the Second Front had been launched against the Germans in France. It was on 6 June 1944 and I was working at a bench in SMAC. Suddenly all the machines were shut off and the music which was always played on the factory radio was interrupted to tell us that an important announcement was to be made. You could have heard a pin drop; and then John Snagge (famous for his Oxford and Cambridge boat race commentaries) came through in that lovely controlled and dignified voice: 'Allied naval forces, supported by strong air forces, began landing Allied armies this morning on the northern coast of France.' The Second Front had begun. We all felt that it couldn't be long now; but in fact it would be almost another year before a final peace in Europe was to come about.

Quite soon after the D-Day landings Hitler unleashed his secret weapon on us, the V1 pilotless aircraft packed full of explosives and directed at London. As if the capital hadn't suffered enough from conventional bombing raids. We used to hear and see those horrible things flying up over the Thames on their way to the capital. You never knew where they were going to land; suddenly the engine would cut out and down they went, inflicting terrible damage and death on the civilian population. Occasionally a bunch of us lads would go up to London for the day and coming back on the train from Fenchurch Street we would see the odd one coming towards the capital, belching a mass of red flames from the back. Our Air Force were trying to find out where they were being launched from in northern France, and were continually bombing the suspected sites. When it was thought that the V1 attacks were lessening the Germans struck again with a V2 rocket-guided missile which would scream out of the sky from a very high altitude on to unsuspecting targets. Both the V1s and V2s did a lot of damage to the south-eastern suburbs in Kent and Essex as well as in central London. The V2s were launched from Germany itself, so it appeared that until Germany surrendered or the sites bombed out of existence – if they could be found – we would not be free from these silent weapons of destruction.

I was called up at the end of 1944 and before going for my medical, the local doctor, who had been keeping an eye on me knowing of my swimming accident in Storrington, told me I must tell the medical board that I had been taking Routinal tablets for a considerable time after the accident.

Early in 1945, having put myself down for the RAF as I was a member of the Air Training Corps, I was called for my medical. I told the chief doctor about the tablets, he put down the details and off I went. Soon after this I received a letter telling me that I had been graded C3 because of the tablets and information they had received from our doctor about the swimming accident. As the war was coming to its close (so everybody hoped) the RAF didn't want any unnecessary pensions on its hands if I should be affected by service life. My mother was very relieved, I can tell you, and I wasn't at all bothered; I went on working at SMAC and enjoying my leisure periods.

Finally the end of the war in Europe arrived, and I think everyone was numbed by the news until it sank in. My mother just cried silently, partly for joy that Fedge had been spared, and in sorrow that the war had taken Jiggy from her. I remember going up to London with a bunch of mates for the VE day celebrations. It was just an extraordinary experience. We walked from Fenchurch Street station to Trafalgar Square. Everywhere people just came up and hugged kissed you and danced in the streets. The small amount of traffic had hooters blaring. Policemen were putting their helmets on civilians who were having their photos taken with their arms round the 'law'.

We stayed up in London all day, walking through the parks and talking to complete strangers. In the afternoon Prime Minister Churchill's message was relayed to the crowds, telling us that hostilities in Europe would officially end at midnight, although Germany had actually surrendered some days before. The evening approached and we lads managed to stay together and find ourselves temporary girlfriends. One of the lads, Alan Mallet, got very friendly with a WAAF and subsequently married her. They took a pub near Maidenhead, although his profession was accountancy. Unfortunately not long afterwards they were killed in a car accident, a real tragedy that.

As we were walking, or pushing, our way up the Mall that evening we didn't realise the crowds were joined by Princess Elizabeth and her sister, Princess Margaret, who had been given permission to go out on that special evening. We of course only found out about this little incident sometime later when it became common knowledge.

We were actually in Trafalgar Square when Big Ben started to strike midnight and there was a silent few seconds before the first stroke of the hour chimed out – and then the crowd went really wild, hats were thrown in the air, people were crying and kissing and laughing, and huge chains of dancers gathered more people around them and did the conga until the group broke up through exhaustion or lack of space. The railways were running, or seemed to be, an all-night service, and although our group had been separated we managed to meet up again at Fenchurch Street for the journey back to Westcliff.

By mid summer the war with Japan was also finally over after the two atomic bombs had been dropped on Hiroshima and Nagasaki. Since then there have been arguments for and against the action of America in dropping these bombs. Perhaps some people didn't realise just what terrible cruelties were being committed by the Japanese on prisoners of war which would have gone on if the war in the Far East had continued, and having talked to some of those ex-prisoners something drastic had to be done, but there are arguments on both sides that have to be respected.

The words, 'It's all over now,' were echoed by everyone at the time – but what did the future hold? We hadn't had time to think about 'after the war' for nearly six years. The war had united everyone in a common cause: now most people had to be single-minded and think about their own future. Rebuilding our cities was one priority, to provide homes for the servicemen and women who would soon be demobbed. Factories and other workplaces would have to be reorganised for peacetime requirements.

It was, however, going to be difficult for the servicemen and women to adjust to a normal way of life. Most had grown up in an orderly service lifestyle where decisions had been made for them; a few had experienced great danger and excitement and would think a normal life rather dull in comparison, which could lead to trouble. Rationing was still in force for many things and this meant that the black market – so splendidly portrayed by Jimmy Beck's character Private Walker in *Dad's Army* – would continue to flourish while there were still shortages.

Women would find the peace equally difficult. They had played a major part in the nation's survival whether as factory or Land Army workers, or whether they were running house and home while the men were away. Women were not content to return to the lives they had lived before the war.

Fashion returned to the streets. Fashion houses and designers responded to the new, peaceful, world order with ideas to bring romance and the sexy look back into our lives. The ladies in their new fashions would catch the eye of the male population and I would be no exception.

# 4 'AND IN THE SPRING, A YOUNG MAN'S FANCY . . .'

The second half of the 1940s was one of the most extraordinary and exciting periods of my life. All sorts of things happened, some of them so quickly that it has taken a while to sort out the sequence of events in my mind. I do advise people to have the patience to keep a diary, it would certainly have helped in several areas of this book, but from my meagre memory and my brother Fedge's very good research notes I hope I have been able to get events in the right order.

In the summer of 1945, now that we had got the war behind us, sports events started again. I was playing quite a lot of cricket as an ATC cadet and one of the corps' officers was Stanley Perfitt-Harvey (P. H.), a great enthusiast of the game. He was the headmaster and founder of Westminster College, Chalkwell, which was between Leigh-on-Sea and Westcliff. His school was very near Chalkwell Park which, amongst other things, was one of the venues used by the Essex County Cricket Club during its annual cricketing weeks.

P. H. had some mid-week matches for his prep school on the ground. Each team tended to include a master or two, but if they were not available he would draft me in, provided I could get a day off work. I learned a lot listening to him instructing his lads and giving them coaching tips when he was umpiring. I also played with him in some ATC matches. He used to say, 'Pertwee, you're trying to hit the cover off the ball too early in your innings; just settle down.' My theory at the time was that if I could start punishing the bowler early on, it would unsettle him, before he could unsettle me. P. H. promoted the idea of treating each ball on its merit and had a very good defensive stroke played with feet and body in the right place. I did manage to take some of his coaching on board and it certainly improved my game.

One day P. H. said, 'I think you could get a county trial if you concentrated on your game.' He obviously made some noises in the right directions because one day I was at Southchurch Park, another venue where Essex played, when a gentleman came up to me after practice and said, 'I believe you may have a trial for the county.' I was pretty surprised at this, but he went on, 'and you'll want to play as much cricket as you can, so I'd like to offer you a job in my business.' As my days at SMAC were obviously numbered now that the war had finished, I asked him what his business was. He replied, 'I'm a stock jobber in the Stock Exchange, you can start as soon as you like.'

Well, anything for a laugh, I thought. I didn't know what the Stock Exchange was about or where it was. Anyway I soon found myself in the employ of Oxley Knox & Co, Capel Court, Throgmorton Street. I had a new suit, the first one I'd ever owned, and a monthly season ticket for the train. It was a major change in my circumstances and I met a completely different type of person working there; they all made me very welcome. The office manager always wore glasses on the end of his nose; he was a real gentleman and I remember every Friday at precisely the same time he would take his bag and go off to Paddington to catch his train home to Newton Abbot in Devon. He stayed in London during the week.

My job was to copy share prices into a ledger; to do this I sat on a high stool at a large desk. I also answered the telephone. One person – a bit of a character – used to love having a flutter on the gee-gees and one day said, 'Do you fancy a bet?' I said, 'OK what's running?' I picked out Happy Knight and put on £1 each way (a lot of money for me). Happy Knight won at 33:1. I was on my way as a gambler, I thought, but in fact I've never got hooked, although I like going to race meetings: to watch and talk to the characters in the racing fraternity.

My gambling has been confined to my theatrical activities! By now my wages were not bad, plus I was part of a quarterly bonus scheme. Up to this time I had only smoked one or two Woodbines a day, but now I bought the occasional pack of Churchman's No 1, in a green packet; these were smoked by the 'nobs' who worked in the Stock Exchange. There was a very well-known restaurant opposite Capel Court and you could see some of the hierarchy of the Exchange coming out of there in the afternoon with slightly redder faces than usual, obviously having had a good, and sometimes liquid, lunch. My more modest venue was the sandwich bar next to the restaurant, and delicious sandwiches they were too.

I also had to take share papers round to the brokers' offices; this was a nice change and got me out of the office for an hour or two. One of the office staff was a Mr Pennel, who just a couple of years ago wrote to me via the BBC and asked me if we could meet. I haven't yet arranged it, but I will.

Of course the best thing about the job was that I was able to play cricket mid-week as well as at weekends. Unfortunately, early in 1946 after seeing me in practice, one of the Essex coaching staff decided that I wouldn't be good enough to reach a really high standard of county cricket and pointed out that there was little financial security unless you were really good: there was no sponsorship in those days and wages were low. I think Tom Pearce, the Essex captain, was also at that meeting and was very pleasant, chatting to me about cricket in general.

I really wasn't dispirited by this decision; I had anyway enjoyed the cricket I had been playing. One particular match stands out – against the British Empire Eleven, a team that toured various venues round the country playing matches in aid of charity. The team I played against included the great West Indian player Learie Constantine, the two Essex brothers Peter and Ray Smith and the side was captained by another West Indian, Dr C.B. Clarke, a very good slow bowler. I didn't get a chance to bat in that match, but it was still a great experience.

I did however play one or two matches against the Army at Shoeburyness Garrison; they were great games and the Army hospitality was always marvellous. One match there included Lt-Col the Hon C. J. Littleton, whose family had all played for Worcester in their time. The Hon C. J., later Viscount Cobham, was a slow bowler, or was in that match, and got me out for a duck. He actually psyched me out even before he bowled. He moved the field about and re-tied his boot laces, while I waited at the batting crease thinking to myself, 'I'll get at this fellow, and quick.' When C. J. bowled I expected he would put a lot of turn on the first one; instead of that he bowled a straight one that went right through my guard. I'd made up my mind what shot to play before it was bowled – a cardinal sin in cricket!

After the decision about my cricket future the position with Oxley Knox & Co was no longer necessary. However no move was immediately made by the firm, instead it was a bit of fun by me that hastened the end of my career in the City. I used to do a few silly impressions, and one day when I was answering the telephone I said, 'This is Raymond Glendenning saying hello and a very good afternoon from Oxley Knox and Co with all share prices of the day.' Raymond Glendenning was a very well-known football and boxing commentator of the period, and he always started by saying 'This is Raymond Glendenning saying hello and . . .' The only problem with my bit of fun was that the person on the other end of the phone was F. P. Knox, who had given me the job in the first place! He wasn't very amused and asked me to see him when he got back. It was decided that I should take a month's wages and disappear quietly.

Another phase of my life was over. The Stock Exchange never was for me really, but I'd had some fun while I was there and I would miss the card games with my pals on the train going backwards and forwards to London. On one or two occasions I travelled without a ticket, if it was getting near to pay day and I was short; when I did I would jump out of the train as it approached Westcliff station, and roll down the embankment. There was a slight incline between Westcliff and the previous station at Chalkwell and the steam engines with their large load of carriages used to huff and puff up the incline so it made the exit from the train fairly easy.

In 1945 I saw a couple of the Victory Test Matches played between England and Australia; nearly all the participants were still in the services but were well known to the cricketing fraternity – players such as Len Hutton, Wally Hammond, Jack Robertson, Cyril Washbrook, Laurie Fishlock (my old acquaintance from the bus episode at Blackheath), Bill Edrich, Doug Wright, Godfrey Evans and Australians Keith Miller, Lindsey Hassett, and others who were to be the stars of postwar cricket around the world.

Walter Hammond impressed me very much with his casual walk to the wicket, a blue spotted handkerchief dangling from his hip pocket. He was already a cricketing legend from way back in the late 1920s. His majestic cover driving was wonderful to watch, and his biography is one of the most interesting cricket books to read. I remember on one occasion I waited for the players to come out of the ground after a match and approached a tall man in Royal Australian Air Force uniform. I thought it was Keith Miller, one of the most exciting Australian cricketers to watch and one who would make a real impact on postwar cricket. However when I said, 'Could I have your autograph please: it is Mr Miller isn't it?' he replied, 'Oh Miller has already left the ground.' I thanked him and someone standing near to me said after he had gone, 'Did you get Keith Miller's autograph?' I said, 'No, the man just told me he'd left,' and the chap said, 'Don't be daft, that was Keith Miller you were talking to.' Miller was obviously a joker as well as a brilliant cricketer. Many years later I was introduced to him at a reception given by a real nice chap, Doug McClelland, the Australian High Commissioner in London, to whom I quite regularly talk on the phone now that he has retired to Australia. When he introduced me to Keith Miller on that evening in question I said, 'I'll make no mistake this time, Keith,' and I briefly told him the story. He said, 'What a rascal I am.' He has not been in the best of health during the past few years, but you wouldn't have guessed it talking to him.

Fedge was demobbed in the early spring of 1946 and what a reunion there was with my mother at Westcliff station when he finally arrived home! It wasn't quite home of course, but it was for the time being. He almost immediately went back to his firm in London which he had left when he was called up in December 1939. It was a long absence but he soon got into the swing of things again, and was obviously pleased to renew his acquaintance with the City – of course very much changed after the terrible bombing it had received.

Fedge managed to get me a job with a paper firm called Marchants with offices just off New Bridge Street, very near Blackfriars Bridge, a stone's throw from Uncle Teddy's office. He worked for a gum paper tape firm, whose products were known as the Butterfly Brand and whose trademark, naturally, was a butterfly. I am not sure with what part of the industry my new firm was connected, but I know that I was given a similar job to that I did at the Stock Exchange, copying accounts into huge ledgers which weighed a ton. The boredom of this job and my passion for cricket led me into another direction.

The first postwar Test Match series in this country since 1938 was to be made by the Indians under the captaincy of the Nawab of Pataudi. When they played Essex at Southchurch Park, Southend, I infiltrated their dressing room and got talking to one of their opening batsmen, Mushtaq Ali. He was very friendly and invited me to come along to the Berners Hotel, their London base, just off London's Oxford Street, and official-ly meet the team. I got to know them all quite well – Vinoo Mankad an all rounder, Hazare and Captain Pataudi. The main-stay of many of their matches was a quiet man called Vijay Merchant, a wonderful player and real gentleman. There was also a very young player called Abdul Hafeez who sometimes got a bit homesick – the Nawab used to ask me to go and sit with him. Hafeez was a fine up-and-coming player, and after the partition of India he eventually became the captain of the Pakistani team under the name of A.H. Kadar.

Mushtaq Ali was always pestering me for clothing coupons (there was still rationing here at that time) as he wanted to take some clothes back to India with him. I got to know one or two contacts on the black market and was able to help him. I did, however, have one hairy moment regarding the coupons. I had gone to the Berners Hotel with an envelope full of coupons and asked the receptionist for Mushtaq. Just at that point another gentleman came in and asked for him and gave his name as Chief Inspector somebody. I thought the game was up, that he'd come to arrest Mushtaq over the coupons, and that I'd end up inside with him too. I said to the receptionist, 'I'm just going to the gents.' I got in there and locked the door but soon afterwards there came a knocking: it was Mushtaq. He said, 'I'll see you upstairs.' I said ,'What about the policeman who's just come in?' He replied, 'He's a friend of mine, I've got him some tickets for the Test Match.' I breathed a great sigh of relief.

I was now spending all my spare time with the Indian team, and some more as well by playing truant from my job at Marchants. I used to help the team with their gear and steal a few hours with them at matches doing odd jobs. They used to call me their assistant baggage boy. A Mr Ferguson, who for many years used to look after all touring test teams in this country, was the official baggage man and confidant of the players.

In that same year, 1946, I was one of a number of ATC lads who decided to start a cricket team of our own. As many pre-war sides were now getting themselves together again, it was going to be hard for a new team like us to get a permanent pitch and fixtures. It was then I got to know the Waud family well again, as son Gilbert wanted to join a side. He was a very useful bowler, so he was enrolled in our team. His father Norman took an interest and, as he had some good contacts in the Southend area, he said he would help us.

We asked Mushtaq to be our first club president – a position he accepted – and we then got a near copy of the Indian team's badge, depicting the Star of India, and had some headed note paper printed with Mushtaq's name on it. This immediately created interest and within a short while we had been allotted a pitch at Belfairs, Leigh-on-Sea. As the phone exchange for the area was Marine, we called ourselves the Marine Cricket Club and those who had managed to afford cap and blazer had the letters M.C.C. on them. This really did the trick, and fixtures started coming in thick and fast. The only trouble was finding the wherewithal to buy the gear and pay the rent for the pitch. So we decided to offer Honorary Membership to people for 10s (50p) a year.

This scheme got going and some of us spent a couple of Saturdays going up to London and back asking people if they would like to participate in the scheme. Once they had agreed and parted with their money we would get out at the next station, wait for the next train and go through the process again in that one. When we got to Upminster, about half way to London, we started the journey back doing the same thing. One of the first people I encountered was a vicar who was pleased to donate but kept me chatting about the evils of women playing cricket. 'Mark my words,' he said, 'they'll be into everything one of these days.' Luckily the method of transferring trains got me out of that conversation. One lady not only gave me her address but also offered her phone number: if she'd been a cracker I'd probably have taken it! We gave everybody a receipt with our club address on it, and by the end of that first day we had enough money for at least half the gear we wanted to start our fixture list.

As you can imagine, what with the Indian cricketers and the time we were putting in to get our club off the ground, including some evening practices in the nets, I was getting a bit tired and sleeping quite a lot at my desk at the paper firm. I used to wake up with my pen shooting up the page leaving a long line from top to bottom with the odd ink stain here and there. By the end of that year Marchants had had enough of me, and I was out of work yet again.

In 1947 my brother fixed up a flat for us to rent in London in the Cromwell Road right opposite Lexham Gardens at Earls Court. The house was owned by an Egyptian gentleman and we had the ground and first floor. So off we went again, Mum, Fedge and I, this time to our own home. My brother had also seen an advert in the *Daily Telegraph* asking for applicants to apply to Burberry's store in the Haymarket for salesmen for the new sports department which was about to open. Burberry's then was one of the most prestigious stores in London, and probably still is, although I haven't been in there for a long time. I went for the interview and got the job, so we were now living in London and I was working again.

Of course I had to leave behind a lot of mates I'd got to know down in Essex – and the Marine Cricket Club which had given me so much enjoyment. My time at Burberry's was, however, a very happy one. The staff were nice people and although there was strict discipline in those days, we used to have a lot of laughs. The sports department wasn't very big, but it was the right size to cope with the small amount of sports' goods available to the public in the immediate postwar years. There were two of us to run the department, a Mr Gordon, slightly older than I was, and a Mr Frame who was in overall charge. Frame was actually running the hat department but was also on call for other departments; he was undoubtedly a great salesman and quite eccentric. Very few people left the store without buying something if he was serving them. For instance, if he was selling a hat and he hadn't got the right size, and it was too big, he would say to the customer, 'You always want a size larger, sir, as they shrink a little in the rain.' If he hadn't got in stock one big enough for the customer he would say, 'Just a moment sir, I'll get you a bigger size,' and he would take the original one behind a coat rail, put his knee in the hat and pull on it. You could sometimes hear the stitching give way in places, and he'd come out again and say, 'There we are sir, that should be your size,' and the customer would go away happy.

There was an old boy called Jack London, who used to work on the reproofing counter. A Cockney, in common with most of the older salesman, he always wore a black jacket and pinstripe trousers. Jack had tender feet and walked as if he were treading on hot coals; if you got too near him he would say, 'Mind my bloody feet,' and hop away. Reproofing was always included in the quote when people brought their Burberry raincoats to be cleaned. Very famous was the 'Burberry'; it was made in several styles for men and women. There was the conventional raincoat in cotton gabardine, and the wool Burberry, and the reversible one, which you just turned inside out to reveal a checked winter coat. Most of them were made-to-measure, and you could always get a made-to-measure deerstalker hat or cap to match your reversible, and even a floppy fishing hat. However, at lunchtime Jack London would eat his sandwiches, which he kept under the counter, in between serving customers. One lunchtime when he was away from his counter for a while, we took the beef out of his sandwiches and replaced it with pieces of brown gabardine from the tailoring shop in the basement. We all watched from behind a coat rail as he set about his sandwiches just as a customer came in. He started taking the particulars down in his order book with a mouthful of gabardine sandwich, which he couldn't take out of his mouth in front of the customer. The look on his face was something to behold! When the customer had left he said, 'Right, who's got my beef.' Well no one could keep a straight face and I got hysterical, so I got the blame. He saw the funny side of it later.

A splendid fellow arrived after me – Freddie Holland, who was engaged for the hat department; he and I immediately became friends. His parents had been killed in the Blitz, but he had married a lovely Scots girl called Greta. I used to visit them at their home in Dulwich and they had a gorgeous baby daughter called Margaret. When, many years later, she got married and had a family, my wife Marion was a godmother to one of her children. After I had taken my early plunge in show business I used to visit 'Dutch' (as I've always called Freddie) and Greta, and she used to give me a good meal and a wonderful apple pie to take home. Her apple pies were superb.

However, let's get back to Burberry's in 1947-48. Freddie was given his marching orders, for what reason I'm not sure, and I was sad to see him go. Incidentally 'Dutch' wrote a wonderful take-off of a racing commentary for me for the first broadcast I ever made. I put various voices to it and, believe it or not, with some slight alterations, I have used it ever since if I've been doing a 'turn' – as we call a stand up spot in cabaret or suchlike. I took a real fancy to one of the girls in Burberry's: she was a tall good-looking girl and she was really the first love of my life.

Her family had a business at Welling in Kent, and I believe at that time also a holiday place at Sidlesham near Chichester in Sussex. Her name was Jeanne and we started spending a lot of time together, lingering over a drink near Charing Cross station before she caught the train back to Welling in the evening, Sunday outings with her brother and sister and days spent in various parks near London. I remember one particular occasion in 1948 when we spent the day at Virginia Water, adjoining Windsor Great Park. We were enjoying a quiet spot behind some green and pleasant shrubbery, getting to know one another even more, when we were conscious of several corgis in the immediate area, being called by their master and mistress. We beat a hasty retreat and carried on meandering through the park. Soon afterwards a couple came strolling towards us with the corgis in tow. I don't think I have to tell you that the couple were the royal newly-weds, Princess Elizabeth and Prince Philip. They both smiled at us as they passed and I often wondered whether they knew there was a couple behind those green and pleasant shrubs when the dogs strayed off course. Everything seemed idyllic at that time.

The sporting world had two new cricketing heroes. Denis Compton, known as the Brylcreem Boy when his face was on practically every available site in the country advertising that brand of hair fixative. Compton in 1947 broke several records with his cavalier batting style, beating not only Tom Hayward's 1906 record total of runs amassed in one season by 300 runs in 11 fewer innings, but also the great Jack Hobbs's 1925 record of 16 centuries in a season. Compton scored a total of 3,816 runs and 18 centuries that year. His Middlesex 'twin' Bill Edrich also beat Hayward's record of 3,518, scoring 3,539 runs. Many of the runs the terrible twins scored were at the expense of South Africa during the Test Match series that summer. They both became my heroes and I had the pleasure of meeting them both on various sporting occasions, including actually playing with Bill Edrich in a charity match in the 1970s. I was at a lunch with Bill the day he died after a fall at his home.

The glorious summer of 1947 followed a terribly cold and

snowy early spring with huge snowdrifts all over the country, and no central heating in those days. The freeze was followed by much flooding everywhere.

In 1947 the Tobin family decided to emigrate to Rhodesia. I think Bill and Gigi wanted to make a fresh start after the war years. They had lost two sons in the conflict and they probably thought a sunny climate in a completely different environment might help. Also, Uncle Bill had become disillusioned with the Atlas Preservative Co where he had worked for the whole of the war under very difficult circumstances.

I am sure my mother was devastated to see her sister go, not knowing whether she would ever see her again: in fact she never did see Bill or Gigi after that. I remember seeing them off on the boat train at Waterloo station – Bill, Gigi and their children, Peter, Daphne, Rosemary and June. It was a sad occasion. I think they settled down in Bulawayo, the capital of the country quite well and the difficult times ahead had not really surfaced in Africa at that point. Bill got a job and continued with his hobby of painting and I'm sure would have made the best of everything. The Tobins were always very adaptable. Bill and Gigi eventually both died in Rhodesia. Peter married and went to live in South Africa. Rosemary is also married, and is still in Rhodesia.

Round about this time I went to see a film which really hit me between the eyes. It was *The Jolson Story*, depicting the life of the great American entertainer who had starred in the first talkie in 1929 – *The Jazz Singer*. *The Jolson Story* starred Larry Parks, who mimed to Jolson's extraordinary, warm and vibrant voice. The film didn't just have an effect on me, a lot of other people were singing all the top songs from the film: *Is It True What They Say About Dixie?*, *April Showers*, *Mammy*, *I Only Have Eyes For You*, *Rosie You Are My Posie*, *California Here I Come*, *Give My Regards to Broadway*, *Toot Toot Tootsie Good-bye* and a host of others. Wherever you went people were trying to impersonate the Jolson voice – what a gift that voice was to all young entertainers who liked to finish their act on a Jolson impression. With the success of the first Jolson film world-wide the producers very quickly cashed in on a sequel – *Jolson Sings Again* – and Larry Parks once more made a wonderful job of it. Shortly afterwards Parks was hounded out of Hollywood during the quite outrageous anti-Communist scourges of Senator Macarthy.

By 1948 nothing could dampen my feelings, I was in love with the lovely Jeanne. We went one evening to the Casino Theatre in London to see the wonderful American singing star Allen Jones, father of the equally famous Jack Jones. Allen Jones was a film star as well as having a great voice and his signature tune, at least the one everyone recognised him by, was Donkey Serenade. On that same variety bill at the Casino, now called the Prince Edward Theatre, was a very funny little man with a tight suit and cap who had a very infectious laugh and did some wonderful 'falls' in his act. He also had a very appealing voice when he sang his popular song at that time – *Don't Laugh At Me 'Cos I'm a Fool*. Yes, it was the London debut of Norman Wisdom, who went on to star in many British films, a lot of which became very popular in Eastern Europe: he's feted when he travels there. He eventually had huge stage successes here and in America. I've known Norman for many years and was delighted to be asked to do a TV series with him for Lew Grade's ATV company in the 1970s. As I write this there are moves afoot for me to do a film with Norman sometime this summer if all goes well. It will be a pleasure if I do, because he is not only a fine professional but also a jolly nice person.

In 1948 the Olympic Games were held in London, which was besieged by people from all over the world. The year also brought the Australian cricketers to England for the first time since 1938. What a side they had, led by the great Don Bradman. They had wonderful batsmen such as Barnes, Brown, Hassett, Morris, Miller and Bradman himself, and an array of bowlers: Lindwall who was superb, Johnson, Toshack and Miller, who was not only a batsman in the cavalier style of Denis Compton but was also a wonderfully inventive bowler. He and Compton became great mates and still are, in spite of their increasing age.

The one sad thing about that series was Don Bradman's farewell to cricket in England in the last Test at the Oval. He made his way to the crease in front of a packed crowd and was given a standing ovation lasting several minutes. Sadly he was bowled second ball for a duck by the Warwickshire spin bowler Eric Hollies, needing only four runs to average exactly 100 per innings in test cricket. I have something in common with Don Bradman: I was also out for a duck in my last appearance at the Oval. I have had the privilege of playing there three times in charity matches, and I've always thought of Len Hutton walking down the stone steps on his way to that massive 364 he scored against the Australians all those years ago, in 1938. It's an extraordinary feeling when you are treading on the same ground that has been trodden by the greatest – and it has also happened to me in the theatre.

We had an idea in the sports department in Burberry's which we hoped might bring attention to our rather small display window. Nearby Lillywhites and Simpsons in Piccadilly had huge displays and were well established, but during that summer there were enough people around for everyone to have a bite of the cherry. What we did at Burberry's was to make a miniature scoreboard and change the Test Match scores every hour or so. I used to ring up the various Test Match venues and say, 'Sime here, Australian Board of Control,' in my best Australian accent. What made me think of the name 'Sime' I don't know, but it's an easy word to say in 'down under' dialect. The people answering the phone at Lords eventually got quite friendly and would say, 'Good morning Mr Sime,' and pass me the score. That scoreboard in the window of our sports department really drew the crowds, sometimes two deep on the Haymarket pavement, it also brought us some business.

I went a step further with 'Sime'. I bet the lads in the store that I could get into Lords using that name. There were pretty strict procedures even then about getting in without a ticket and I promised that I would get in through the hallowed Grace gates. The bet was on, and I took a tube to St John's Wood and then hopped in a taxi. I got out at the Grace gates, went straight up to an official and said, 'My name is Sime, Australian Board of Control.' No problem, I was in, and after spending about half an hour walking round the perimeter chatting to people in my Aussie accent, I bought a programme, asked the fellow on the gate to sign it, adding Grace gate entrance, and left. It had all been very easy. Most of the lads believed me when I got back to the store and we had a drink on it after work, on them.

Boxing also came in to the reckoning as one of the great sporting occasions in 1948. The likeable Freddie Mills won the World Light Heavyweight Championship in London. A few years later Freddie died in what most people thought were mysterious circumstances in a shooting incident. A young Lester Piggot also won his first race at the age of 12 in that year.

While I was at Burberry's I had my first skirmish with show business. One evening, just before closing time, a familiar figure came in and asked for a raincoat: it was the great Sid Field. I recognised him straight away from his pictures outside the nearby Prince of Wales theatre where he was appearing in *Piccadilly Hayride*. The assistant he approached couldn't be bothered to serve him so near to closing time and said, 'Sorry sir, we have nothing in your size.' I was shocked at this and when the store closed I asked the manager if I could take a couple of raincoats round to the theatre for Mr Field to try on. I was allowed to do so and Sid was very grateful and bought one from me. I went to see him again when he said he might like some other garments. He was a charming man and we had a long chat and he introduced me to Jerry Desmond, his wonderful feed. Sid offered me tickets to see the show – a revue. He also said that if I ever thought of going into show business I was to go and see his agent Archie Parnell & Co. I told him I was quite happy at Burberry's and pleased to serve him.

Anyway, I saw the show at the Prince of Wales and was quite mesmerised by his performance. He had various stooges with him apart from Jerry Desmond and the laughter that greeted his antics on stage was unbelievable. I actually witnessed people falling out of their seats. I won't go into details of his golfing, photographers, cinema organist and snooker sketches, amongst other little gems, as they have been covered in other books. Laurence Olivier went to see him and afterwards wrote in his *Evening Standard* review, 'Every actor should go and see Sid Field for his natural timing, comic genius and overall acting ability in controlling an audience.' Sid really was the toast of the town and fêted on both sides of the Atlantic by other great comedy giants like Bob Hope and Danny Kaye.

Sid had been travelling round the provinces for several years before the great George Black brought him to London, something which should have happened much sooner than it did. I also saw Sid in the play *Harvey* at the same theatre, and he brought such warmth to the character of Elwood P. Dowd, it was another great triumph. I also saw the American Joe Brown who took over from Sid when he wasn't well. It was a terrible shock to the whole of show business and his admirers when Sid died at the age of 45. What a loss he was. The sudden surge of hard work when he hit the big time, his nervous approach to keeping at the top and a slight drinking problem occasioned to hide his nervousness, contributed to his death. I went to his funeral at Putney Vale with a friend; practically everyone in show business was there, plus many members of the public who had come to say good-bye to a genius. My friend and I walked from Barnes station to be there, quite a long way, but we would have walked twice as far as we were such great admirers of the great Sid Field.

Many years later I had the pleasure of working in a film with Sid's son, Nick Field, who looked just like his dad, tall and with the same facial expression, a nice boy indeed. Sid's wife eventually spent her last years at the EABF retirement home, Brinsworth, in Twickenham. Being on the committee of the Entertainment Artistes Benevolent Fund which administers Brinsworth, I often used to see Mrs Field – a great pleasure. I will add that my second agent when I entered the entertainment business was a partner in Archie Parnell & Co: George Knapman, a sweet man and very thoughtful to his charges. We used to talk at length about Sid Field. George is now also a resident at Brinsworth since his wife died, and at 80 is still very sprightly with a fantastic memory of the business going back many, many years. He still plays the occasional round of golf.

My second introduction to the theatrical scene in 1948 happened when I met up with my second cousin Jon Pertwee for the first time. He was then doing a lot of radio work and had a big following through one particular programme, *Waterlogged Spa* written by and starring Eric Barker. Jon was doing all sorts of wonderful character voices in that show but perhaps the most popular was his Devon postman: 'What does it matter what you do as long as you tear 'em up,' in a lovely West Country accent. Jon was also featured in another popular programme: *Up the Pole* starring Jimmy Jewel and Ben Warris, two very funny men on both stage and radio.

*Waterlogged Spa* was recorded at the Paris Studios in Lower Regent Street, just a couple of minutes' walk from Burberry's, so one evening I decided to go to there and introduce myself to Jon. After a short introduction – he was just about to record the show – he invited me to see the recording. During it they had a short audience spot – the 'Double or Quits' cash quiz. It was conducted by actor Harold Warrender and when he asked for volunteers, cousin Jon jumped up and said, 'My cousin will come up,' and so I did, without much hesitation. Either I was afraid to say no or I'd gone potty, it was leaping in to the unknown for me. You could choose your subject, so I chose cricket, got all the answers right and won £1, my first radio fee. Little did I know then that several years later I would be a part of so many radio shows from that delightful studio. The Paris had originally been a small cinema showing risqué French films and the BBC had taken it over on a long lease. Sadly the BBC relinquished the premises in 1994 and an historical period in sound broadcasting had finished. I think the general public were as sad as the many entertainers who had worked there when the doors finally closed. Its fame was known all over the world.

Getting back to Jon. He came to visit us at our flat in Earls Court and he charmed my mother, but seemed a little eccentric and theatrical. He drove American cars and knew everybody and talked about people whom we had only read about –

like the J. Arthur Rank film starlets, male and female, who were being groomed for future stardom: Jean Simmonds, Michael Rennie, Barbara Murray, James Mason and a host of others. Jon was then living in a basement flat in Chester Row, a flat I was to get to know well in the 1950s.

During that summer of wonderful sporting events Fedge decided to take my mother and me to the West Country for a holiday. He booked up at a guest house in Dartmouth, Devon. It was a wonderful journey down from Paddington by G.W.R. (God's Wonderful Railway) passing through the deep red sandstone cuttings at Dawlish Warren where the trains run along beside the sea wall and thence to Newton Abbot, Paignton and finally Kingswear, then transferring to the ferry for Dartmouth.

I'll bore you now with a little bit of railway history. A single track loop line inland used to exist between Exeter and Newton Abbot so that trains could be diverted that way when the seas were running high along the Dawlish coast throwing up water and debris over the trains. There was a signalbox on the loop and the signalman who manned it was a keen gardener and put his produce in buckets by the line. As trains approached, he put his signal to red, telling the travellers the delay wouldn't be long, and in the meantime would they like to buy some flowers? Now there's enterprise for you!.

Today the main line trains from London only go as far as Paignton where you change for the delightful journey into Kingswear by steam train on a line run by the Paignton and Dartmouth Railway Co, one of the many preserved railways in the country. Thank goodness there was some enterprise around when Dr Beeching got the knife out in the 1960s. I tell you there is nothing quite like that coastal journey particularly when you catch sight of Kingswear, Dartmouth, the River Dart and Dartmouth Naval College – bliss!

Early in 1949 my romantic days with the lovely Jeanne were coming to an end. I think I probably got a bit too possessive and Jeanne probably felt I was on the point of getting really serious. Of course we were both too young for that, so a break was decided upon. I was heartbroken for a while, not just for the parting of the ways with her, but also because I had got to enjoy her widowed mother's jolly company. Her mum was the lady who introduced me to tea. I had never drunk that awful smelling liquid, or coffee, before, but after some protest I tried it and from that time drank the occasional cup. Aunt Amy had tried to get me to drink it in my early teens at Roundabouts but I flatly refused, and she sent me to my room for a day to try and make me see sense. I didn't, and I had no intention of doing so, just over a silly cup of tea. Perhaps Jeanne's mum was a little more persuasive, or did I think in those heady days that my courtship of her daughter might be marred if I didn't drink it?

It was about this time that a customer came into Burberry's and we instantly recognised one another. It was George Goodliffe. the window and office cleaning company director, whose family I had met during the wartime years. After a few pleasantries about our families Goodliffe asked me how much I earned at Burberry's. I told him £6 a week and one percent commission (it took a heck of a lot of sales to earn that one percent I can tell you!). Goodliffe told me his business was expanding by leaps and bounds with all the offices and shops in London being rebuilt in the aftermath of the wartime bombing 'So,' he said, 'I can give you more money than that if you came to work for me.' I discussed it with my mother and brother and thought about this rather drastic change of direction. It would mean starting at about six in the morning, finishing about three or four in the afternoon and working out of doors, which appealed to me – as did the extra money which would allow me to enjoy the increased leisure time I'd have in the evenings.

I accepted George Goodliffe's offer, and, suddenly, I was a window and office cleaner. The move also meant I would be working apart from Jeanne who was still at Burberry's – probably a good thing for both of us. In fact, we lost contact with one another until 1974 when I was in a play at the Criterion Theatre in Piccadilly. Jeanne and her husband David came to see me afterwards and that was a treat. She hadn't changed at all really. She and David had two children, a boy almost the same age as my son Jonathan (who has become known as James for theatrical reasons when he came into the business). Jeanne and David also have a daughter and granddaughter now. Several of us from Burberry's have had a reunion during the past few years: Nina Griffin who, after Burberry's, worked for Freddie Laker Airways for some time and is now in partnership in a very good eaterie and pub; Pat Castle, who is a fine artist, had exhibitions of her work, and the last time we met was at a super lunch party at Jeanne and David's house near Chichester in Sussex just a year ago.

It took me a while to adjust to my new environment with the cleaning company, but I soon learned how to 'scrim' a window (a scrim was a large coarse sort of mesh cloth used for removing the initial dirt) and then leathered it off to take away the smears and give it sparkle. Everybody always seemed to be rushing about in the pre-fab buildings of the cleaning company in Eagle Street, Holborn and, as I've said, work was coming in from all directions with the new building works. The three brothers, George, Gilbert and Tom, were the main directors of the company, but it was a real family affair amongst the management, which included in-laws, cousins etc; they all worked hard and had a cheery word for everyone.

My immediate boss was one of the 'family' with a dry sense of humour and who used to laugh at his own shaggy dog stories. I was soon out on the road as a rep under the guidance of a nice man called Louis Brewer. He and Pat Connett were particularly helpful in pricing jobs. You got to know pretty quickly how long it took to clean a window, depending whether it was a weekly, monthly, or quarterly clean. A lot of shop fronts were done daily. One of the first contracts I obtained for the firm was a string of Dolcis shoe shops all over London. That brought in a nice little bonus! Dolcis shop windows and door surrounds were all chrome and that had to be done as well.

We had our own areas to 'police', mine was from New Oxford Street to Marble Arch and their surrounding areas. All of this was done on foot every morning and early afternoon. One of the directors, Gilbert, used to come on the round with me sometimes and he was a real master at it all. He knew all the window and office cleaners on the rounds and, it seemed, their family's Christian names too!. He always kept a packet of ciga- rettes on him and would offer the cleaners one, and ask them how they were getting on. It made me realise that if you kept the workforce on the ground happy, that was half the battle. You could be walking along with him past a building and he'd say, 'They haven't got a window cleaner, let's find the caretaker.' He probably had a flat in the basement and once Gilbert found him he would engage him in pleasantries and then give the caretak- er his card saying, 'If we can help at any time.' That was all: not, 'What about us cleaning your windows.' About a week later he'd walk past that same building, judging when the caretaker might be around, and once again exchange pleasantries with him. You can bet your life that either then or after a third visit he would have obtained the cleaning for the whole building. At Christmas the caretaker would get a bottle of something and his wife a box of chocs.

I learned a lot about salesmanship with the firm. If any employee was not well, they would instantly be visited by one of the management to see if they needed anything. That's when Governors really knew and cared about their workforce. Some still do I'm sure, but I'll bet they're outweighed by those self- centred 'fat cats' we hear about nowadays who don't.

My social life seemed to be going quite well. I'd joined a club, the Olympic in Gerrard Street, now the centre of the Chinese food and trade business, very near Leicester Square. The Olympic was a social club for people living in or near London. Amongst other things they had a drama group, which I didn't get involved in but enjoyed watching. One of those folk, a Patrick somebody, eventually went to America and I saw him in a few movies when they were repeated here on TV. I also saw from time to time James Booth on TV – I used to play cricket with him at Westcliff when I lived there.

I met a girl at the Olympic who was to have some effect on my eventual theatrical career. Her name was Joyce Davis and she was Kenneth Horne's secretary at Triplex Safety Glass where Ken was a director. Joyce had a super family – widowed mother, sister Betty and a charming brother. They lived in a lovely house out at Barnet in Hertfordshire. In due course Joyce and her sister Betty set up an amateur concert party called the Startimers and insisted I should be part of it. Amongst other things we did sketches and singing routines. Betty had a very good singing voice and Joyce was no slouch either, singing the Joyce Grenfell numbesr. For my part, I was hopeless, and they decided that I should have a permanent 'L' plate on my back which caused a giggle. We took the concert party out to village halls and such-like to raise money for charity. We had a marvellous pianist called Florence, an old friend of the Davis family.

The biggest bonus for me in being a Startimer was that I got to meet Kenneth Horne who used to come and see a show or two. Like millions of people I was a fan of *Much Binding in the Marsh,* written by and starring Ken Horne and Richard Murdoch, and here I was, meeting Ken socially. If anybody had told me then that I would eventually spend the best part of 10 years working on radio with him, I would have said they were off their rocker. The Startimers eventually disbanded, but Joyce and I remained friends. We always met outside Swan and Edgar's store in Piccadilly, Joyce straight from work and me after I'd got home from the window cleaning company and had a bath. I was invariably a little late for our meetings and always said, 'I went home to have a bath.' Joyce would say, 'You must be the cleanest person in London.' Well it was only natural I should want to spruce myself up after a day's cleaning.

Brother Fedge got married in 1949 to a very sweet Swedish girl, Lizzie Palmertz. Lizzie's family lived in a small town called Forshaga in the western part of Sweden, just north of Karlstad. It must have been traumatic for her in the early days, coming from a different culture and a small community into central London with all the things one has to cope with in a big city. Lizzie seemed to adjust well, but it must have been a difficult time for both of them in the early stages of their married life.

We then moved virtually across the road to Lexham Gardens. It was a big flat in a large house that was owned by a friend of Amy Heilbron, and this was where Fedge and Lizzie's first child,

James, was born. He was a lovely looking baby with big eyes, and this was a marvellous event for everyone. I was probably too busy doing my own thing to have realised how difficult it must have been to bring up a baby in a flat, with the constrictions of two female parents, my mother and Lizzie sharing kitchen space etc. They were both good cooks and Lizzie still turns out some wonderful Swedish dishes.

I had been left a small legacy by one of my father's sisters and decided to blow it all on a trip abroad. A friend in the travel business fixed me up with tickets and a contact in Paris to spend a holiday there. This I did, and I had a great time seeing all the sights, eating wonderful meals and drinking the odd glass of wine on the pavements in the evening sunshine. Pavement restaurants had not yet come to London, so it was all a completely different way of life for me. I think the thing that most stuck in my mind was the incessant noise of cars and cabs hooting all the time.

I particularly remember from the early 1950s two other holidays – very different from one another, but nevertheless both enjoyable. We all went over to stay with Lizzie's parents in Sweden and found Forshaga a lovely spot, the hospitality marvellous. We were introduced to meals that had six, seven or maybe more courses, all taken very slowly with different drinks in-between. I remember my mother being given Schnapps and told you drank it straight down followed by something else. The first time this happened her eyes glazed over a bit, but she came to enjoy it and became very talkative, part of her conversation being in her mother tongue of Portuguese. With several people speaking Swedish, and me trying to cope with a conversation in English which was being translated by Fedge and Liz, meal times were made even longer. This mixed with my mother getting merry and laughing at everything whether it was funny or not must have made Lizzie's family and friends think they had inherited a lot of crazy people.

We went swimming in a lovely lake that had cabins all round, used by the people living in the area in the summer months. We had travelled to Sweden in a Swedish ship from Harwich to

Gothenburg and thence by train to Forshaga. What impressed me most, apart from the scenery, was the cleanliness of the trains. We just weren't used to it in Britain at that time. There was drinking water available in each carriage if you wanted it and the coaches were light and airy. We travelled back the same way after a most enjoyable time, full of food and hospitality, but as we left Gothenburg an almighty storm blew up. Most people were affected by this, but not my mother; maybe she was so used to the crossings backwards and forwards in her young days to Rio and back that she was immune from seasickness. While the other passengers were staying put in their cabins or walking about with green faces, Mum would be wondering what was on the menu for the next meal. I don't recall the storm bothering me too much either.

The second holiday was with Pat and George Castle in Spain. George had an open-topped car and we decided to travel via Rouen, Paris and the Pyrenees. The weather was good but it still took a whole day to drive over the top of those mountains. There was a slight breeze, enough to disguise the heat of the sun, and at the end of the day I collapsed with sunstroke. We stayed the night, above a small cafe, whose proprietor and his wife were very helpful and gave me some Aspro. I crawled into bed and slept solidly for about 12 hours. Afterwards I didn't seem to feel too much the worse for wear so we carried on, eventually reaching the Spanish border where a lot of shouting took place while we got our travel papers sorted out.

We had booked into a hotel about nine miles inside Spain in a small coastal resort called Rosas. It was really lovely, and you could practically see the bottom of the ocean bed, with fish swimming about everywhere. The hotel cost us £3 10s (£3.50) each a week including all meals, which were just snacks in the daytime, but the evening meals were like banquets. Our bedrooms had stone floors and a shower that was part of the room, the water just drained away across the stone floor and that was it. Of course the stone floors kept the bedrooms pleasantly cool.

The first morning after arriving we went swimming, and when I came out of the water I found myself surrounded by

Spanish police all dressed up in exotic gear, shouting and pointing towards my swimming shorts. I couldn't make out what it was all about, but I was marched off to the local police station. Pat and George went to the hotel and asked the manager to come to the police station and sort it out. He could speak a little English and explained to me that by Spanish standards my trunks were too brief. Everything was quickly sorted out and I bought another pair locally. My own trunks were perfectly respectable, and by today's standards were almost Victorian, but there you are.

We went on a trip round the harbour in a fishing boat equipped with a strong light on the front with which the owner showed us craters deep down on the sea bed. The captain claimed that these had been caused during the Spanish Civil War. That had been back in the late 1930s so I'm sure they would have filled up by the time we were there, but we pretended we were suitably impressed with his information. The hotel had dancing at night in the open air until the early hours; they also staged a boxing match one night accompanied by more shouting and a lot of fist clenching from the spectators.

We stopped in Paris for two nights on the way and I got rather drunk on one of them. Pat and George suggested I sample a brothel next to the hotel, which I did. As soon as I got into the young lady's room, I fell asleep on the bed. I woke next morning with a bit of a headache and found my watch, money and wallet all laid out on the table beside me, and the young lady offering me a cup of coffee. She said in very broken English that I had been a bit drunk the night before and she let me sleep it off while she had gone into another room next door She showed me it, all very nicely furnished with frilly curtains round the bed. I told her we were leaving for England that morning and offered her some money, but she refused. So much for my attempt at brothel visiting, but what a nice girl. I could have lost everything that night with a dishonest one.

Light-hearted radio shows in the early 1950s were dominated by programmes such as *Variety Bandbox* which brought the two compères of the show a huge following. Frankie Howerd and Derek Roy alternated each Sunday night and eventually nobody went out on those evenings, as no one wanted to miss not only Howerd and Roy but the whole programme which was always discovering new talent, among them 'confidentially' Reg Dixon, Dick Emery and Robert Moreton (with his *Bumper Fun Book*') – the list was endless.

Charlie Chester's *Stand Easy*, which he devised and wrote himself, included some of the artistes who had worked with him entertaining the services in 'Stars in Battledress' units during and after the war. In the mould of Tommy Handley's *ITMA*, quick-fire material from Charlie and characters flying in and out was accompanied by noisy sound effects. From the mid-1940s Charlie Chester established himself on radio and in lavish revues at the Palladium and in the provinces, a career that spanned 50 years as one of this country's favourite entertainers; he was a lovely fellow to know and work with, and I have first-hand experience of doing so.

There were other wonderful radio programmes that ran from the latter part of the 1940s right through the 1950s and into the 1960s. *Take It From Here* featured Jimmy Edwards, Dick Bentley, Joy Nichols and later June Whitfield. *Ignorance is Bliss* was entertaining with a different format – a sort of potty quiz full of banter and gags supplied by the resident team of Harold Berens, Gladys Hay and Michael Moore, who incidentally was later one of the extras for the whole of the *Dad's Army* series. Michael was a very good impressionist amongst other things. *Bliss* was compèred by Canadian Stewart Macpherson who had come to Britain and become a great radio boxing commentator.

*Happidrome* was also a popular series, with its opening song from the three stars, 'We three in Happidrome, working for the BBC, Ramsbottom and Enoch and me' (Harry Koriss). The other two were Cecil Frederick and Robbie Vincent. *Hi Gang* and *Life with the Lyons*, written by and starring American film stars Bebe Daniels and Ben Lyon, became very popular with British audiences who really took the husband and wife team of Bebe and Ben and the children Richard and Barbara to their hearts, and entertainer Vic Oliver regularly contributed his own great style to the series. *Ray's a Laugh* was another series, starring Ted Ray, one of the greatest quick-thinking gagsters in the business and included Australian Kitty Bluett, a young impressionist called Peter Sellers, and two lovely blokes – Bob and Alf Pearson ('My brother and I'). Bob Pearson had a wonderful wit and I wish I had been able to get to know him better. His brother Alf is a charming fellow, whom I see quite regularly. I am always delighted to listen to his funny stories about the variety theatres and the artistes that played them. At a later stage *Ray's a Laugh* also included Kenneth Connor, and yours truly.

About 1951 I joined another amateur group through a friend of mine that I'd met at the Olympic Club. It was called 'The West B's', as they had apparently been formed from the nucleus of an ARP post down at Sydenham, South London, the location being the West B post in that area. The chap who introduced me was called Bob List. He was a pianist for fun, but a very good one, and he earned his living working for the Moss Empires Theatre Group, who at that time not only owned the London Palladium but also a whole string of variety houses in London and throughout the country. Bob used to get me tickets for all the big shows in London. I saw the opening night of *South Pacific* and wish I'd kept the programme because in the chorus credits were Larry Hagman and Sean Connery. They've both done quite well since then! Hagman's mother, Mary Martin, was one of the stars of the show, and sang one of the show stoppers – *I'm Gonna Wash That Man Right Outa My Hair*. What a show it was, all the songs were memorable.

I also saw the opening night of *The King and I* – when the house curtain stuck as it was going up and just showed the actors' knees – and many of the variety bills at the Palladium: the first night of Judy Garland, when she nearly slipped into the footlights on her entrance, and Johnny Ray, with his big hit *Cry*. On his opening night you couldn't move for youngsters in Argyle Street seething round the stage door with policemen trying to control the crowds. Johnny Ray was the first of what was then an unusual breed – the pop singer – and had already sold millions of records.

The visits to the Palladium were quite something because you saw the really big names that the boss, Val Parnell, brought over from America: Bob Hope, Jack Benny, Dean Martin and Jerry Lewis (a great double act), Betty Hutton, Tony Martin, Cyd Charisse, Frank Sinatra and so on. Unfortunately I never did see Danny Kaye who was perhaps the greatest hit of all at the Palladium. Those variety bills were made up of some wonderful acts from all over the world as well as our own home-grown entertainers like Max Bygraves, Frankie Howerd, Morecombe and Wise, Tommy Cooper, Ted Ray and many more. There were always a couple of great speciality acts on show – acrobats, illusionists, impressionists and those wonderful John Tiller lines of dancers with their precision routines.

In 1951 I remember listening on the radio to one of the greatest boxing contests to be staged in London when Randolph Turpin beat the American World Middleweight Champion Sugar Ray Robinson. I remember the words of commentator Raymond Glendenning as the referee raised Turpin's hand at the end of the fight: 'It's Turpin. Randolph Turpin-is-the-new-Middleweight-Champion-of-the-world.' The rest of his comments were drowned in roars of cheering from the Earls Court Arena.

Early in 1952 some of the West B Players were invited to take part in a week of talent competitions at the Forest Hill Capitol Cinema, between Sydenham and Dulwich, a sort of 30-minute interlude between the films. We went on on the Monday night and won our heat. However, next day the cinema cancelled the rest of the week's programme, not as a result of the West B's appearance, but because King George VI had died. I heard the news when I was sitting in the manager's officer at the cleaning company on the Tuesday morning. He said to me rather gravely, 'The King has died.' It was a shock to the whole country, more so because I don't think anyone had realised just how ill the king had been for some time. We now had a young queen on the throne, the first for over 50 years, and a widowed queen mother. I was destined to meet both of them more than once in the years to come.

Fedge and Lizzie's second child was born in October 1952 – a girl, Ingrid. She was lovely, and didn't seem to be any bother as a baby from what I can remember. However, it was obvious that we could not now all live together in the flat in Lexham Gardens and so Fedge and Liz went house-hunting, eventually finding their first home at Oxhey in Hertfordshire. It must have been wonderful for them to get into their own place away from the roar of London's traffic. That phrase was used as the beginning of a very popular weekly radio show called In Town Tonight, which introduced interesting people in London from home and abroad. The programme started with all sorts of traffic noises and flower-sellers and paper boys shouting out their wares. It suddenly stopped and a voice said, 'Once again we stop the mighty roar of London's traffic to bring you some of the interesting people who are in town tonight.'

I was actually in hospital when Ingrid was born. I had had what was diagnosed as a boil on my coccyx for about a year, and I was having regular treatment but it didn't seem to be getting any better. I sometimes couldn't even sit down to eat, and walking about all day in my job with the cleaning company was proving difficult. It all came to a head when I went to stay with some friends from my days at Roundabouts and we went out in a car which hadn't got the best of springing in the back where I was sitting. I suddenly felt a rush of liquid springing from the lower part of my back and when we stopped I found that I was covered in blood, but some of the pain I had been experiencing on the journey had subsided. One of my friends said, 'Oh I expect you've got cancer, my mother's talked about cancer.' I didn't know what to think, I just wanted to get back to London and get it looked at.

I telephoned Aunt Amy when I returned home and told her about it, not wanting to frighten my mother too much. Amy said to go and see Dr Rau, the man who had treated me when I had my swimming accident. This I did the very next day going to his consulting rooms in Grosvenor Square. He took one look at the problem, rang up Westminster Hospital and got me a bed for the following day. Apparently the official term for what I had was a Pilanidal Sinus Cyst. A hair had got under the skin just inside the bottom of my spine and was growing up inside which was causing the continual inflammation. I was operated on almost straight away, stitched up from just under my crutch to the small of my back, given tablets to stop me going to the toilet and put on a sort of pulley contraption to stop my body putting any weight on the bed.

I was like this for about a fortnight and at the end of that time the nurse who looked after me said, 'This is the big day, you're going to have an enema and we'll all stand clear.' This reminded me of the old gag, 'What do you give an elephant with diarrhoea? Plenty of room!' Once I was active again I was sent to a wonderful convalescent home at Lingfield near East Grinstead. It had beautiful grounds and I spent a very pleasant two weeks there. During my stay in hospital and for a few weeks afterwards the directors of the cleaning company were most generous and paid me. So a few months later when I got itchy feet and decided I ought to have a change of job, I felt guilty about the thought of leaving, not only because I felt I owed them loyalty but also because I knew the governors as friends as well as bosses. Their sons were now coming into the business and anyway if I left the firm what would I do for a living? So I put off the thought for the time being, and got back into the old routine.

# 5 THE FOOTLIGHTS BECKON

By the beginning of 1953 I had done quite a few shows with the West B players at Sydenham. Their producer was Ernie Lower, a real theatre enthusiast, who encouraged everyone around him. He had known Ralph Reader, the instigator of the Boy Scouts' gang shows and later the RAF gang shows during the wartime period and just after. I know quite a lot of the lads, most of them now in their 70s but still imbued with the zest for life that Reader had. Ernie Lower was in the same mould. The West Bs had one show a year at the Catford Town Hall, very different from the smaller venues where they normally performed. I took part in one of these shows at the town hall and was frightened to death, even though I was only doing a couple of quick impressions and appeared in a sketch. But the excitement of it all was probably good for me as I was getting rather bored with the window cleaning business.

The biggest event of the year was, of course, the coronation of Queen Elizabeth II, and what a day it was. The whole world and his wife seemed to have arrived in London for the celebrations, and the great occasion was watched by the biggest television audience ever up to that time, and for a long time after.

Another very important event, at least for cricket enthusiasts was the Test Match series against the Australians. The result was decided in the last match at the Oval. I remember walking back to the office during the afternoon of the final day and seeing groups of people standing outside radio shops or offices listening to the commentary. England was almost certainly going to win, barring mishaps, and when the winning runs were scored a big cheer went up. Who scored those last four winning runs needed for victory? – that man Denis Compton; and batting with him at the time? Bill Edrich. Perfect! The two Middlesex players who had brought such a sparkle to the game were together for England's postwar triumph. Captain Len Hutton had proved what a good 'professional' skipper he was. Trevor Bailey, Willie Watson, Jim Laker and my old mate Freddie Trueman had all played their part in the series that brought back the Ashes to England for the first time in 20 years.

It was altogether a good year for sporting occasions. Footballer Stanley Matthews won his first FA cup winners' medal when Blackpool beat Bolton Wanderers in the last minute at Wembley, and on the turf Gordon Richards won his first Derby on Pinza.

Nearly everyone who listened to the wireless at that time thought the BBC had gone potty, because a programme called *The Goon Show* was making its mark. It was anarchic for that period, very fast and combined the talents of a new wave of original comedians – Spike Milligan, who also wrote it, Harry Secombe, Peter Sellers and Michael Bentine. There were some wonderful sound effects and ridiculous voices from the cast, and it was destined to turn radio comedy upside down. It is very gratifying nowadays to know that we can buy some of those early shows of the Goons and other popular programmes such as *Take It From Here*, *Educating Archie* and many others from the BBC radio collection of audio tapes.

By the end of the year Mum felt she couldn't carry on at our flat in Lexham Gardens. I think she was feeling lonely amongst other things: I was out a lot with what seemed a busy social life quite apart from my working hours. Fedge and Liz suggested she should live with them at Oxhey, so we moved out and I got a room in Ebury Street, Victoria through, I think, a friend of Aunt Amy. It was very small but suited me.

The situation must have been difficult at Oxhey; Fedge and Liz had two very young children and now they had the responsibility of Mum as well. Of course Fedge wanted to do his best for her, but he also had to take into account Lizzie's position with all the problems one has in bringing up a very young family. Only they know what this meant at the time.

I was coping well in my one small room at Victoria. I had a

gas ring in my room and kept a frying pan under the bed and had the occasional fry up, blowing the dust off the frying pan before starting. I got to know a young lady who was the daughter of a famous family food company business. The young lady in question shared a flat with a friend and I remember a party there one evening. She and I disappeared into her bedroom but after a few minutes there was a knock on the door; it was her flat mate saying her regular boyfriend had arrived. There was only one thing for it: I climbed out of her bedroom window, walked very gingerly along the parapet to the bathroom window, let myself in and locked the door. I came out after a few minutes and was introduced to the boyfriend as if I were a complete stranger. It was a near thing and I was glad of my window cleaning training.

On the international scene at that time people were worried about relationships with Communist Eastern Europe: what became the 'Cold War' started almost immediately after World War 2 had finished. In 1949 the Russians blockaded Berlin. Policed after the war by four nations – France, Great Britain, the USA and the USSR – the Russians pulled out of the agreement and refused land entry into the city. The Allies responded with the Berlin Airlift flying food and essential services from this country to relieve the situation. On the other side of the world, in 1951, war broke out in Korea, when the Communist North invaded the South, and a UN force of primarily British and American troops was drafted in to defend South Korea. As this war dragged on it was decided to send out some entertainers from this country to cheer up the lads. This was done under the banner of the Combined Services Entertainment's Unit, the CSE which had been organised in Germany during the final fighting and the aftermath at the end of the war in Europe in 1944 and 1945.

Cousin Jon Pertwee was one of those artistes who went to Korea. His group also included a young, up and coming comedian called Bill Maynard, who has since become a very good television and film actor. While Jon was away he asked me to keep an eye on his flat in Chester Row, into which his young fiancée moved while Jon was in the Far East. She was Jean Marsh who later reached heady heights as the writer and one of the stars of *Upstairs, Downstairs*, a huge hit all over the world. She was about 19 when I first met her, a quietly spoken girl who seemed quite shy, taking a little time to answer any question you put to her. She was good looking and seemed a bit regal when she walked. She always called me Billy and seemed relaxed when we had a cup of tea together. I'm sure she was in love with Jon, but perhaps she was too young to cope with the married life that was to come.

The wedding was an eventful day near the Thames at Shepperton. Jean had stayed the night at a hotel opposite the church and her mother called me to see the bride-to-be just before the wedding. She was lying on her bed in full wedding gear trying to recover from a few drinks the night before. She said to me, 'I'm so nervous, I don't know whether I can cope with it all.' Happily, after a few words of mature wisdom from me (I'm sure it was a lot of rubbish!), she made her way over to the church.

Some members of Jon's family were there: playwright Michael – Jon's brother – and their father Roland amongst them. Roland was a long-standing writer who had written short stories for *Strand* magazine and, of course, plays including the successful *Pink String and Sealing Wax*. In his early days Roland produced several of these plays in the theatre on the Palace Pier at Brighton. He was then living in Brighton with one of his wives. I'm not sure how many wives Roland actually had: I think most of his family gave up counting! He also wrote, in co-operation with Michael, *The Paragon* – a very successful play that was eventually made into a film, retitled *Silent Dust*. He and Michael also wrote this country's first television 'soap', *The Grove Family*. Jean Marsh also has a sister called Yvonne, with whom I had the great pleasure of working for four years from 1988 until 1992 in David Croft and Jimmy Perry's television series *You Rang M'Lord*. Yvonne is a really very capable actress and lovely looking with it.

A lot of Jean and Jon's friends would stay at the flat in Chester

Row for the odd night or two while Jon was away in the early 1950s. I used to go round there to see if any mail had to be dealt with or such-like and the door would often be opened by someone – Joan Collins, Simone Lovell and, memorably, Diana Dors, who greeted me one morning in the nude and said, 'Oh sorry, we were expecting someone else.' I was sorry I'd disappointed her!

Diana was a very nice girl with a great sense of humour; I got to know her reasonably well much later on when I worked with her in concerts. I particularly remember one at the King's Theatre in Southsea when her boyfriend at that time, Troy Dante, and his guitar group were also on the bill. They played their first note and plunged not only the theatre into darkness but the whole block of shops and offices. I went out in front of the curtains with a torch and chatted and gagged with the audience until light was restored. One thing I said was, 'Business hasn't been too good here lately, last week they shot a stag in the circle.' Diana thought this was hilarious and repeated it to friends and fellow artistes for years to come.

Another fairly regular visitor to the flat was a merchant seaman called Vos, whom Jon had known for many years. Vos used to like a drink or two and on several occasions I found him asleep in the shower or even the coal cellar after a particularly heavy night. Another visitor was Bonar Colleano, an American entertainer with a wonderful personality living in England. He worked in variety with a most original approach to story telling and a lovely routine which included back flips that always went wrong until the last time when he would do three or four on the trot finishing his routine to great applause from the audience. Bonar was also a fine actor and appeared in many films in this country: I often see him on TV in a repeated film of that period.

Bonar was a bit of a character. His family came from a famous circus background and I think circus folk always have the daredevil in them as well as being generous and warm people. One story sums it up: Cousin Jon was always very happy to entertain at police concerts in aid of charity, so there was a good rapport with the Chelsea 'law'. He had a Vespa motor scooter amongst his mechanical vehicle collection and one day I had a call from the police saying, 'Bill, would you collect Jon's Vespa from the lounge of the Royal Court Hotel, as Mr Colleano drove it into the hotel last night through the front doors.' Some years after the hotel incident, Bonar was a passenger in a car driven by another actor in a hurry to get to Liverpool for a filming engagement. The car took a roundabout a bit too fast and Bonar was killed in the accident. It was a sad end to a great talent.

In spring 1954 I decided to leave the cleaning company and take pot luck at anything that came along. The little I had saved from my job soon dwindled and my dear mother used to come out from Oxhey once a week to visit me, a difficult journey for her. She would always go to the local grocers and stock me up with food – she really was some mum. I also used to borrow cousin Jon's Vespa and drive out to Oxhey for a good feed-up once a week. Lizzy certainly knew how to replenish my rumbling tum! I also used to visit a coffee stall at Victoria late at night: if you went along there between 11.30 and midnight the fellow running it would give you a snack and a drink for nothing before he packed up. I remember a well-known actress of the time, Joan Greenwood, also being there on several occasions. She seemed to have a rapport with the local tramps who gathered around the stall. She told them all sorts of stories in that fascinating low husky voice of hers. She seemed a nice person, very polite and chummy.

I took on several odd jobs at that time to keep the wolf from the door – one of them was at the Richmond Hill Hotel as pantry boy (boy!) and hors d'oeuvres chef, with a little clearing-up thrown in. The wage was £5 a week, all meals found. I had got a little behind with my rent and, knowing the landlady was mad on smoked salmon (oh yes, Ebury Street was a posh area: I know Noel Coward at one time resided not far from where I lived at No 78), I asked the head chef whether I could have some salmon. He, obligingly, gave me a packet almost every day. The landlady seemed to forget about the rent arrears every time I brought her a few more slices!

In the middle of the hotel's large kitchen was a huge boiler, rather like the upturned dome of a steam engine. It hung from the ceiling by chains and had a small pilot light under it 24 hours a day and contained the soup of the day, whatever day it was and whatever soup it was. The chef used to walk past it and if he saw a piece of meat or half an onion or a potato lying about, he would throw it in the boiler. I often heard a waiter coming into the kitchen and saying, 'Customer, he say compliments to the chef for good soup.' I used to have a bowl occasionally and it was certainly OK.

Another job I had for a short time, although my mother and brother didn't know about it, was as a Westminster City Council road sweeper. I think I was rather taken with the uniform: tan brown jacket, a large brass badge on the front with my number on it, and topped off with an Australian-type bush hat. My area was at the back of the Army and Navy stores in Victoria. You were generally given a sandwich by the owners of local cafes as you passed by and waved a greeting. I wished most passers by a good morning, and most of them responded likewise, particularly the ladies. One of them took my photo one day as I leaned, ever so nonchalantly, on my cart. She said she'd buy me a pint when she saw me next but I'd probably given the job up by the time she came back. I wonder if she ever dreamt about her road sweeper acquaintance! I was only at it for about six weeks but it had been an outdoor job and there wasn't so much pollution in those days.

Early in summer 1954 cousin Jon said he was going on a variety tour of theatres around the country: would I like to come with him as his 'Man Friday'? He had a caravan in which we would live and he would pay me £5 a week, all found. I jumped at the chance. We started at the Theatre Royal Portsmouth. Apart from helping to keep the caravan tidy, I was to help him in the theatre with his stage entrance, which was very unusual and very funny. The act before Jon was performed in front of the curtains. During it, he would climb up a rope ladder fixed to the fly rail. When he was announced the curtain would open revealing the rope ladder; Jon would then climb down on to the stage, look up and say, 'There's a bloody silly place to put a dress-ing room.' Big laugh and applause. He followed this by saying, 'It's very nice to be back in this lovely old garden city (or what-ever town we were in) but there seems to be something miss-ing.' He toured with a life-sized dummy of a musician holding a violin which I placed in the theatre pit before the show start-ed. On his saying, 'There seems to be something missing,' I would blow a huge raspberry on a little mouth piece from a crouching position in the pit. He would then say, 'That's it, who did that?' and pick up a large farmer's pitchfork which I had previously set in the footlights and thrust it into the pit at the dummy and heave this huge dummy out of the orchestra and hurl it offstage to a tremendous gasp, laugh and eventual applause. To pick that dummy up from a deep pit and haul it offstage all in one movement was quite a feat. Jon had very strong arms. But what an opening to any one's act, it really was tremendous.

The tour took in, amongst other places, Newcastle, Leeds and the Winter Gardens, Margate. As the shows at that resort didn't start until about 8pm, one day we went over to the Hippodrome Theatre there, a beautiful little Victorian building, to see the first house of a show called *Hot from Harlem* starring a double act, Woods and Jarrett. Soon after the start a young lady singer was introduced. I should think she was about 17. She had a tremendous voice and really made us sit up in our seats. Her name? Shirley Bassey!

I met a lot of people during those few weeks with Jon: Dorothy Squires, a bit of a handful at times with some fruity language but with a heart of gold; the Radio Revellers, a singing group of four jolly lads, very popular with the audience; ventriloquist Saveen with his shy lady puppet Daisy May and two outrageous dogs, one of them a real live one. The dummy dog did all the talking and Saveen's act finished up with the real dog uttering his only line, 'Shut that bloody dog up.' This always brought a huge laugh of surprise. It was done with a false chin which, when it dropped, looked as if the real dog said the line; it was, of course, Saveen's voice in true ventriloquial fashion.

Concert pianist Semprini was hugely popular at that time with his broadcasts at the piano, 'Old ones, new ones, loved ones, neglected ones.' He and his wife Consuello were a charming couple and often invited us into their caravan to sample Consuello's wonderful cooking. Semprini towed behind his caravan a large van which housed his piano; he would practise on it every morning. Usually we all parked on farmland near the town or city we were playing and the odd cow or two used to come up to the windows of his van to listen to the music. They probably found it relaxing!

The young Bill Maynard was with us and had a good sense of humour off stage. He said to me one day, 'If you ever go into this business proper you ought to do an act dressed in a pin-stripe suit, bowler hat, and briefcase. Say to the audience when you come on, 'I'm not really suited to this business but because my name's Pertwee the family think I should have a go. I don't want to do it so I'd be much obliged if you didn't laugh at my jokes and then I could prove I'm a failure.' This was Bill Maynard's quirky mind working overtime, and we had a few laughs talking about it.

Needless to say I didn't try the idea, but when eventually I turned pro I did play some dates when I didn't get laughs – not because I asked the audience not to, but because I was doing the wrong material or it was too sophisticated and they didn't understand it. I particularly remember one date at the Empire Theatre, Middlesborough, where the audience sat in stunned silence while I went through an impression routine of Noel Coward, Jack Buchanan (a London matinée idol) and Charles Laughton. I don't think word of any of these artistes had reached Middlesborough at that time. But the incident didn't put me off: I wasn't going to change my routine – at least not then, not even for the musical director in the pit who always slept through my act and whom I had to wake up when I was ready to do any musical bits. There was a local comedian/singer on the bill who used to tear the audience up every night; one evening when I had come off to the sound of my own footsteps he said, in the lovely Geordie accent that still fascinates me, 'You don't have to be a success in Middlesborough to be a success you know.' Words of wisdom from an old pro.

All that was to come as I was still having fun touring round with Jon in the summer of 1954. He always made me laugh when he was trying to be serious. When we were doing a week's variety at the Palace Theatre in Blackpool, we parked the caravan in the large grounds of what was a holiday camp, and probably is again. It had been commandeered by the RAF during the war as a training centre, but at the time we were there it was empty. Jon invited a few folk to lunch one day: Beryl Reid, Semprini and his wife, and Jack Warner who was in a play at the Grand Theatre in the town. It was decided that soup would be a good starter – and plenty of it, so the folks wouldn't want much of a main course. I had left the caravan to get a tin of corned beef, a few radishes and half a lettuce, which was bound to be enough for six people after having had pints of soup poured down them!

I got back to the caravan and opened the door straight on to Jon who was just turning round from the tiny Calor gas cooker. He was very tall and he – and an enormous metal tureen full to the brim with hot tomato soup – went flying. Soup everywhere, on the floor, on the ceiling, on the bunk beds. There was silence for a few seconds and then the fun and games started. You can imagine the language. Jon stormed out of the van, still carrying the empty tureen and covered in soup, and started to chase me round the camp. The abuse continued, and the more he carried on the more I laughed. He was shouting, 'Stop laughing all the time!' The more he said that the more I laughed. When we got back in sight of the van, our guests had arrived. Jon slowed up to a walking pace, put his arm on my shoulder and said quite seriously to the waiting group, 'Billy and I always go for a run before lunch.' And do you know, no one commented on the picture of two orange gentlemen standing before them. While Jon poured everyone a drink I was sent out to get another tin of corned beef. Luckily it was a very hot day and we were able to eat outside.

I have left until last the description of one significant person, because meeting her was to influence my future life in the theatre in no uncertain manner. The lady was Beryl Reid. She was very funny in those days with her monologues as 'Marlene from the Midlands', dressed in the outrageous styles of the day with huge earrings, and her 'jolly hockey sticks' schoolgirl with plaits, gym-slip and straw boater. She talked to us about a television series she was going to do and she wanted to try out new material for it in a revue for a few short weeks at the Watergate Club Theatre just off the Strand in London. In my naïvety I suggested I could write something for her, which I did. It makes me go hot under the collar now thinking of my cheek.

When the tour with Jon was over I had to find a job of some sort, and I got one in Daniel Neal's school outfitters in Portman Square. As I had worked at Burberry's and knew something about selling, it suited me fine. Once again I had a weekly pay packet and the money, though not a lot, put the dusty frying pan to work again. Come the autumn and I had a phone call from a producer called Ronnie Hill; he asked me whether I would like to come into Beryl Reid's revue which he was producing at the Watergate. It would be for eight weeks only, and I would be working with Beryl and four other people, and doing a solo piece.

I didn't want to leave Daniel Neals as I'd got used to a regular pay packet again, and when it transpired that the revue was only on in the evenings, I decided to keep the day job as well! The theatre pay would be £6 a week, plus £3 for the material – everyone was on the same money, but I had the extra three quid as a writer: combined with the pay from Neals, I was doing quite nicely.

I got particularly friendly with two of the people in the show, Douglas Argent and Barry Sinclair. Douglas went on eventually to become an executive television producer and director. We have met many times since, and he's never changed from those days in 1954. He and his charming wife don't live far from me now. The other, Barry Sinclair, had already had a distinguished career playing the lead in various West End productions, taking over from Ivor Novello when all those great musical plays of

Ivor's London productions went on tour around the country.

I remember that first night at the Watergate Theatre. There was I, a very raw recruit and suddenly in London's theatreland. I saw the other lads putting on their make-up with the greasy sticks used in those days and lots of eyeshadow. I didn't have any of these things, so I asked if I could borrow some. Well, you've never seen such a mess in all your life. I looked like a Red Indian in a fit! I started to whistle to cover up my embarrassment and this caused a rumpus. Barry Sinclair took me outside, turned me round three times and smacked me on the cheeks. I thought this was part of some sort of ritual you underwent before you started in the theatre and said, 'Thank you very much.' Well, I thought, I'm a professional now, although to this day I'm not sure that I really understand the reason for not whistling in the dressing room.

However everything seemed to pass off quite well, and I'd made a few new friends. Ronnie Hill was a nice man and advised me gently of a few do's and don'ts; Barry Sinclair I saw frequently – he had a great sense of humour and was a most handsome fellow. I went to several parties at his flat in Marylebone. We lost touch after the revue for some time but, would you believe, several years later when my wife Marion was in hospital at Brighton having just had our son Jonathan, Barry's wife was in the next bed having just had a baby.

I have jumped ahead a little because when the tour with Jon had finished, towards the end of the summer, I was walking back to my lodgings through Victoria Station one night and who should I see sitting on a seat but my cousin June Tobin. You could have knocked me down with a feather. The fact was that we were practically the same age and had been close when we played together as kids – seeing her quite unexpectedly in London, believing she was still with her family in Rhodesia, really was a joyous meeting. I of course hadn't seen her since the family emigrated there in 1947.

June had been doing a little broadcasting in Rhodesia and had come over here to try her luck in the UK. I asked her where she was staying and she said in a nearby hotel, but it could only be for a short time as she was running out of money. Unfortunately I was in no position to help her financially, so I phoned my brother Fedge and told him of the position. He said June must come over to Oxhey while her future plans were sorted out. The problems for Fedge and Liz, with a young family and my mother to look after, were now to be increased with the arrival of June. It must have been pretty worrying for all, but naturally June had to be looked after in the immediate instance.

My mother was delighted to see her niece again, and as Fedge and Liz had the same caring instincts there was no question that they shouldn't help. Eventually June found a new home with a large family not far away from Oxhey at Watford. Eventually she moved nearer London and worked for the BBC radio repertory company which was run by Val Gielgud, brother of Sir John. June eventually married writer and producer Peter Luke who had a very big success with one of his plays, *Hadrian VII*. The family moved to Spain some time ago and June is still there. Peter died a few years back. It is quite ridiculous that we haven't met up in recent years. June's eldest sister, Rosemary married a Geordie, John Dods in Rhodesia and, along with her elder sister Daphne, is still there. Brother Peter is now living in South Africa.

I carried on at Daniel Neals after the revue with Beryl Reid in 1954 and didn't really have any thoughts at that time of making show business my full time occupation, but I think the bug had bitten me subconsciously because early in 1955 I spoke to cousin Jon and said I thought I would have a go. He told me he thought I was potty, but if I felt strongly enough about it I must start at the bottom and get some proper experience in whatever form I could, either in repertory, which was still at that time in full swing round the country, or in a small seaside revue somewhere. He suggested I join the Concert Artiste Association as they had Monday night introductory spots and an old pro friend of his, Fred Hugh, could probably get me one.

This he did, and I duly did my Monday night with a take-off of a village cricket match. I was dressed in whites, carrying stumps, bat and all sorts of paraphernalia. The audience must have thought a madman had been let loose in their midst. There was I swinging a cricket bat around this tiny platform stage, narrowly missing the pianist, the overhanging lights and the front row of the audience who were practically on stage with me, all the time shouting out cricketing terms at the top of my voice. Nevertheless I got two offers that night, one from a gentleman accordionist called Carlo who would be presenting a summer season at Morecambe, and an agent called Robert Layton who said to come and see him in his office in the morning. Carlo offered me £8 a week so I waited to see what the agent had to offer. When I got to his office he said he could fix a season for me at Gorleston, near Great Yarmouth, with two weeks before that at Bognor Regis. He offered me £9 a week, which I got him to push up to £10: I was now in 'The Business' proper.

The name of the show I was to join was *Summertime*, with eight performers and a pianist. I met most of the company at Victoria station for the journey to Bognor and had decided that I should make them think I had all sorts of funny props that I would use. I had a huge fishing net, a large biscuit tin full of stones, cricket bat, stumps and a large broken down suitcase. Apart from the cricket gear and the biscuit box I had no idea what I was going to do with the rest, but thought I could probably dream something up, such was my faith in my professional future. Little did I know what a hard time lay ahead.

The gentleman putting on the show was Henry Lutman, who had been a well-known singer both in summer shows and London musicals. He would also be the male singer in our show. His wife Flo was the wardrobe mistress, and the stage manager-cum-props girl, scenery painter (what little there was of it) and general factotum offstage was Henry's daughter Pam. It was a real family affair, full of enthusiasm. The experienced principal comedian was Clifford Hensley, who had done summer shows all over the country. He had a ton of material, most of it written on faded bits of paper which he would hand out to me as previously described in Chapter 1. Cliff had a smiling face and was always ready to help where needed, and was basically in charge of all the comedy for the show.

Apart from a solo spot of about eight minutes duration, which all the artistes had to do, I was also to feed Cliff in the sketches. What I didn't know, because I hadn't read the contract properly, was that we would be doing five changes of programme, eventually changing every Tuesday and Friday. What a bombshell this was to me; I was going to have to find about 40 minutes of material in all. I can tell you there were going to be plenty of sleepless nights ahead. We had two dancers, Pam Lethay and Dinah Kaye, a lady pianist, Mary Gale, an accordionist, Alice Dells, and a soubrette, Marion Macleod, who was a singer and dancer, and would also be joining in the comedy items with Cliff and me. We would also be joined by Henry Lutman himself, who would not only be doing the male singing but would also join in the comedy bits when needed. Our pianist for the whole show was a young and inexperienced girl called Margaret White who was a member of the Bassett Liquorice Allsorts family!

Rehearsals started to get under way, and it was obvious from the start that I was going to be out of my depth as far as the production numbers were concerned. The singing was OK in that I could hit the right note, but my sense of rhythm was dismal as I either came in too early or too late; and as far as the little bit of dancing (or movement as they called it) was concerned, well I had three left feet and a constant habit of bumping into people. The other artistes headed by Marion Macleod and Cliff Hensley called a meeting and said to the boss, 'This fellow Pertwee will have to go, we can't afford to carry a passenger in a small show like this.' Mr Lutman said, 'I will not be able to find anyone as cheap at this stage, even if anyone were available. And anyway Bill fits the costumes,' (always a bonus for a small management!). In those days everyone in the business was working somewhere in the summer. So I was reprieved and the cast set about trying to sort out my left feet and lack of rhythm.

We finished our two weeks at Bognor and moved on to Gorleston for the main season. Now came the hard grind of trying to sort out all the extra solo material. By this time I think the rest of the cast was starting to feel sorry for me and was suggesting ideas. One of them was for me to dress up as a schoolboy watching a film; I would face the audience and give my reaction to the film. I went out and bought a pair of shorts, a cap and loads of crisps, nuts, bananas and oranges to eat. I had been told that a small lad would eat the whole time and I should mime it. The trouble was that I didn't know what the word mime meant, so I bought the real thing. I tried it out in the next programme and didn't come off until I'd finished the crisps, nuts, bananas and oranges, half of which were strewn all around the seat in which I sat. This was accompanied by shouts from the rest of the cast on the side of the stage like, 'Get him off,' 'Look at the mess,' 'He's gone crazy.' Eventually I did come off and was promptly sick – that was the end of the 'boy in the pictures'. However, with a little coaxing from Marion Macleod, I joined her in some singing, including a duet from the musical *Show Boat* called *Make Believe*, and did some impressions, and I managed to get by after a fashion. In the meantime I was still coping by 'covering things up with a cough'.

As the summer was turning into one of the most wonderfully hot seasons on record, there was time for relaxation. We went swimming every day in the warm sea, and met up with some of the other pro's in the big shows in nearby Great Yarmouth – Charlie Chester, the Beverley Sisters, Ronnie Ronalde (the brilliant whistler and singer), a very funny comedy act – Billy Whittaker and Mimi Law– and Tommy Trinder. We used to play a lot of tennis with Tommy's wife Toni.

I had changed digs a couple of times since reaching Gorleston, the last when my landlady brought my tea in one morning and decided she'd get into bed with me! I thought I'd got enough on my plate with three left feet, coping with my lack of rhythm and covering things up with a cough without taking on more problems, so I moved out and found yet another temporary home. I'd forgotten to tell the others my change of address and, after moving in, went to sleep after lunch.

The conditions of employment were that we would have 'matinées if wet'. Apparently, while I was asleep, three spots of rain fell on Gorleston and Henry Lutman rushed out with the board announcing 'matinée this afternoon'. He was able to get in touch with the rest of the cast, but not me as I had moved. When I got to the Pavilion for the evening show Henry said, 'Where were you for the matinée?'

'Matinée?' I replied, 'But it's a lovely fine evening. I'm sorry, I was sleeping in my new digs.'

'We took £3 10s this afternoon,' he told me, 'You must keep in touch in future.' He was a lovely fellow Henry, if a little absent-minded. One night we heard laughter coming from the audience during his solo singing spot, which was quite out of order as Henry's songs were mostly serious ballads. We rushed on to the side of the stage and there was Henry still dressed as a vicar from a previous sketch. He'd been so busy counting the evening's takings in the dressing room he'd forgotten to change.

Marion and I were getting closer romantically: a difficult situation as she was already married. At one point her mother came up to stay with her for a couple of weeks and twigged something was starting to happen between the two of us. I got on very well with her mother, Maud, who was a really lively person. I thought she was reasonably well off – I don't know why, not that it was any of my business. However I soon realised she wasn't because she asked me to buy her some fish and chips after the show one night. Marion's husband also arrived for a short stay; he was a merchant seaman engineer, a quiet chap and we all got on well together. Although it was to be a sad parting for everyone at the end of what had been a wonderful season for the whole company, it was going to be particularly difficult for Marion and me. However, it would not be the end of our professional and romantic partnership, just a temporary farewell.

We did have one marvellous occasion at the Pavilion before we left: BBC radio in those days used to do live outside broadcasts of shows round the coastal resorts and, thanks to some suggestions from Tommy Trinder and Charlie Chester, our little show was to be included in the one from the Great Yarmouth area. We were all going to have a chance to be on the radio. I did my sporting impression of a horse racing commentary and the others also did a short item each. The broadcast was heard by a producer in London (yes, they used to listen to them then) and when the season was over and I was back in London I got a call asking me whether I would like to take part in *Midday Music Hall*, a popular weekly programme. I was to have four minutes along with some other regular broadcasters. The show went out live, so you couldn't make a mistake, or if you did it would be heard by millions of listeners – remember, it was 1955 and radio was still hugely popular.

I have broadcast many times from the Playhouse since then, and appeared there in stage plays, but that first London broadcast for me was a milestone. I bumped my head quite hard on a low arch, going up to the stage, but soon forgot it in the excitement of just being part of what was a new experience for me. If anyone ever asks me what was the first real turning point in my career, I always say it was not getting the sack from that little show at the Gorleston Pavilion in 1955. If I had, I would probably have forgotten about having any future in the theatre and gone back to being a salesman of some sort.

When I got back to my room and that dusty frying pan in Ebury Street at the end of the season, I had to take stock of what I would do next. At that time there were auditions going on in small buildings all over London for various jobs, but more particularly for Rediffusion Television, which was presenting shows for the London area for the new commercial channels. Rediffusion had to find writers and performers to fill air time, which was not a great deal yet but audiences were growing with increasing sales of TV sets. Through a contact I met at the Express Dairy Cafe in Charing Cross Road – a popular meeting place then for performers and agents who operated in the industry – I did all sorts of auditions, along with other artistes trying to get their foot in the door: Rolf Harris, Ronnie Corbett, Charlie Drake amongst them.

Sometimes rushing from one place to another we would all pile into a taxi and share the fare. I did get a couple of jobs from this careering around the town. One was for Rediffusion TV for a short afternoon spot in a sort of magazine programme. You can guess what I was doing . . . yes, the cricket routine . . . stumps flying all over the place, worked with strings operated by someone behind a curtain, and of course the flailing cricket bat accompanied by a lot of shouting. My spot was sandwiched between someone talking about flower arranging and a lady giving tips on how to make apple chutney with windfalls. I don't think I made much impression on London's viewers, but at least I'd been on the telly!

The second job I got from my contacts was in cabaret at the 21 Room just off Curzon Street. All the nobs used to go there: Debs, young army officers and regular West End night clubbers. This job was arranged by a lovely lady called Phil Rounce, who was a partner in a new agency – International Artistes. Phil's senior partner was Major Bill Alexander, who had been responsible, along with Captain George Black and Colonel Basil Brown, for originating the wartime entertainment unit 'Stars in Battledress', a unit which nurtured many of the early and raw talents of entertainers who eventually became household names in the theatre – Terry Thomas, Tony Hancock, Janet Brown, Cardew Robinson, Arthur Haynes and, as I've already mentioned, Charlie Chester. These were just a few who took advantage of their time in SIB. Phil Rounce told me that when International Artistes first started money was short, and she remembers sitting on the floor typing the contracts. The firm is now truly international in a big way.

My first night at the 21 Club was something quite new for me, and a bit of a shock. The cabaret room was quite small and people were dining at tables. I was, naturally, presenting my cricket sketch – not easy in a small room which also housed a large grand piano. The customers must have thought a lunatic had come into their midst with cricket stumps flying, flailing bat and the usual shouting that accompanied everything. One night when I was in the middle of performing a tall gentleman diner, a little the worse for the golden amber, came over and kicked my stumps down, shouting in a loud voice, 'How's that.' Well I wasn't having someone interfering with my cricket match, so I punched him in the stomach as I told him so. He was instantly sick over the piano, and I was promptly marched off the floor by the head waiter and thrown down the steps of the club, followed by stumps and bat and shouts of, 'The customer is always right.' Not as far as I was concerned he wasn't!

I made my way back to Ebury Street, which wasn't that far away, thinking I'd probably have to go into another business. I always walked to and from the club every night in full white cricket gear with bat, stumps and pads under my arm. The first night a policeman on his beat said, 'Off to Lords are we sir.' He and I met on various occasions after that and had a little chat.

Phil Rounce phoned me the next morning after the fracas at the club and asked me what the hell I'd been up to. I explained what had happened and she said she would phone the club. As a result of this they said I could continue my two week stint there if I behaved myself. The first night back, would you believe, the tall gent was again in the audience. I thought to myself, 'If he starts anything tonight he'll get my bat across him.' As soon as he saw me he came over and said, 'I apologise for messing up your performance, I'd like you to have a drink with me.' At the end of my spot on that occasion he led the applause with murmurings of 'Bravo'. A small audience, particularly diners, are never very outgoing, so I suppose their response then was quite good.

Meanwhile Marion used to come up to London for the day to see me and would bring me goodies to supplement my food store. I think she was trying to wean me off the dusty frying pan, which I had told her about. We had now decided to form a double act to try and get some dates in variety theatres. We used to hire a rehearsal room and rehearse various items that we thought might be suitable. Marion came from a theatrical family and therefore had the general experience I lacked. Her mum and dad had worked in the West End and the provinces in various shows. Maud, her mother, had actually worked with Caruso at Covent Garden. Her dad, a Scot, had understudied Sir Harry Lauder and when Lauder's shows went out on tour, James Macleod (dad) used to take over Lauder's part. They also worked together at the Old Shaftesbury Theatre in Shaftesbury

Avenue (next to the fire station) in a revue called *Three Cheers*. Marion's brothers Johnnie and Norman were part of a hugely successful singing act the 'Maple Leaf Four'. I first saw them at Worthing in 1955. They made many records, and broadcast regularly, eventually having their own radio series – *Smokey Mountain Jamboree* – for several years. The act had been formed towards the end of World War 2 when, along with two other lads, Johnnie and Norman were entertaining in the services, a lot of it for the SIB unit. Their big break had come in 1947 when they were engaged for the Henry Hall stage show at Blackpool. So Marion came from good show business stock.

In 1956, under the title of 'Comedy Cocktail', we were launched on the unsuspecting public. We had done a sort of audition at the Nuffield Centre near Charing Cross. It was a club for servicemen and women who could spend an evening there once a week for tea, coffee, sandwiches etc. and see a show, mostly by very new artistes. Agents were also very welcome to come and see if any of the new talent on display might be worth taking on their books. One lady thought the 'Comedy Cocktail' might have a future and decided to get us some dates. Her name was Eve Taylor, and she shared an office nearby with another agent, Joe Collins – father of Joan Collins – and Carol Levis, the Canadian who presented his discoveries on radio and in the theatre. Eve thought Marion was very good and thought that if I dressed well (in fact she actually said, 'You've got to look a million dollars') I might get by with the odd impressions we had included in the act. Marion was doing some dancing and we would sing a couple of upbeat current songs, one of them I remember well called Relax-a-vous, which had recently been made popular by Americans Dean Martin and Jerry Lewis.

Marion had come to the conclusion that she had to make up her mind and I, of course, hoped it would be the right one for us. In the end she left her home in Hove and threw in her lot with me. In my circumstances I really wasn't much of a catch but we were obviously going to have to get by. Marion's mum stayed in their flat at the coast together with her ex-husband Billy, who at this point, incidentally, decided to give up the sea and look for a job on the technical side of the theatre. We have both been very close to Bill and his second wife Clare ever since, but I'll come back to Billy later.

1956 was to be our first summer show as a double act and we appeared in various production numbers as well. Before that we had to find temporary accommodation and this we did in Putney, south-west London. We got our first radio engagement when we were there and Marion bought a new dress for it at Richards in the High Street. I think it probably cost more than we were getting for the engagement! We only had to do a short act, but it would include a song which we got from one of the song pluggers in Denmark Street. If you sang one of the songs they were just publishing then you could get a whole orchestration for the BBC Variety Orchestra, which was very large, for nothing. As I've already related, I had a problem with timing when it was just piano accompaniment, but with a large orchestra it was almost impossible. This is where Marion's elbow was to come into service. At intervals she would dig me in the ribs and off I'd go. I was OK on pitching the right note and could hit it practically every time so our first broadcast seemed to go passably, I had a few sore ribs, but at least we'd got 'Comedy Cocktail' on the air!

Our summer season at Newquay in Cornwall was very good because the bosses, John and Adele Berryman, allowed us to experiment with new material. We did a take-off of Bill Haley's *Rock Around The Clock* which was then being played on radio and in all the juke boxes. The principal comedian in the show was Jack Francois, a super, jolly chap, with some original material and we all worked well together. Marion and I lived in a caravan on a small farm outside the town and we hired bikes, not just to get backwards and forwards to the theatre but to see the beautiful surrounding countryside. We used to visit the local pubs with Jack and his wife and play table football etc. There was a super pub in Newquay called the 'King Mark' where you could get wonderful Cornish pasties.

On one notable occasion there was a huge storm early one morning and the caravan started to rock really badly. I got up about 6am and saw tents from the adjoining camp sites flying over the roof of the farmhouse; we made haste and got into the large nearby garage. We'd hardly been in there five minutes when our caravan was lifted off the ground and hit the corner of the house. Luckily not much damage was done but it was a bit frightening while it lasted. Next day we went to the top of the cliffs and saw that the sea had risen and was thundering against the cliffs which usually were well above the usual level of the sea.

Before the season finished we had been booked by the Berrymans to play for them the next year, although they didn't know then at which resort we would be. I remember the excitement amongst the cricket fans in the show during that 1956 season when Jim Laker took 19 wickets in the Test Match against the Australians at Manchester; an unbelievable feat.

When we got back to London we had a phone call from Reg Brightwell, who was then running Combined Services Entertainment, asking whether we would like to go out to the Middle East to entertain at various service garrisons in the area – Alexandria, Aden etc. It would not be worth a lot of money, but it would be better than trying to eke out a meagre existence in Putney, where we had to spend a lot of time walking around or wrapped in blankets playing scrabble, as we hadn't got enough money to put in the meter for the small two-bar fire. Additionally, of course, it would mean travelling to foreign parts which we had only read about. Unfortunately, however, about a week after the first call we had another saying problems were boiling up in the Middle East and all entertainment in the area had been cancelled for the time being. The Suez crisis had boiled over and it would lead to war, so I'm glad we weren't caught up in that!

Marion and I managed to get a few variety bookings in the autumn of that year, notably at the Plaza, West Bromwich, which was a converted cinema. We arrived in the town on the Sunday night after a long train journey (railway services were pretty bad on Sundays then and I have to say they are not much better now) and we hadn't booked any digs in advance. There was no stage-doorkeeper on hand so we went to the pub next door. They couldn't help and sent us to the police station where it was suggested that we get a bus into Birmingham and try there. We walked around the 'pro's' area for a while without success, and eventually returned to the police station at West Bromwich. It was now getting late, and we had had enough of lugging our cases around. The police suggested an address we might try, which we did, and when the lady opened the door a terrible smell of sour sausages hit us. The landlady directed us to a room at the top of the house and when we got up there to the one large room, there were two blokes asleep in it snoring their heads off. Luckily there was a large chair on the landing in which we took turns to doze. Next day we found some accommodation in nearby Dudley.

During that week we went to see a matinée of the pantomime Dick Whittington at the Dudley Hippodrome. It starred Morecombe and Wise, Marion's brothers with the Maple Leaf Four and Mrs Shufflewick playing Sarah the cook. Shuff as he was known (real name Rex Jameson, although he never appeared as a man) was a very funny person, and had started his career during the war with the RAF Gang Shows.

Later in the week we had to do a broadcast in London so we left Dudley by coach at about 5am and afterwards got back to West Bromwich in time for the first performance at the theatre at 6.15pm. In the show there was a very funny comedian – Jimmy French – who apparently hadn't got any money and used to sleep on West Bromwich station. He used to walk straight on to the stage in his outdoor clothes and do a different comedy routine every night. I remember talking to impresario Bernard Delfont many years later about him. Delfont said that if someone had been able to discipline Jimmy he would have been one of the comedy greats; there again, as we agreed, if you had you might have taken away some of his magic.

We also had a nudist on the bill – most of shows at that time included a poser of some sort because management then thought that it might help the already waning business in the number two and three touring theatre dates. There were plenty of titles for the shows then, all supposed to titillate the male population. There was *All Tits and Tinsel*, *We're Taking Off Tonight*, *Bareskins and Blushes*, and Marion and I played our fair share of them. The management didn't tour the girls who were to pose nude, they would go round the town the week before asking the girls in the big stores whether they would like to earn a few extra pounds in the evenings – generally about £5. Their normal week's wages in the store were probably not as much as that. They reckoned Boots Chemist shops were the best recruitment centres, particularly in Nottingham.

The girls used to pose at the back of the stage and the announcement off stage would go something like this:

**Announcer:** 'Daphne is now in Switzerland' . . . and the curtains would open revealing her in a Tyrolean hat and close again.
**Announcer:** 'Now Daphne is in Mexico' . . . and the girl would be revealed in a Mexican hat, and so on.

The announcer at West Bromwich was also a rather gay piano player, doing an act in the show. One night he had a row with one of the girls before the show, and on the final announcement said, 'And by the way Daphne can be seen during the day serving behind the perfume counter at Boots in the High Street.' It made us laugh when we heard it over the tannoy in our dressing rooms but I'm sure Daphne wasn't amused – although she might have done good business at Boots next day!

Another date we played that autumn was at the Newcastle Palace, a small theatre where audiences were generally scarce. We arrived in Newcastle in the pouring rain but at least we had booked digs. It was very dark and cold, and we had a room at the top of the house; in the night we were woken up by a roaring sound and found ourselves covered in soot – it was everywhere. The rain had cleared the chimney all right. The landlady thought I'd been looking up the chimney for her cash box.

The week's variety at Newcastle included four young lads called the 'Railroaders' and the gentleman who came in with them on the Monday night asked me whether I would keep my eye on them until he came back to collect them after the show. They were nice boys and sounded good on stage, playing guitar and drums. Many years later, in the 1960s, I arrived at Manchester Palace to compère a week's show and found the police keeping order while hundreds of people were clamouring for tickets at the box office in the morning. When I got into the theatre one of the star acts of the bill, alongside Frank Ifield who had just shot to fame with the song *I Remember You* and his famous yodelling in the middle of it, were The Shadows, who had been backing Cliff Richard but had now gone solo for a while. One of the Shadows came up to me and said, 'Remember us? We met you at Newcastle; we were the Railroaders then.' A nice bunch of lads and they've consistently kept a high standard of performance.

1956 had come and gone, and we hoped 1957 would see audiences waiting for our Comedy Cocktail; we certainly did not think the audiences would be the Americans in Germany, with all the adventures that brought. A British agent who had never actually seen our act booked us to play the American service bases near Mannheim. We had a girl singer with us and a couple of Latvian (I think that's where they came from) acrobats. We were booked into quite a comfortable hotel, except that local building work went on all night under floodlights – the Germans were very quickly picking up the pieces after the war.

We were transported to the first base, and it became obvious that the Americans were not yet ready for our Comedy Cocktail. We had only been playing to British audiences and the Americans didn't know what we were talking about. In fact the lads didn't seem to take any notice of anything that was going on. They were playing the fruit machines, which completely drowned out anything that was going on on stage. Those who were not playing the machines were shouting across the floor at one another. I think we did about three or four shows before the end of the second week by which time the hotel manager said, 'What about your accounts.' I told him that we were being paid by a representative but unfortunately nobody knew where he was. The manager told us we would have to leave if we couldn't pay the bill so far.

I got the address of the representative whose office was in Frankfurt and off I went, only to find cobwebs over his door and rubbish piled in the doorway. I managed to make myself understood to one or two folks nearby and they told me he had left sometime ago. Apparently he was the Coca-Cola rep in that part of Germany as well as being responsible for paying the acts who were playing the bases, and as far as they knew he had gone back to Canada where he lived. Whether he had or not, or had just changed his address in Germany, I don't know. At any rate when I got back to the hotel I explained the situation to the manager who said we couldn't leave until we'd paid the bill for all of us. I contacted the British Consul who luckily agreed to settle our bills and let us have enough money for the fare home.

We left on an overnight train which seemed to stop everywhere accompanied by lots of shouting. The longest wait was at the Belgian border where everyone had to show their papers. The two acrobats, who had decided to come to England to try their luck, looked a little worried through all this. As soon as we were on the move again they got their large and very heavy canvas bags down from the rack and started to unpack some of their equipment – in particular the various-shaped metal pieces that they used in their balancing act. They unscrewed bits and pieces to reveal hollow insides that contained cameras, camera lenses, and various other things that I presume they were going to sell in the UK to see them through until they found work. When we eventually arrived at Victoria station after the journey across the Channel from Belgium the acrobats disappeared and we never heard of them again. They were never going to give up, and we thought good luck to them; they'd survived the war years in what had probably been a pretty hard time, presumably moving from country to country as circus and variety entertainers did. They never spoke a great deal about it, mainly because we could hardly understand them.

I rang Fedge and my mother when we got back to Victoria station and I remember the first thing my mother said was,

'Fancy ringing from Germany, it must be costing you a fortune.' I said, 'No Mum, we're home at Victoria, and we've only got half a crown between us (12.5p). Marion got in touch with her mother in Hove, and her brother Norman who lived nearby. He and his wife Bunty were just leaving for a summer show with the Maple Leaf Four at the Gaiety Theatre in Ayr, Scotland, so they suggested we have the use of their flat while they were away. Before we left for Germany we had confirmation that our summer show was to be at the Marine Gardens Theatre in Folkestone, so we knew we would have some money coming in a bit later. Marion's mum worked for a doctor nearby in Hove, including making his lunch. She decided she would cook far more potatoes than he could ever eat and would bring the extra ones round to us each day; we used them for salads. To this day, when somebody suggests we have potato salad my mind goes back to those days at Hove.

Marion's mum, Maudie, used to 'do' for another gentleman at Hove who ran a wine bar opposite the Theatre Royal at Brighton. He offered Marion and me a job making the sand-wiches and doing odd jobs around the bar. Horace Grice, the owner, was a really very, very nice man, and we remained friends for many years after. He married a really lovely girl called Pat and they had four children. We had contact with one of the grandchildren only a couple of years ago.

We had to pay back the British Consul the money we had borrowed to get home from Germany; we did this during the season at Folkestone, so there was little money left at the end of it. We had a small cottage in the town and we were able to relieve Fedge and Liz of some of the pressure of looking after Mum, something they had been doing for some time now , by bringing her down to Folkestone to stay with us. It was quite difficult in the little cottage and of course my mother wanted to help, which was not always possible as Marion had things pretty well organised, as she had to, working in the show as well. But we did have some fun there, and I particularly remember a party we had, the whole cast squeezed into very little space. I was opening a cheap bottle of fizzy wine outside in the garden and the cork flew off and hit the dog next door fair and square on the bum. He yelped and jumped in the air and a golfing enthusiast we had in the show said, 'Blimey, a hole in one!'

We made a lot of friends in the show – like Phyllis 'Podge' Haynes, a lady singer with a big voice and her husband, Francis, who was the pianist/organist of the show. There was a young lady called Dorothy Wayne who sang, whistled and played guitar and went on to appear in various TV shows. The principal comedian was Chips Sanders. He was very tall and had a lovely line in patter which accompanied his non-stop conjuring tricks and illusions. During that season I had been engaged to appear in a radio programme that we pre-recorded for broadcasting on Saturday evenings. The programme, *Variety Playhouse*, had a resident compère, Kenneth Horne, and included a short excerpt from a play or specially written sketch performed by the wonderful husband and wife theatre team Jack Hulbert and Cecily Courtnidge. I just had a short spot doing a couple of jokes using different voices and a couple of impressions. I did not know then – why should I?– that this short spot would eventually open the door to my big break in radio. Kenneth Horne I had met socially; the writer of the programme was Eric Merriman and the producer Jaques Brown. I was to join forces with all three of them in 1959, but more of that later.

Marion went to Torquay for pantomime in 1957 to play the name part in *Aladdin*, after an agent Harry Harbour had seen her at Folkestone. I went down to see her at Torquay and she brought terrific energy to the part as she was very athletic anyway, a good tennis player and swimmer. It was even more shocking when, soon after I returned, I was amazed to get a phone call from her mother to say that Marion had been taken to nearby Brixham Hospital to remove a small lump. At the same time her joints had started to seize up and had become terribly painful. The problem was diagnosed as the early stages of rheumatoid arthritis. This was a blow, as you can imagine, and, although she coped with it, from that time on and for the next few years it was to restrict her stage work.

During the autumn of that year I used to spend as much time

as possible sitting in the reception area of the BBC Light Entertainment headquarters at the Aeolian Hall in Bond Street with a tape of different voices I had made. Whenever a producer came in to go to his office I would try to accost him. One of them was a large gentleman called Leslie Bridgemont; he had produced more comedy shows than practically anyone: *Mediterranean Merry-Go-Round, Ray's a Laugh, Meet the Huggets* and many more. Leslie had also discovered Jack Warner when Jack was doing cabaret at the Headland Hotel in Newquay. Leslie happened to be staying in the hotel and gave Jack his first broadcast; I think he said he paid him £4 for it. Most people only think of Jack as Dixon of Dock Green, but he was much more than that. His cabaret act was very good and his impression of Maurice Chevalier was marvellous. He was the brother of those radio favourites Elsie and Doris Waters, and he had also raced in some of the very early motor track events. I worked with Jack on several occasions and he was a real gentleman.

But back to my first meeting with Leslie Bridgemont. He asked me to come into his office, which was not very big: most of it was taken up with a large grand piano. Leslie told me to sit down and then went over to the piano and played all sorts of familiar tunes; he was a very good pianist. When, eventually, he'd finished he told me that he always played the piano after lunch. He practically dismissed my tape: 'Leave it on my desk, it's been nice to meet you,' and ushered me out. I wasn't in the happiest mood, but at least I'd been able to see a producer, even though it had taken me a couple of months, during which time I had drunk many glasses of orange juice and eaten a quantity of sticky buns in the BBC canteen.

When I got back to our then temporary accommodation at Balham, south London, the landlady, a very sweet woman called Berna, said an agent had called. I rang him back and he asked me whether I'd like a week's work in a pub just outside Leeds. Apparently there was a cabaret room at the back with a Chinese menu. As I had literally run right out of money I said I'd go. Before Marion went to Torquay our financial resources were almost non-existent. She used to make porridge for breakfast, leave some over and add an Oxo cube in the evening to make thick soup. We also played a lot more Scrabble and walked for miles over the surrounding commons, sometimes quite near the Bolinbroke hospital where my mother had once been and my father had died.

Anyway, I did not know how I was going to get to Leeds without any money, but Berna turned up trumps and lent me the fare. It was near the Christmas holiday period and the train from London was absolutely packed. I found a space in the corridor next to a nice young girl who was returning home for the holidays from university. She was worried about her horse, and wondered whether it had been looked after and fed in her absence. She asked me whether I was going to have something to eat and I said I wasn't hungry – it wasn't true but I couldn't chance having to pay for her as well; in any case, I don't think I had the money to get myself anything. She asked me to look after her case while she tried to find the buffet car. It seemed to take her ages in that crowded train but she eventually got back and said, 'I can't eat in front of you without you having a bite so I've got something for you as well.' I ate the sandwich very slowly; had I been on my own I would have wolfed it down!

The owner of the pub, Jack Showers, met me at Leeds station and told me the BBC, a Mr Bridgemont, had been on the phone and would I ring him. This I did as soon as I arrived. Leslie said, 'Hello. Can you come into *Ray's a Laugh* on Friday'.

'Oh no,' I replied, 'I'm in Leeds doing cabaret for a week.'

He simply said, 'OK, goodbye,' and hung up.

Can you imagine how I felt? After all the waiting I couldn't grab the chance – and what a chance *Ray's a Laugh* was. It only had one or two series to go so my opportunity had gone. Still, I had a good week with eccentric Jack Showers, who had a wife and a live-in lover, both of them living in the place together quite happily. When I was doing my act if anyone should dare to make a noise – even a cough – Jack would shout, 'Silence please or you'll have to leave.'

My accommodation was in a caravan adjoining the pub; of course I was getting fed and so would return to London with some money in my pocket which would let me pay Berna back. She had a very young son and was soon to emigrate to New Zealand. Just a couple of years ago a large gentleman and his wife knocked on our door one day and he introduced himself. It was Berna's 'little' son. How we talked, finishing up phoning his mum in New Zealand. She didn't stopped talking and there was a bit of crying going on as well. The couple had found us by asking at Gatwick airport, 'Do you know where the Warden from *Dad's Army* lives.' They were surprised to find out we were quite near. The same question was asked by another New Zealander at Gatwick quite recently, and he too was told where I lived, or at least the area. This lad, Dave Homewood, is now the secretary of the New Zealand branch of the *Dad's Army* Appreciation Society.

The following year, after the Leeds pub cabaret, I had been booked to do a season with the famous summer revue, the Fol-de-Rols – the cream of summer shows since they started in their present form in the 1920s. Very well disciplined, wonderfully dressed, they had great music and lyrics, nearly all of them written by the Governor – Greatrex Newman, who had written for the Crazy Gang in London. He also wrote the book for the original production of *Mr Cinders* starring Bobby Howes, the father of that lovely actress Sally Ann. The principle comedian in the 'Fols' was Jack Tripp. He was also a wonderful dancer – nicknamed 'Plymouth's Fred Astaire' after his home town. He had some marvellously eccentric dance routines, send-ups of things like Swan Lake, and his tap routines were brilliant. Through the years he has become a great pantomime dame, perhaps the leading one in the country today. His sketches with his partner, Australian Allen Christie, were always funny. Allen was also a featured singer in the show. Sadly he died a few years ago, and was a great loss to the business.

Others in the show were Joy Jackley, sister of the great comedian Nat 'rubber neck' Jackley, Bonnie Downs and Lee Young. The Fols had two pianists, only one of which played the opening chorus of the show, the other one's job was to check that all the gentlemen on stage had done up their flies. We did a pre-tour, before the main season at the Winter Gardens Theatre in Eastbourne, taking in Worthing, Hastings and Margate. After the first night at Margate Rex Newman announced that another comedian would be joining the show next day. He obviously thought the input as far as the comedy was concerned, of which I was part, was not adequate enough! A small slight gentleman arrived the next day and introduced himself as Ronnie Corbett.

Now the Fols had a 'uniform' which was a fairly long Edwardian coat with waistcoat and tall hat all in a tan colour. There had been no time to alter anything for the new comedian; anyway, until he'd had time to rehearse he would only be in the opening and finale, and perhaps one production number. The first night for Ronnie when the curtain went up revealed him in a coat much too long and a hat much too large. I immediately laughed, and so did the audience. I thought to myself, 'This is good, and he hasn't done anything yet, so we're in for a few laughs this summer.' Well something did happen after the show that night, although I'm not sure what it was. I imagine a member of the cast suggested to the Governor that Ronnie was trying to be too funny, not too difficult with an oversize uniform. I got to the theatre next morning to start rehearsing with Ronnie and there he was with his suitcase. He told me, 'I'm on my way home. They're paying me two weeks' money and I'm off.' It was never talked about again. That pay off didn't do him much harm in the long run: his partnership with Ronnie Barker has given hours of pleasure to TV audiences.

When we were at Worthing the lighting batten at the top of the proscenium arch overheated and the curtains caught alight at the start of the second half. Everybody disappeared, it seemed, except me. Rex Newman said, 'Go out and stand on the piano and talk to the audience until they put the fire out.' This I did by the light of a torch on my face held by one of the pianists. As I was the only sort of story teller in the show I took it on and was out there for about half an hour.

During the main season at Eastbourne, when we were packing in about 1,500 people a night, Kenneth Horne, Jaques Brown (the producer from *Variety Playhouse*) and Kenneth

Williams had come down to spend the weekend in the town with Gladys Young's son. Gladys was a stalwart of the BBC radio repertory company for several years. For want of something to do on the Saturday night they came in to see our production (I only found this out afterwards). After the performance they knocked on the various dressing room doors to say how much they had enjoyed the show. I don't think I saw them as I was washing at the time. However they had discussed me during the show, and at the end of the year I got a call from Jaques Brown saying he thought I might be right for the series they had just started on radio, *Beyond our Ken*. I had heard one episode and thought it was really good. They had done the first series of six but wanted to slim down the cast as it was difficult to give everyone enough to get their teeth into in half an hour. So out would go Ron Moody and Stanley Unwin, the double-talk character; I still see him occasionally now, and what a lovely fellow he is. I could, if I fancied it, start in the second series in 1959. I couldn't wait to say yes as you can imagine.

I had auditioned several times for the Windmill Theatre, the theatre that boasted even during the war years 'we never closed', but the answer was always the same: 'Thank you, we'll let you know.' However I stuck at it and passed the fourth time – I think I just hated taking no for an answer. Of course it was a wonderful showcase to be seen in. There were six shows a day starting at midday and finishing about 10.30 at night, so there was no excuse for agents to say they hadn't got time to come in. Before starting at the Windmill, Marion and I moved to a flat in Wimbledon, and at the same time we decided to go our separate ways professionally. It was time to say, 'he or she who travels alone travels fastest'. I also thought that if I was going to have to play in theatres around the country which were not being kept in the best possible condition, and take dodgy digs, it would be no life for Marion. Soon after arriving in Wimbledon that Marion was asked to join the cast of the now very famous *Boy Friend* musical at Wyndhams Theatre. So she had beaten me into the West End! I used to meet her some nights at the theatre – I was turning into a real stage door Johnnie!

Fedge, Liz, James, Ingrid and Mum had in the meantime all moved from Oxhey to Sunbury on Thames. The children were now growing up and were at a school in Nursery Road, Sunbury – a school I pass on many occasions when I'm travelling by car to London.

After our short stay in Wimbledon Marion and I also moved, to Hove in Sussex, quite near her mother. It was a nice flat near the sea and shops and large enough for us to have my mother with us. This would give Fedge and Liz a break and be a nice change for Mum who loved the sea anyway.

1959 was really the start of all sorts of exciting things for both of us.

# 6 ANOTHER ROLL
# OF LINO

When I did my fourth and final audition at the Windmill Theatre for Vivian Van Damm there was no, 'Thank you very much,' after 30 seconds and, 'We'll let you know.' I went right through it and the Governor, as he was known, said, 'OK, you can do a season here if you like, but why didn't you do that sort of material when you came here the first time.' I said, 'I'm not sure,' a rather silly answer really. The reason for my remark was that I had done the acceptance material when I went there the first time, but either Van Damm had forgotten or wanted to see, as he had done with some other would-be Windmill performers, whether I was so keen to play the theatre that I would keep trying, and so give him the loyalty he always asked of his artistes.

The summer of 1959 was very hot and doing six shows a day, starting at midday and finishing about 10.30pm, was pretty tiring. The dressing rooms, being high up in the building, were very hot and I particularly remember one day sitting near the window every time I came off stage because there was a bit of a breeze. Perspiring and going from hot to cold several times each day brought on a severe cold, and trying to do so many performances in a week with a cold resulted in loss of voice.

The Governor told me to pack it in for a bit and sent me, at his own expense, to a Harley Street specialist. He was a caring bloke beneath his disciplinarian attitude. He was wonderful to the girls and would send them down to his house by the sea in Sussex for the weekend to relax. There were always two teams of girls working a show, one day on, one day off. The production generally lasted for eight or 10 weeks and during that time, while one group was playing, the other would be rehearsing upstairs in a huge room across the top of the theatre.

When the male performers first started the Governor used to tell them to wait on the stairs until the tableaux nudes were off and into their dressing gowns. You then made a bolt for the stage as your entrance music was being played. After a while he would casually tell you that you could help with the dressing gowns now. I suppose he was confident we wouldn't start any nonsense with the nudes as they came off. Actually there were several reasons why we blokes wouldn't really have thought of doing anything. First of all, we were scrambling to get on as soon as the girls were off. Then there were the girls themselves: good types, some of them coming from well-to-do families, and anyway as we worked with them for long hours each day, we were all friends together. Some of them were married and a lot of others had boyfriends. The Governor always liked to get to know the boyfriends; I thought it was a good idea, that way he knew the types that his 'girls' were going out with.

I remember taking a shower one day in the main large shower room and a couple of the girls came in, not in the least embarrassed, and said, 'Phew, it ain't 'arf hot, how are they out there for you today Bill?' One of the girls said to me one day, 'You don't want to worry about us, but don't drop the soap if the boy dancers are up here!' The girls felt very secure working at the Windmill and certainly didn't mind the heavy workload or the discipline the stage manager demanded of everybody.

I went back for another long season in 1960 and by this time had learnt a lot about keeping my head when I got no reaction to my act for most of the day. The last two performances at night brought in a mixed audience, so this brought a different reaction, and I generally went home feeling I'd won some of the folk over. Every Saturday we had a party of West Country farmers who had queued from early in the morning to get front row seats. Every time the male performers came on they would open their sandwiches and pass a ketchup bottle along the row. No one was asked to leave after one performance because it was called continuous revuedeville so of course people would come in half way through a show and see it round again, but the attendants all had a keen eye and if anyone was spotted in their seats after two whole performances they were gently asked to leave. As soon as the male performers started there would be a clatter of seats tipping up as one left and the person behind jumped into his seat to get nearer the stage. Everything at the Windmill was done with artistic flair; eventually this would be its downfall as several clubs were opening in Soho where this wasn't always the case, and nudity became rather coarser.

One evening a couple of us went to one of the nearby clubs during our break and there was a nude doing an act with a snake. Well the snake got a bit excited when she came down into the small audience space and wrapped itself round her bum. We started to laugh and were asked to leave. We never did find out what happened to the snake, never mind the girl.

The night the Windmill finally closed a lot of the people who had worked there over the years were invited to the last night party. It was quite a sad occasion for many of them. They included Harry Secombe, Bill Kerr ('I've only got four minutes'), Sheila Van Damm (Vivian's daughter), Des O'Connor, Arthur Haynes, Michael Bentine, Jimmy Edwards, Alfred Marks, Arthur English, Bill Maynard, Bruce Forsyth and many more, all recollecting their own memories.

The first male comedian to be engaged by Van Damm way back in 1932 was a gentleman called John Tilley, who later became a great radio favourite doing monologues. One of them was about a scout rally and his routine about this was punctuated with 'Rally boys rally'. Tilley was such a favourite with the Governor that when he left Van Damm locked his dressing room up just as he'd left it, and it was still locked when I was there. I asked to see it one day and I was not allowed to. It had become a bit of a shrine as far as the Governor was concerned. Sheila was a well-known saloon car racing driver and had taken over the reins at the Windmill after Vivian died. She was loved by everyone there. But the theatre, whose motto was 'We never closed', finally did. It was the end of an era.

During that summer Marion had a call from an agent asking whether she could take over at Bognor Regis in the summer show there. The lady she was to replace was part of a double act and had to leave for a while due to ill health. The act was Charlie Stewart (whom Marion had met) and Ann Mathew.

They were very successful in variety, summer shows and pantomime. After a short rehearsal with Charlie, Marion went into the show and then went up with him to Glasgow to do another revue. Stewart was a Scot, and very popular north of the border. The pair of them worked very well together and Marion stayed on to do pantomime in the city with him. I was practising for my driving test while Marion was at Bognor, and with an authorised driver I used to drive to Bognor from Brighton on some evenings to collect her. The long runs there gave me a lot of practice but I still failed the first test after hitting a lamp post as I was reversing. I passed at the second attempt and got my first car, a light green Austin 12.

I had been engaged by a very well-known pantomime management, Emile Littler, for Christmas 1959. Emile, along with his brother Prince, also presented some of the big musical shows in London and between them also controlled several theatres. This was to be my first panto engagement and I was cast with a young man who was also making his debut in Christmas entertainment. His name was Roy Hudd. We were to play the broker's men in *Goody Two Shoes* at the Empire Theatre Leeds. I made arrangements through the management to give Roy a lift up to Leeds in my car. A few days before we were due to leave I got a call to say that someone who was taking part in a sketch in the live weekly TV show *Sunday Night at the Palladium* had been taken ill and would I like to do it. It was only a few lines, but of course to be in that show, watched by several million every week, was very good and, although the fee was small, it meant another roll of lino or some other item for the flat.

The show that night was at the Palace Theatre Cambridge Circus (now owned by Andrew Lloyd Webber) as the Palladium was getting ready for its pantomime season. I arranged to meet Roy Hudd after the recording and we would then drive to Leeds up the old A1 overnight ready for the start of our panto rehearsals the next morning. It was a bitterly cold night, my car didn't have a heater, and Roy had no overcoat, just a thin suit. Anyway we made our way to Leeds and half way there, with a shivering Roy beside me, it started to rain and my windscreen wipers packed up. We finally arrived at about 6am and I dropped Roy at his digs and drove off to mine, right in the heart of Leeds. Next morning I asked Roy how he'd got on, and he said when he knocked at the door of his digs the landlady said, 'You're too early, I wasn't expecting you until 9 o'clock,' and shut the door on him. Oh the glamour of show business! But Roy, with his tremendous enthusiasm for the theatre which he loves and which has never waned, laughed it off.

*Goody Two Shoes* was a lovely company and we all got stuck into our new environment. We had a wonderful company manager called Algy More, who had a terrific sense of humour; he became a great mate to us all. We remained good friends until he died a few years ago at the age of 89. The stars of the pantomime were Charlie Carolli and company, the great clown from the famous Tower Circus at Blackpool ,and Ken Platt, a well known broadcasting comedian with the catch phrase 'I won't take me coat off, I'm not stopping'. The dame of the pantomime had worked with Carolli before and was very experienced and quite wonderful. His name was Henry Lytton; he came from a well known theatrical family.

We had a midget in the show playing the dog. Was he good? He didn't miss a trick getting the children on his side! His name was Kenny Baker and since then he has made a name for himself in films, particularly for playing R2D2 in *Star Wars*. Kenny was always fond of the girls and was very chummy with the Tiller Girls, those great lasses who have graced so many pantomime and musical productions. Alas, few shows nowadays have precision dancers like the Tillers. Managements believe they are an added luxury and prefer to save money. I remember going into the Tillers' dressing room one night. They were bathing little Kenny in their washbasin. Kenny said, 'A bit good this, dad.' He always called everyone 'dad', I don't know why. I think the girls were enjoying themselves as much as Kenny.

The principal boy (played by a girl in traditional pantomime for those who are not aware of this) was a West End artiste called Joyce Mandre. The villain was a real character – Stewart Pearce. He played the yellow dwarf in *Goody Two Shoes* for 11 years on the trot. He was a real actor laddie, wearing his coat slung over his shoulders and a stylish trilby hat turned up at one side. He had a dry sense of humour and Roy and I shared a dressing room with him. He had what he called an L. Boiler. It was a sort of open kettle he used for making tea, always the best, which he had sent up from London by his girlfriend. I lived near him in Leeds in what had obviously once been a well-to-do estate of small houses called Cobden Place. We used to have a few late night parties during the run, and one Sunday evening, when we'd been out, Stewart's landlady had left a cryptic note for him. Stewart said, 'I've had enough of her,' went into his room, brought out his po and emptied it down into the base-ment where the landlady lived saying, 'Take that you old cow.'

It was, as I've said, Algy More who provided us with so many laughs, telling us stories about variety artistes he had worked with through his career. He had started as a pierrot in beach shows at the seaside and later went into the music halls as part of a musical act called 'Vine, More and Nevard'. I wrote about many of his experiences and life with his eccentric father, who was also a performer, in my book *Promenades and Pierrots*.

I mentioned that Marion was playing pantomime in Glasgow that Christmas; she often came down to Leeds on the overnight train. I used to meet her in the early hours. I remember at the end of her run in Scotland she arrived with a terrible cold which turned to pleurisy. She still remembers Roy Hudd bring-ing her a bunch of snowdrops to help her get better.

We had a long season at Leeds and my mother came up for a few days. I took her to a matinée of a pantomime at the Bradford Alhambra to see Ken Dodd. I thought Mum would fall out of her seat when at one point in the show Ken threw a pair of corsets into the audience: she really loved him. We made friends with some of the artistes in the other pantomime in Leeds, at the Grand Theatre, singer Ronnie Hilton and the wonderfully funny Peter Butterworth, husband of that lovely impressionist Janet Brown. Peter was playing the dame in that panto. I'm delighted to say that their son Tyler has made his way as a very good actor, and this year will probably be in a new comedy in the West End. After what seemed a very long season (well we didn't finish until April), we arrived back in Brighton.

Before going to Leeds I had started in the radio series *Beyond our Ken* with a contract for six shows. I went to the bank manager and told him I had a long BBC contract which I laid out in front of him, being careful to cover the words 'six weeks'. I said I wanted overdraft facilities as we needed carpets and some furnishings for the new flat; it wouldn't be for long, just until the money started rolling in! I think I started at £15 a show. The bank manager was quite happy to help. That six-week engagement turned into eight years in all with *Beyond our Ken* and *Round the Horne*. Joining the show was absolutely wonderful. I used to walk from Victoria station across St James's Park to the Paris studio in Lower Regent Street on Wednesday mornings with a real spring in my heel. The cast made me very welcome, with the exception of Ken Williams who, in a jokey way and always in front of me, used to say things like, 'Why have we got him in the show, we can do all the voices,' etc. We did manage to get back at him once, and Ken applauded the gag!

Although I was really the utility man in the show I was pleased to do anything: odd voices that came up from time to time plus a few send-ups of personalities who were popular broadcasters at that time, such as Frankie Howerd who came out as Hanky Flowerd, Fyfe Robertson (who was a resident on the *Tonight* TV programme and was always outside somewhere and used to start off by saying 'I'm standing now. . . '). Robertson became Ryfe Hobertson in *Beyond our Ken*. Hugh Paddick and Kenneth Williams had regular characters, Charles and Rodney, two slightly precious upper class twits gossiping about their latest ventures. Betty Marsden did a send-up of the cookery expert Fanny Craddock, rewritten as Fanny Haddock. Hugh Paddick was pop singer Ricky Livid, Kenneth Williams was Arthur Fallowfield ('The answer lies in the soil') and the show's resident singer was a lovely girl called Pat Lancaster.

But the whole thing revolved around the star of the show, Kenneth Horne. A real help to everyone, his own timing and style was a tremendous asset to any programme. The partnership of Horne, writer Eric Merriman and producer Jaques Brown, actually started with the Saturday night *Variety Playhouse* series. Eric was asked to come up with an idea which would follow it, and so *Beyond our Ken* came about. Barry Took partnered Merriman in the first couple of series and then Merriman carried on and wrote over 100 episodes. Eric came up with ideas such as send-ups of the American Western television serial *Wells Fargo*, which became Tunbridge Wells Fargo. *Kitty From Kensington* was a musical piece based on some of the rather twee musicals, around London's theatreland for many years.

Then there was 'The Twinkle Dolls' episode which came about when Eric and I went over to see Sandy Powell's *Starlight* summer show on Eastbourne Pier. During the performance you could actually hear the sea lapping under the pier. We went round to see Sandy and his wonderful feed Norman Meadow after the show and they recalled all the funny instances that happen in a seaside show. This gave Merriman the idea of writing about a seaside concert party in the early days of rehearsal, and the result was a hilarious send-up of the whole business of trying to put on a show at the seaside, with all the arguments, etc, that had been repeated around our coasts for years.

When we recorded 'The Twinkle Dolls' in the studio, Sandy Powell and his wife Kay were invited to join the audience and they laughed louder than anybody. Sandy was one of the most experienced and wonderfully inventive comedians you could wish to see. He had been a hugely popular music hall and radio comedian before and after World War 2 with the catch phrase, 'Can you hear me mother?' He was, I think, the first recording artiste in this country to sell a million records. Unfortunately the Pier Theatre burned down in 1970 and that was the end of Sandy's reign. His feed Norman was asked to take over as pier manager when it was refurbished and proved very successful. Norman still lives in Eastbourne with his wife Peggy.

Early in the 1960s Eric Merriman and I joined forces with a girl singer called Danny Clare to present *Don't Look Now*, a late night revue on Southern Television, and it ran for several weeks, late in the evening.

*Beyond our Ken* rolled on, getting more popular all the time. Audiences waiting to get in to the lunchtime recordings used to queue right up Lower Regent Street. I witnessed people offering money to buy tickets from those that had them, despite the fact that BBC shows were free on application to the BBC ticket unit. Kenneth Williams would regale us with stories and was very funny. He also told us of the latest show business gossip and a number of outrageous stories, one of which I still remember very well. The story concerned a convent where one of the nuns goes in to see the Reverend Mother.

**Nun:** 'I'm sorry Mother, I've got to be leaving the convent.'
**Reverend Mother:** 'Why, child?'
**Nun:** 'I'm pregnant.'
**Reverend Mother:** 'Get out of here at once you wicked girl.'

This is all repeated when another nun comes in and says the same thing, with a similar reaction from the Reverend Mother. Then a third nun comes in saying she's going to leave.

**Reverend Mother:** 'Oh God, you're not pregnant as well.'
**Nun:** 'No, but there's an awful lot of fornicating and scrubbing going on around here and I'm doing all the scrubbing!'

'Hornerama', a magazine style send-up of the popular TV series *Panorama*, ended each show.

My regular appearances on *Beyond Our Ken* got me some theatre concert work as a supporting name. I used to come back after these outings, put the cheque down and say to Marion, 'Well, there's another roll of lino.' Every bit of money earned went into the house we had bought in Hove. Lino, for those who don't know what it is, is a sort of oil-cloth floor covering, which, having been in existence for years and years, was eventually taken over by plastic, and plastic tiles which were fairly easy to lay, but messy as the adhesive was a sort of black tar.

Our house in Hove was an old Victorian semi-detached on three floors. It had been empty for ages and was almost derelict inside, but the thought of putting it right really excited us. I remember the first time I was given the key to have a look rounde, I found an old tramp in the living room. I asked him what he was doing and he said, 'I come in here a lot, it's very nice.' I told him I was going to be the new owner, and there wouldn't be room for him as well. I didn't see him again after that, I suppose he thought his privacy had been disturbed.

When my mother first saw the house she went to church and lit a candle and said a prayer hoping we wouldn't buy it. It certainly needed some attention: the entrance hall had collapsed. We couldn't afford a builder to do the work so Marion's brother Norman, who never shirked a challenge, suggested we jack up the stairs. With much creaking and cracking, we replaced all the timbers, joists and floorboards. We also had to rebuild most of the brick pillars. To finish off, Norman said we ought to spray it all underneath with anti-worm spray. This we did, but unfortunately the spray seeped through to the adjoining house. The neighbours came rushing in to say that they were experiencing the smell and their eyes were smarting from the spray.

At one point I was appearing for a couple of weeks in cabaret on the other side of Birmingham. I used to down tools at about 5pm, have a bath at the flat and drive up to the Midlands, do my cabaret performance at about 10.30pm and get back to Hove in the early hours; then, after some breakfast, get back to the house for more work. As it got more habitable we moved in and decided that there was enough room for my and Marion's mother to come and live with us, each having their own room. Maud, Marion's mother, had to move out of her flat because Marion's ex-husband had left the sea, had gone into the theatre on the technical side and was going to live in London.

We got married in April 1960. I had been able to get on with the house while Marion was away doing pantomime in Cardiff. Our mums came with us on our short honeymoon at Westcliff-on-Sea – well, they didn't want to be left out! Marion's divorce had been quite amicable and we kept in touch with Billy Rose. In fact while looking for more suitable accommodation back in Brighton he came to live with us for a few weeks.

Aunt Amy and a whole lot of folk came to stay for our first Christmas in the new house at Hove Park Villas. We had a marvellously festive gathering, but I do remember we had a fall of soot in the lounge at one point, which even those not quite used to our slightly eccentric life style had to laugh at. I remember sister-in-law Bunty's baby was asleep with our dog on the hearth rug and they both received their fair share!

Amy decided to make a gift to us of a nice sum of money. She also did the same to Fedge and Lizzie, which helped us all considerably. Amy had lived a pretty ordered life and I'm sure she thought we were all potty. We called the house Pertwee Towers. It was a joke on our part, of course, because it was a long time before we got it into any order. Some people actually took Pertwee Towers seriously when they wrote to us. I titled myself 'The Laird of West Sussex'. This was a title I had cribbed from my sister-in-law Bunty's father in Scotland. He was a very well known comedian north of the border, his name was Harry Gordon and he was known as 'The Laird of Inversnecky'.

We had all sorts of folks coming to 'Pertwee Towers'. Little Kenny Baker stayed with us when he was playing in an ice show at Brighton, and others from the touring stage version of the popular TV *Black and White Minstrel Show*. We were having the old parlour turned into a kitchen at the time, most of it was being done by brother-in-law Norman and myself, so Marion had to cook the Minstrels' breakfast on a primus stove in the hall. Every now and again we would hear voices from upstairs saying, 'Are you doing our breakfasts?' It was our two mothers.

Jack Tripp and Allen Christie, with whom I'd already worked at Eastbourne for a season, lived nearby. When they came to visit Jack would call upstairs to the mums, 'Won't be long number 8 (or whatever number came into his head). Tea's nearly ready,' just as landladies used to do in the theatrical digs we had all known. So after our camping-out breakfast sessions in the hall we used to call out, 'Breakfast is ready number 6. Bring your dirty dishes down and don't forget to empty your pos.' You could hear the mums saying, 'That boy is so rude, supposing someone heard him?' We would then pretend we had been talking to someone in the hall, and you'd then hear further conversations from above, 'Oh my God, whatever will people think'. It was all part of the fun we had at home.

We also made a second bathroom out of the pantry and coal store. I finished it off by putting polystyrene tiles on the ceiling. I didn't know you just put a blob of glue in each corner and one in the middle, and I smeared it all over. I was the first one to have a bath when it was finished and as I was lying there, all the tiles came off the ceiling and into the bath. What a mess that was, the worst advert possible for do-it-yourself.

Agent George Knapman, whom I have mentioned in connection with the great Sid Field, booked me into a series of one-night stands with cookery expert Marguerite Patten. These shows were sponsored by companies including Ovaltine, Creda Cookers and Pearce Duff custard powders. Marguerite did a fairly long spot in the middle of these shows, giving the audience tips on making various simple dishes. One of her regular presentations was icing a cake, or perhaps a stupendous ice cream sundae that was a bit different. The decorations would include my contribution in Marguerite's spot; of course I got it all wrong, with most of the contents of the icing bag going on to the floor. This would bring some laughs or groans from the audience. Marguerite would then show how it should be done.

I was principally engaged to compère the whole show, which included some of the best current entertainers in the business: Tommy Trinder, Arthur Haynes, Pearl Carr and Teddy Johnson, plus the big band of Eric Delaney making the whole production really swing along. I had a lot of fun on those trips round the country. We sometimes did a matinée performance in one town and then moved on to another for the evening show. One day we did an afternoon performance in Middlesborough and the evening show in Wolverhampton, and afterwards drove back to Brighton, where Marguerite also lived; on those occasions we did the journeys in my car, Marguerite always insisting we stopped half way to have a light meal as she said it would give energy when you're driving. She was right of course.

One announcement from Eric Delaney when he introduced

a solo spot during the band interlude has stuck in my mind ever since. A tall black guy called Herbie Goynes was a regular contributor, playing an instrument, tap-dancing and throwing in a few quick one-liners. Eric used to say, 'And now, Ladies and Gentlemen, I want you to meet and greet Mr Herbie Goynes.' Don't ask me why I remember that so well. Eric was a super drummer and led his band through a selection of great numbers. The audience for these shows came in free on production of a wrapper from a tin of Ovaltine or a Pearce Duff box.

An incident at the New Theatre, Oxford, sponsored by Ovaltine gave us all a laugh. At the end of the show Tommy Trinder stepped forward to thank the audience and said, 'Don't forget to take your cup of Horlicks before you go to bed.' It was a genuine mistake and the audience joined in the laughter. I don't think the sponsors, there in force, were terribly amused. Marguerite and her husband Bob, Pearl and Teddy, and I became good friends during those tours; we still keep in touch with one another. The shows were hard work combined with the travelling, particularly for the stage staff and technicians moving around the country, one day here, one day there.

We will always remember fondly living in the Brighton area in the early 1960s. It certainly was a time that I'm sure the whole of society will look back on and say it was a major turning point in social and historical terms. President Kennedy was the new man in America, only to die two years later from an assassin's bullet. Russian Yuri Gagarin became the first man in space. We all believed we might be on the brink of a third world war with the Cuban missile crisis, and the disaster of the Vietnam war was shaking the Americans to their roots.

On the home front there was the Profumo affair: how we all felt for John Profumo and his lovely actress wife Valerie Hobson. They have since carried themselves with great dignity and profound affection. The great man Winston Churchill died and was truly honoured as a great wartime leader. And who can forget the Great Train Robbery? It caught the imagination of the public, and, if it hadn't been for the injury to the train driver, would have been regarded as one of the most daring deeds in the annals of crime. There was the awful Aberfan disaster in Wales, when many children were killed in a terrible coal slip that engulfed their school.

In entertainment, the film *Lawrence of Arabia* quite rightly picked up many awards for excellence. I can still watch it today with great admiration of its cast and director David Lean.

In the same year Charles Laughton died at the age of 63. He was a huge personality on the screen: his portrayal of Henry VIII as early as 1933 raised him to the heights of film stardom. I remember seeing it in my teens. I loved the routine with the chicken bone, throwing it over his shoulder, which in somebody else's hands would probably have meant very little. Then there were his larger-than-life facial expressions as Captain Bligh in *Mutiny on the Bounty* with those immortal words to Clark Gable's Fletcher Christian: 'A midshipman is the lowest rank of animal life in the British Navy.' His portrayal of Quasimodo in the *Hunchback of Notre Dame* was, I think, his most moving film performance, although other people will probably have their own favourite. The humour he brought to *Witness for the Prosecution* as QC Sir Wilfrid Roberts was wonderful. I never saw him on stage but I did meet him very briefly when I went to the New Theatre in London to get his autograph. He hardly looked up until I said I was going to appear in the *Fol-de-Rols*, which I believed he used to see as a young boy in Scarborough. He looked at me and said, rather slowly, 'The *Fol-de-Rols*, wonderful days.' That fine actor and director Simon Callow wrote a wonderful book about Laughton; it is well worth reading and gives a real insight into this great actor.

Four university lads, Peter Cook, Dudley Moore, Jonathan Miller and Alan Bennett, turned stage revues upside down with *Beyond the Fringe*. Television's *That Was the Week that Was*, presented by David Frost and introducing artistes who found fame overnight, liberated broadcasting to the point almost of anarchy. They didn't mind who they lampooned, the monarchy, the church and politicians all came in for ridicule. Television and radio would never be quite the same again.

Perhaps the biggest turnabout in entertainment, certainly in

6 ANOTHER ROLL OF LINO

the pop world, was provided by the Beatles. I remember going to do a concert on the Isle of Wight before Beatlemania had really got under way. Driving through Portsmouth I saw mounted police out round the civic hall controlling crowds of youngsters. When I asked what was going on someone said, 'It's the Beatles.' It could have been a horde of insects let loose on Portsmouth for all I knew about them. A great pal of ours in Tin Pan Alley, Eddie Rogers, had been offered the Beatles music and he turned it down. The boys went across the road to Dick James, himself a well known singer, and he took them on. Very soon Dick was in the really big money.

In 1960 I had done a summer season revue at the De La Warr Pavilion, Bexhill, and this brought about a deep friendship that was to last for a very long time. The two singers in the show were husband and wife team, Ronald Evans and Joan Danson. They were very popular with audiences in the resort having appeared there before. They had also recently bought a house in Barnet, Herts, and Ronald and I spent most of our spare time making things for our respective houses. At times we'd both be working in the basement of the theatre, sawing and hammering in full evening dress ready for an entrance on stage, and Ron would say, 'Oh Bert, there's our entrance music.' We'd dash up and just make it in time. Joan would always be in a state, waiting for him to turn up in time to go on stage. The minute he joined her they would go straight on and into their opening number. I remember one night Joan brushing sawdust off his dinner jacket as they were singing.

One Saturday night Marion and I were going back home with them in their van-cum-car. Ron asked me to help him with some deckchairs he had just taken from the beach, lettered all over with Bexhill Corporation. I asked what the hell he was doing and he said, 'We've only got two chairs at home so I'm borrowing these until we get back here on Monday.' Ron was really harum-scarum, a Welshman with a healthy appetite for adventure. He'd break into song at the drop of a hat, and had no nerves as a performer. He had, and still has, a great voice.

The principal comedy act of the show was Billy Whittaker

and Mimi Law. They had a lot to put up with with Ron and me. One night we were talking in my dressing room with our stage cues coming up and I couldn't find my dress trousers. Everything else I had on – evening shirt, bow tie, dinner jacket – but no trousers. We turned the dressing room upside down until I suddenly remembered that I had taken them to the cleaners and had forgotten to collect them. Ron fell on the floor in hysterics and, of course, I couldn't go on just in under-pants. Bill Whittaker really got cross that night. However we remained great friends with both of them until Billy died just a couple of years ago. We still keep in touch with Mimi at her home in the Isle of Wight.

I carried on doing one night stands and radio. I remember one afternoon concert I was compèring at the East Ham Granada and the top of the bill was American singer and gui-tarist Duane Eddy. When I arrived at the theatre there was pan-demonium outside with crowds of excited youngsters chanting, 'We want Duane, we want Duane.' I saw the stage doorkeeper and he suggested I park my car as far away as was convenient and make tracks out of the theatre as quickly as possible once I'd introduced 'this Duane fellow'. The first thing I noticed when I went on stage at the beginning of the show were two burly guards with Alsatian dogs standing at the bottom of the steps on either side of the stage. The girls in the audience kept up a continual screaming and chanting and at intervals during the performance would throw knickers on to the stage. I could have opened a lingerie shop with the amount of underwear that was flying around. You can imagine the noise when I eventual-ly announced the man they'd all come to see. I did what the stage doorkeeper had suggested and dashed out to find my car and make my quick getaway.

I was travelling all over the country at that time doing con-certs and the odd week of variety. I did several of the latter with the Billy Cotton Band Show. Bill and his band did most of the second half of each bill. At the New Theatre, Oxford, one of the supporting acts was singer Frank Ifield. He was about third act on, doing about 12 minutes. During the week his recording of

*I Remember You* broke into the charts and was being played on every radio station in the country, so by Friday the management changed Frank's spot with the radio group 'The Keynotes' who were closing the first half. Ifield then had to extend his act very quickly to about 20 minutes, but still the audience wanted more. Frank was a really nice guy and had a great following everywhere he played.

*Beyond our Ken* finished in 1964 because Eric Merriman was being wooed by television. He thought it would be marvellous to transfer *Beyond our Ken* to television if he was going to make a move in that direction. But the controller of radio at that time refused to let the programme go, so Eric decided to make the move anyway. He made the transition very successfully, writing regularly for Norman Vaughan when he took over the compèring of *Sunday Night at the London Palladium*, and also writing, in partnership with John Chapman, the very successful TV situation comedy *Happy Ever After*, which starred Terry Scott and June Whitfield.

Eric has now come full circle writing, with his son Andy, a delightful programme called *Minor Adjustment*. On several occasions I played cricket with Eric and the very young Andy in their garden. Andy has become an accomplished writer. I appeared in one of the episodes of *Minor Adjustment*. It's always a pleasure to do good material: there isn't too much of it around nowadays. Andy Merriman is the third generation of his family to be involved in the entertainment business, as his grandfather Percy Merriman was a concert party proprietor with his company 'The Roosters'.

When *Beyond Our Ken* finished we, the same cast, almost immediately returned to a regular spot with a fairly similar show called *Round the Horne*. It carried on where *Beyond our Ken* had left off and was just as eventful, running for another four years. The writers were Marty Feldman, an eccentric comedian in his own right, and Barry Took. For me it meant we could still have several rolls of lino when it was needed.

Marion and I were booked that year for a summer show on the Isle of Wight. I, for the first time, was to be the principal comedian. It also included a second comedian/conjuror in Frankie Holmes, two experienced principal dancers, Leon and Eunice Bartell, Bette Gilmore – a girl singer who had recently arrived from New Zealand – a musical act and a line of dancers. This booking had come about after a friend had asked me to come over to the island one night just before Christmas 1963 to do a spot in a special bingo evening at his cinema in Sandown. Afterwards I met the entertainment manager for the area and he said, 'I hear you went well tonight. Would you like to come here for a season at the Pier Pavilion?' He went on, 'I understand your wife Marion is a comedienne/singer – would she like to come as well?'

What a season we had there in 1964! The weather was hot – too hot to do really good business at the theatre, but it meant we were able to do a lot of swimming and accept the many invitations we received from the hospitable islanders. Every night after the show we used to go to a nearby hotel on the front owned by the Holland family, Reg, Vera and son David for a drink or two. I, as principal of the show, was driven round until the early hours, mixing with hotel proprietors and coach tours promoting the show. This was very tiring and by August I called a halt to some of these late nights. I had the show to do at night and nearly every Sunday was spent compèring the Sunday concerts which were headed by big name artistes like Dick Emery, Jon Pertwee and Adam Faith.

We struck up a real friendship with the two folk who had originally invited me to go to the island in 1963, Tony and Sybil Snelling. This friendship has grown over the years and we have spent many, many happy times with them at their lovely house on the island and at various functions. We saw their businesses expand and their children grow up from babies. After they retired from their business commitments Tony and I joined forces in a small film company. Their children, Deborah and Timothy, are now adults; Deborah is married to Matthew and they have a lovely daughter. Timothy is a writer of no mean ability. Sybil was recently awarded the MBE in recognition of her great work for the NSPCC.

I remember when Jon Pertwee came over to top one of the Sunday concert bills. He stayed with us at our flat in Shanklin and during the night our dog Bilko apparently kept trying to get into bed with him. When we woke in the morning Jon was curled up in the dog's basket. Well he was a big dog and he had a large basket.

Frankie Holmes, the conjuror in our show, was very popular with the audiences and as I always liked feeding in sketches and comedy items we used to change characters although I was always supposed to have the comedy part as I was the principal. This turn around worked very well and, as I was only interested in the show and not who got the laughs, the management came to accept my ideas. Marion was in nearly all the sketches and did some double material with Frankie.

Before we left for that season we put our house in Hove on the market. Would you believe it, two young lads wanted to buy it for the asking price straight away. It was impossible to move at that point because of our commitment to the season on the island – and, anyway, where would our mums go? So the sale was delayed by agreement until we had finished. We then bought a fairly modern house a little way out of town. It was quite a job, moving from a large house with big pieces of furniture, which of course we had to get rid of.

In 1965 Marion did a season on the West Pier at Brighton for Alan Gale, an old friend she had worked for many years before. He and his wife Patty presented *Old Time Music Hall* which was very popular at that time. I was still recording *Round the Horne* for radio and doing concerts and cabaret, including the Bailey's club circuit in the north-east, Newcastle, Middlesborough, Darlington and Sunderland, with Sunday concerts in between as far afield as Torquay, Margate and the Isle of Wight. Because of the travelling I was not eating properly and started to get various pains about my body. The doctor I went to see said, 'You must pack it up for a while, your digestive system is all up the creek.' This I did and things immediately improved. Our new house didn't have the character of the old Victorian one we had left, but we settled into it quite quickly.

While we had been moving house we had seen little of Fedge and Liz, or the children who were growing up fast. They themselves had had two moves, from Oxhey in 1959 to Sunbury on Thames, and in 1962 to Ashford in Middlesex. Fedge had really climbed the ladder with his firm and was travelling all over the world in his directorial capacity.

1966 was pretty memorable in many ways. The biggest sporting event was the World Cup Football competition which England hosted and won, setting the nation alight. The controversy over the third goal against the Germans in the final is still talked about today.

I followed Marion's season at the West Pier in Brighton in 1965 by going there as chairman in a new edition of *Old Time Music Hall* in 1966. It was a lovely summer and we did wonderful business. Alan Gale was a real character to work for. He took part in the show itself and when he was doing one of his monologues, he sometimes forgot his words. He would walk to the side of the stage, where he had his lines pinned up on the scenery, have a quick look, and carry on as if nothing had happened. He also used to come out at the beginning of the interval and say to the audience, 'We shall start the second half just as soon as all the ice creams are sold.' He had a percentage of the sales, and he wasn't going to lose on them if it was possible.

There is a true story about Alan when he was presenting pantomime, which he did regularly, at Middlesborough. The pantomime was *Red Riding Hood* and the night before they opened the Stage Manager, who was also playing two parts in the production and doing a double speciality with his wife – fire-eating or something (everything fitted into a Gale pantomime) – went to Alan and said, 'There's no costume for *Red Riding Hood*.' Alan said, 'Go into the town and get some red crêpe paper.' The stage manager came back empty handed, saying, 'Everywhere is sold out of it for Christmas.' Alan said, 'Oh never mind, we'll do *Dick Whittington* instead.'

On 19 July, in Brighton Maternity Hospital, Marion gave birth to our son Jonathan. Oddly, in the weeks leading up to his birth Marion's arthritis appeared to have got better. The night before he was born she had actually been out to a party having a glass of wine or two and dancing the night away. During the show that evening I rang the hospital a couple of times to see how things were going but there was no sign of the baby.

Just after the second half started Alan Gale came on stage and interrupted what I was doing, took the microphone from me and literally with tears in his eyes announced to the audience, 'At 8.30 this evening ladies and gentlemen, Bill became the father of a bouncing baby boy.' Well the place was in pandemonium, the audience starting sending up drinks to my chairman's table until there was no room left. I passed them back stage and to the band who were on stage on a rostrum behind us. The show had got under way again during all this and it was an extremely merry cast and band who finished the performance, which ended with me singing *What Kind of Fool Am I?* The rendering of it that night, and the band's accompaniment, was slightly different from usual, but the audience applauded as if I were Pavarotti in full flight.

I dashed up to the hospital after the show and was met by a nurse who said, 'Phew, you've had a drink or two haven't you! Put this mask on.' I went to see Marion, who looked quite chirpy, and then went to see Jonathan, who was screaming the place down, being manhandled by a couple of nurses. He had bright red hair, which eventually turned to blonde as he got older. My mother had an extra glass of sherry that night, and I phoned up as many of the family as I thought would still be up and told them the good news.

Some of us habitually went over to a gay club across the road from the Pier after the show, and the lads used to make us a snack or something. They were very hospitable and good fun to be with. Outside the stage door on many nights during the World Cup was a very attractive girl with a portable radio and she used to relay the scores of the matches to me, and I would give the audience the news during the show. One night when I came out she was just leaving the Pier and I asked her if she had far to go. When she told me I said, 'That's on my way home, I'll give you a lift.' She lived in a block of flats and invited me

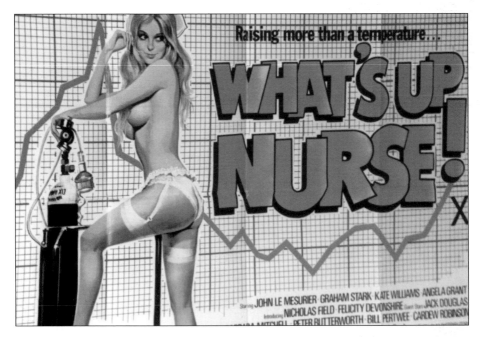

Raising more than a temperature...

WHAT'S UP NURSE!

X

Starring JOHN LE MESURIER · GRAHAM STARK · KATE WILLIAMS · ANGELA GRANT
Introducing NICHOLAS FIELD · FELICITY DEVONSHIRE Guest Stars JACK DOUGLAS
BARBARA MITCHELL · PETER BUTTERWORTH · BILL PERTWEE · CARDEW ROBINSON

*Above: What can I say?
One of several inconsequential films I did in the
1970s.*

*Right: Here I am playing
the Dame in* Babes in the
Wood *in 1971. Fancy a
grown man doing this sort of
thing for a living!*

*Far right: What a 'Carry
On'! Julian Holloway, topless Bunny and me. I was
in three of these uniquely
funny films – this one is*
Carry On Loving.

*Previous page: It's all
'Beyond Our Ken'.
Clockwise from top: Betty
Mardsen, Douglas Smith
(Announcer), Eric
Merriman (writer), Kenneth
Williams, Kenneth Horne,
Hugh Paddick, me.*

*Above: 'Put that light out.'*

*Left: Cartoon by Jeff Holland.*

Issue 5
April
1996

# COMIC HERITAGE

*Inside: Interview with Bill Pertwee*

*Comic Heritage raises money for charity and is well patronised by show business people. Its April 1996 issue included an evening with . . . me! The picture is taken from the* Dad's Army *episode 'The Honourable Man'.*

# SHAFTESBURY THEATRE

Shaftesbury Avenue, London WC2. Phone: 836 6596/7

LICENSEES: MARTIN GIBSON AND BRIAN RICHMOND-DODD FOR CHARTERGATE ESTATES LTD.
BERNARD DELFONT and RICHARD M. MILLS (for Bernard Delfont Organisation Ltd).
and DUNCAN C. WELDON and LOUIS I. MICHAELS (for Triumph Theatre Productions Ltd).
present

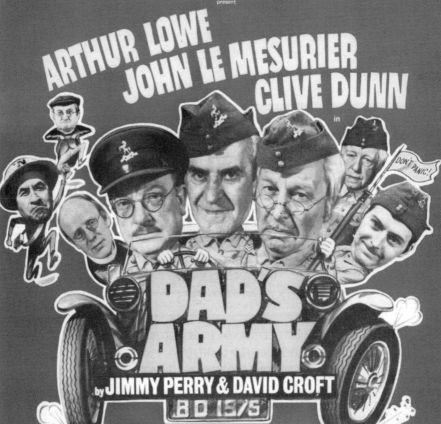

## ARTHUR LOWE JOHN LE MESURIER CLIVE DUNN

in

# DADS ARMY

## by JIMMY PERRY & DAVID CROFT

BD 1975

## A NOSTALGIC MUSIC & LAUGHTER SHOW OF BRITAIN'S FINEST HOUR

featuring

# ARNOLD RIDLEY · IAN LAVENDER · BILL PERTWEE
# FRANK WILLIAMS · EDWARD SINCLAIR
# JOHN BARDON and HAMISH ROUGHEAD
# JOAN COOPER · PAMELA CUNDELL and JANET DAVIES

Directed by
## DAVID CROFT & JIMMY PERRY
Staged by
## ROGER REDFARN

Designed by TERRY PARSONS
Choreography by SHEILA O'NEILL
Costumes by MARY HUSBAND

Musical Director ED COLEMAN
Lighting by ROBERT ORNBO
Sound by DAVID COLLISON

A FORUM THEATRE BILLINGHAM PRODUCTION

*Above:* Dad's Army *stalwarts with writers Jimmy Perry and David Croft.*

*Far left:* Dad's Army *takes to the stage.*

*Left: A scene from the stage* Dad's Army: *Jeffrey Holland as a mad inventor and who's that suspicious looking German general wearing a monocle?*

*Above: John Laurie and I show off our horsemanship in the* Dad's Army *episode 'Two and a half feathers'.*

*Above right:* Dad's Army *v Hayfield, Derbyshire – Arthur Lowe's home team. 'A good time was had by all!'*

*Right: For the cricket lovers in the cast the episode 'The Test' was particular fun as it featured a special guest star – Freddie Trueman, the greatest English fast bowler.*

*Above and Left: 'The Royal Train' included an epic chase sequence on a pump truck. I had a close shave when the lever caught in my pocket and threatened to spill me out over the front under the wheels.*

*Above right: 'Gorilla Warfare': me and the verger, Edward Sinclair.*

*Below right: In a nice touch the wives and girlfriends of the cast with Equity membership took part in the final Dad's Army episode as guests at Corporal Jones's wedding to Mrs Fox.*

ON PARADE: The team who became tops with viewers.

# DAD'S ARMY DISMISS!

## After nine years a final salute

### By KEN IRWIN

THE lads of Dad's Army are hanging up their boots and turning in their rifles after parading for nine years among the leaders in the TV ratings.

Captain Mainwaring's Home Guard platoon reported for duty yesterday to start filming their last six shows. After these are screened in the autumn, the team will be demobbed by the B.B.C.

Arthur Lowe, who plays Mainwaring, was all dressed up as St. George for one of the episodes.

He said: "It's a sad time for all of us. But it was inevitable that we'd have to finish some time."

#### Show

John Laurie — the gloomy Private Frazer — said: "The trouble is, we're too damned old to carry on. We've all grown old together."

The oldest is Arnold Ridley, at 87. Then come John Laurie, 81, John le Mesurier, 65, Arthur Lowe, 62, Clive Dunn, 54, and ARP man Bill Pertwee, 50.

The baby of the outfit is 31-year-old Ian Lavender, who plays Private Pike.

He said: "I was a lad when I joined the show. My whole professional life's been wrapped up in it."

...ARD: Arthur as St. George yesterday.    Picture: ALBERT FOSTER

*Above:* Daily Mirror *of 13 June 1977.*

*Left: 'Some of the* Dad's Army *cast relaxing in Arthur Lowe's dressing room' – from* Woman *magazine.*

*Top: Photo taken in 1976 when the Chamberlain family entertained the cast of the*
Dad's Army *stage show. Our hostess is second from right. General Roosevelt is centre*
*back and at the front is Arthur Lowe with Jonathan.*

*Above: Frank Williams, me and Ian Lavender at the launch of my book*
Dad's Army – The Making of a Television Legend.

Patrons
Her Majesty The Queen
Her Majesty Queen Elizabeth The Queen Mother

we the undersigned tender our sincere congratulations to

*Phill Perture*

on being one of the representative artistes selected to appear before

Her Majesty The Queen
on the occasion of the

Royal Variety Performance
held at the

London Palladium on Monday, November 10th 1975

the performance being in aid of the Entertainment Artistes' Benevolent Fund

President          Vice-President          General Secretary

*Above: My invitation to appear at the Royal Variety Performance in 1975.*

*Below: 'All together in the Floral Dance.' Choir practice for the
Royal Variety Performance.*

*Above: Appearing as Sergeant Beetroot in* Worzel Gummidge, *with cousin Jon and Una Stubbs at the Cambridge Theatre in December 1981.*

*Above right: The original London cast of* Run For Your Wife *at the Shaftesbury Theatre in 1983. Left to right, back row: Peter Blake, me, Royce Mills. Sitting: Carol Hawkins, Richard Briers, Bernard Cribbins and Helen Gill.*

*Below right: The cast of* See How They Run *at the Shaftesbury Theatre in 1984. Back row, left to right: Royce Mills, Peter Blake, Michael Denison, Christopher Timothy and Derek Nimmo. On the sofa, left to right: Lisa Goddard, Carol Hawkins and Maureen Lipman. But who's the M.P. Sergeant in front?*

*Above: A proud moment – being made a Freeman of the City of London. 'I can now drive sheep over London Bridge!'*

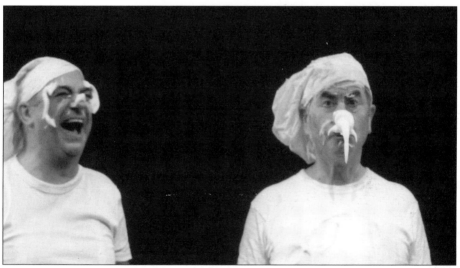

*Top: Meeting the Princess Royal at an Army Services Charity Concert.*
*Left to right: Sir Harry Secombe, HRH, Paul Shane, Jeffrey Holland, me and*
*Bill Waddington.*

*Above: Another fine mess – in pantomime with my old friend Roy Hudd.*

*Top left: 'I'd rather sit here with the Martini, than doing that cabaret tonight.'*
*With Norman Macleod in the early 1980s.*

*Below left: From left, me, Ray Cooney, Peter Blake and John Quayle*
*in* It Runs in the Family.

**Max Miller**
*Dressed like a peacock, his cheeky face beamed under a white trilby. His jokes were outrageous and his act was breathtakingly fast. Dozens of comedians have followed his style, but Miller, born Thomas Henry Sargent in 1895 – he died in 1963 – was the master original. Bill Pertwee (right) re-creates his act.*

*9–15 February 1985* TVTIMES

*'Now here's a funny thing; now that is a funny thing.'*
*Me as Max Miller in* Super Troopers, *a TV series which ran in 1985.*

*Above: Looking down on Piccadilly Circus – the last production at the Criterion Theatre London before it closed for refurbishment. Left to right: Terry Scott, me and Colin Baker.*

*Below: One of my favourite pictures. In pantomime with Spike Milligan and Evelyn Laye.*

*Above: Another great cricketing night at Sheffield. From left to right: David Drabble, John Arlott, Norman Yardley, me and Peter Parfitt.*

**10.55–6.30*pm** *MW*
**Test Match Special**
England *v* West Indies
*Fourth Cornhill Test*
Commentary on the third
day's play at **Headingley**
by BRIAN JOHNSTON, DON MOSEY
and TONY COZIER, with expert
comments by FRED TRUEMAN
and COLIN MILBURN.
**1.05 News**
**1.10 A View from the Boundary**
**Brian Johnston** welcomes
actor **Bill Pertwee** to the
commentary box.
**1.30–1.40*; 3.45–4.00***
**County Scoreboard**
Producer PETER BAXTER

*From John Arlott*

The Vines, Longis Road, Alderney, C.I.
Tel. 2656

~~The Old Sun, Alresford, Hampshire, Alresford 2307~~

19th April, 1981.

*Dear Bill,*

What a very kind thought. Many thanks indeed – just
my kind of book – and the one my old friend, Maurice
Willson Disher never quite wrote in his sequence of
histories.    How desperately nostalgic it all is.

It was good to meet you – and I am glad you enjoyed
Charlie Brett's as much as I did – and, I think, Bill
and Dick.

Have chuckled several times since about your story of
the theatrical landlady at Leeds.

If ever you are in the Channel Islands come and see
us – our fish and chips may not be as good as Headingley but
we have our compensations.

*Kindest regards,*
*Yours,*
*John*

Bill Pertwee, Esq.,
The Old Rectory,
Ockham Road South,
East Horsley,
Surrey.

*Above: A real thrill, appearing on Test Match Special alongside Brian Johnson during the Fourth Cornhill Test at Headingley when England were playing the West Indies.*

*Left: A lovely letter from John Arlott.*

*Above: Actor Norman Mitchell, Veronica and Freddie Truman. We were gathered at the Imperial War Museum to celebrate 25 years of* Dad's Army.

*Below: Being presented with a special commemorative coin at the Imperial War Museum. From left to right: Me, Steve Race, Dame Vera Lynn and Charlie Chester.*

*Right: With Doggie in the TV series* Woof. *He was prettier than I .*

*Below: Playing trains filming an episode of TVs* Woof. *Director David Cobham looks on at the Great Central Railway.*

*With June Whitfield working for Kingston Hospital radio — a very popular community radio service promoted by programme presenters Alan and Sandy Baccolini.*

You Rang M'Lord!
*Giving Su Pollard a bunk up.*

*Above: The cast of* You Rang M'Lord *during a night filming shoot.*
*From left to right: Barbara New, me, Brenda Cowling, Jeffrey Holland, Su Pollard, Paul Shane, Katherine Rabbet, Donald Hewlett, Susue Brann, Michael Knowles, Mavis Pugh and Yvonne Marsh. Kneeling in front is Perry Benson.*

Many a cook has lost her mutton talking to a copper.

*Left: The type of humour which inspired the series as shown in a contempory postcard.*

*Above: Meeting a Dad's Army fan at the Queen Elizabeth Foundation in Surrey – the Queen Mother is patron of the foundation.*

*Right: A book signing reception with General (Stormin') Norman Schwarzkopf at the Imperial War Museum.*

CLARENCE HOUSE
S.W.1

28th August, 1990

Dear Mr. Pertwee,

Queen Elizabeth The Queen Mother bids
me say how delighted she has been to receive
the good wishes from yourself and the Cast of
the BBC television series 'You Rang M'Lord'
on the occasion of her 90th birthday, and
the most attractive card signed by everyone
you have kindly sent.

Her Majesty truly appreciates the
warmth of your message, and sends you all
her sincere thanks.

Yours sincerely,

*Frances Campbell-Preston*

Lady-in-Waiting

Bill Pertwee, Esq.

*A note from Clarence House.*

*Right: Farewell to the old BBC The Paris Studio — the home of comedy, music and light entertainment for six decades.*

*Below: The impressive cast list.*

## BOB HOLNESS PRESENTS .... FAREWELL TO THE PARIS

The Paris Studio, Regent Street, London

1940 - 1995

Recorded 26th February 1995 7.00 pm.  TX: Saturday, 11th March 1995 7.33 pm  Radio 2

A CELEBRATION OF SIX DECADES OF COMEDY, MUSIC AND LIGHT ENTERTAINMENT

featuring

BARRY FORGIE and the BBC BIG BAND
and
THE STEPHEN HILL SINGERS

Cast (in order of appearance):
* JUNE WHITFIELD * FRANK MUIR * DENIS NORDEN * JOHNNY MORE * MOLLY WEIR * MAURICE DENHAM *
* HUMPHREY LYTTELTON * JOHN BARNES * PETE STRANGE * KENNY BAKER * BILL PERTWEE *
* BETTY MARSDEN * NICHOLAS PARSONS * PETER GOODWRIGHT * PETE MURRAY * CLIFF BENNETT *
* LYN PAUL * LESLIE PHILLIPS * JON PERTWEE * ROY HUDD * CHRIS EMMETT *

Announcer:  ALAN DEDICOAT

Written by MICHAEL COLEMAN
Additional material by BARRY TOOK, MICHAEL DINES and PETER GOODWRIGHT
Research by MICHAEL COLEMAN and ALISON HARBERT
Production Assistants:  ALISON HARBERT and JULIE PEARCE
Studio Managers:  JOHN WHITEHALL, ALICK HALE-MONRO, MARTHA KNIGHT and SUE TEMPLEMAN
Produced by RICHARD WILLCOX and ALED EVANS

*In 1992 Dad and son were joint compères at the* Russ Conway Show *in Bristol. He's a good-looking lad, isn't he? (Father or son?)*

*My role in* Candida *was my first in a George Bernard Shaw play.*

in to meet her mother and have a coffee. As I didn't have to rush home as Marion was still in hospital I took her up on the offer. I chatted to her mother while the girl disappeared into another room. When she came out again she wasn't a 'she' but a young man, smartly dressed and not in the least embarrassed or ill at ease. We all chatted for a while and as she/he saw me off at the front door he/she just said, 'Surprised?' I never saw him/her again at the West Pier. I did think on the way home how glad I was that I hadn't tried to get too friendly in the car; that would have been a surprise!

Jonathan was a very good baby, we never heard a peep out of him. I used to bring friends home some nights after the show and he would just lie on a chair gurgling and smiling. We seldom went to bed before midnight and Jonathan slept through until late most mornings. One night when he didn't seem to want to sleep and just lay in his cot blowing raspberries, I got a small tape recorder and hung it on the cot and we played it back next day. I wish we still had that tape, but I fear it has been lost during our several later moves.

For Christmas that year I was engaged to play the baron in Cinderella at the Theatre Royal, Brighton, a home booking for me of course. I was with some lovely mates, Norman Vaughan, singer Craig Douglas and a jolly company manager, Alec Myles. I am not quite sure why, but we seemed to have a succession of ugly sisters in the show. I know the first one lost his voice for a while and was replaced, I think, by Barry Howard, and then another left and Alec Myles took over for a few nights, using the book for his words. The 'ugly' he was replacing was very tall and Alec is quite small, not much over five feet: you can imagine what he looked like wearing those long costumes, frequently tripping over them.

Norman Vaughan and I had two wonderful scenes, one the George Truzzi/Laurie Lupino Lane paper-hanging routine using different coloured pastes in buckets and basins. The pastes were based on shaving soap and used to take the stage management ages to make for twice daily performances. We had ladders on stage, trestle tables and yards and yards of wallpaper.

When it is done properly, it is a real pantomime winner. Some nights Norman used to hurry the routine which you can't do, and I would suddenly receive the splosh, either all over my head or down my overall trousers when I wasn't expecting it. The only problem with the paper-hanging routine is it has to be placed in the right position in the production to give all the actors at least 10 minutes to shower and re-dress ready for the next routine. In our panto we had a lot less time than this, so it was a question of dashing off stage straight into a shower warmed up by the dresser, letting yourself be hosed down and re-dressed very quickly.

During the pantomime season you generally get a back-up of students ready for emergencies, and at one performance a young girl who was new to the production finished by getting more water on her than me. We finished up on the floor of the shower amidst foam, clothes and the shower head with the water getting warmer and warmer and the stage manager shouting, 'Hurry up, you've got 60 seconds to get back on.' And people who don't know, say, 'I'll bet you have fun in the theatre.' They ought to just try it sometime!

Another routine we had was Pierre Picton's comedy car, an old circus favourite. It is quite wonderful, and the kids loved the antics we got up to. You had to be careful to push the various effects buttons in the right order and at the right time. For instance, after the radiator boils over, one of the two driving the car gets out to look at the radiator and gets a jet of water full in the face; or when you close one door, the opposite one falls off. The finale of the routine would be when I had decided to sit in the back and at the push of a button the whole of the rear of the car fell backwards with a big explosion. It was all over very quickly, but to hear the shrieks from the children, and the grown ups, made it all worthwhile.

Norman Vaughan got a bad cold at one point and lost his voice. Yet another person had to join the cast at short notice. He arrived and got stuck in to the part of Buttons straight away. It was John Inman, long before he made it big in television. John is a real pro.

Marion's arthritis returned in several joints after Jonathan was born; it was bad enough to force her to have hospital treatment. Our local doctor suggested we should consider moving to another area, as perhaps Brighton wasn't good for her condition, so the following year we decided to put the house on the market and see what happened. I was due to do a summer season at the Esplanade Theatre, Bognor Regis; this turned out to be a lot of fun and I stayed most nights in the resort. As a cast we made a lot of friends, particularly amongst the hoteliers, caravan and camp owners, and the shopkeepers who, we hoped, would put the word around if they enjoyed the show themselves. Betty Lunn presented the show. She was the daughter of Wilby Lunn who had presented many shows at resorts in the 1940s and 1950s. The singer of the show, and also responsible to the management for the running of the day-to-day rehearsals, was a Scottish lad, Roy Murray. He was a tower of strength and nothing was too much trouble to him, arranging the purchase of any props and so on that we needed for the productions. He always had a smile on his face, and it was no surprise to me when he eventually went to the Theatre Royal, Norwich, to be producer Dick Condon's right-hand man. Dick turned the Norwich theatre into a real money-spinner when he took over there, and made it a delightful venue to play as a performer. Since Dick's death Roy has taken on the job of production manager for that live wire and hugely successful magician (perhaps illusionist is a better word), Paul Daniels.

At Bognor I met a family with whom Marion and I were to get very close – Paul and Stella Wills and their son Tony. They loved the theatre and Paul got involved with the Esplanade at Bognor as front of house manager. He was a gregarious character and treated all the theatre customers like old friends. I've always thought that the front of house staff at a theatre are terribly important: if they do their job properly, they can have a real effect on the audience. They are the first people the customer meets when entering the theatre, and if there is a friendly greeting from them, the show is well on the way to being enjoyed before it starts.

I did a very small part in a TV show for a producer called David Croft that year. It was in an episode of *Hugh and I* with Terry Scott and Hugh Lloyd. I only had a couple of lines and had to push Terry Scott out of the way in a cinema queue. It was to prove an important small part in years to come, as we shall find out. I was booked again for the following year, 1968, at the Esplanade, this time as part of the management as well as performing.

At the end of the 1967 season I had found what I thought would be a nice home for us in the resort. It had once been a guest house but needed a few things doing to it. Marion saw it and liked it, and we both thought it would give us plenty of room for the mums as well. We put a bid in for it and it was all arranged. On the morning we were to exchange contracts I got a letter from the BBC saying there was going to be another series of *Round the Horne* (in fact it was to be the last) in conjunction with some different writers as Marty Feldman had gone to America to make a film. It had been decided that I would not be included in the new plans and the letter finished abruptly: 'Thank you for your past contributions. Yours sincerely, etc.' When I showed the letter to people they wondered how anyone could be dismissed with such a short letter. To be quite honest it didn't upset me, although the money would have been nice for another 16 weeks, particularly as we were just about to move. My thoughts were that my run in *Beyond our Ken* and then *Round the Horne* had started with a six-week contract and had lasted eight years, so who was I to grumble? It had all been beyond my wildest dreams anyway.

We moved to Bognor and immediately started making the house more habitable, with central heating, new carpets and so on. We had the whole of the ground floor, which would be better for Marion with her increasing arthritis problems than having to climb stairs; we fixed our mums up with two nice rooms on the first floor with their own small cookers and fridges. We also let one room to a retired businessman, which was to cause a few problems, I'm sorry to say. He started taking our mums' underwear hanging up to dry in the bathroom. We had to ask him to leave. However this did leave us room to take one or two of the cast of the summer show that year. One lovely girl, Pamela, asked me one day whether her fiancée could come down for a few days. I said yes and when he arrived I was delighted to recognise Eli Woods. He was an integral part of the great comedian Jimmy James's act. Perhaps Jimmy's greatest and best known sketch was 'The Lion in the Box'. I have worked with Eli many times since then.

I wrote to several TV producers and directors during this period. One of them, Alan Tarrant, replied to a jokey letter I had sent him saying I had nine children and 10 dogs to support. I had met Tarrant, or 'Big Al' as he was known, when we played a few charity cricket matches together. In his return letter he indicated he was about to do a series with Sid James and Victor Spinetti called *Two in Clover* and there was a regular part of a country policeman I might like to do. I had some very happy weeks with Alan, Sid and Victor, and the two writers Vince Powell and Harry Driver.

Sid was trying to give up gambling which had got him hooked in a big way; he was restricting himself to the occasional, brief visit to the bookmakers in Teddington High Street for a small flutter. Sid's wife would phone up to see how he was and we'd tell her a porky, saying he had just gone to the loo and would ring her back. I'm sure his missus didn't believe us.

Just before that season at Bognor started I was rung up by producer David Croft, who said he was just starting on a programme about the Home Guard called *Dad's Army*. There were a couple of lines in it for me as an air raid warden if I would like to do it. So I said yes (well it was another roll of lino). The programme had originally been titled 'The Fighting Tigers' but changed by Michael Mills, the head of BBC comedy, to *Dad's Army*. Whatever Michael produced or was involved in afterwards, that title must go down as his greatest stroke of genius.

The controller of BBC TV was not ecstatic about the idea of a programme on the long forgotten Home Guard of the 1940s but David Croft and the originator of the programme, Jimmy Perry, thought it had great possibilities. With the backing of

Michael Mills and the head of BBC1 Tom Sloane, it was decided to do six programmes as a trial.

Anyway, there I was in the very first episode rehearsing with a cast I had never met before. The BBC's reluctance to give the programme too much prominence was made obvious as we were sent to a back room of the 'Feathers' pub on the Hogarth roundabout at the beginning of the M4 out of London. I met Jimmy Perry for the first time that morning and he asked me at lunchtime what I thought about the idea. I said from what I had witnessed, watching these lovely actors working together, I thought it would be a success. Jimmy said he had been down to Bognor for a weekend and seen my show at the Esplanade Theatre, and was pleased to meet me in person.

I was given another small part as the air raid warden in the sixth and last episode of the first series and then didn't hear any more from anyone. During my brief encounter with the actors I felt I had got on well with them, although I was from the variety side of the business. Clive Dunn had been on the lighter side of entertainment, doing seasons at the Players Theatre in London, and it was nice to have a warm greeting from John Le Mesurier on the first day of rehearsal, inviting me to have a drink with him at the lunch interval.

I went back to Bognor and did the season. All went well in the new house – and we were very involved – as all new parents are – having lots of fun in his early toddler years with Jonathan, our pride and joy. Through the latter part of the 1960s I did cabaret and concerts, several of them at Butlin's holiday camps. I had a contract for Sunday guest appearances and also for Easter and Christmas seasons. These were quite hectic because you played at one camp – like Minehead in Somerset – two days before Christmas, then on Christmas Eve at, say, Clacton in Essex and then, on Boxing Night, at somewhere like Bognor Regis in Sussex. Driving from one venue to the other in wintry weather could be very unenjoyable.

The summer Sunday concerts were quite tiring as the theatres at the camps were built to hold something like 2,000 people, and the big camps themselves would have a weekly intake of

8,000 holidaymakers. You played the first house at about 6pm to 2,000, and they would then be replaced by another 2,000 and so on until you had done four shows during the evening playing to 2,000 people each time. The theatres were well equipped with a full pit orchestra, so there was everything to support the artistes. A big notice on the side of the stage said, 'We do not allow swearing or blue jokes to be used in our theatres.' I suppose there are a few performers who could still abide by those rules today, and still be able to entertain audiences without offending them, but not many.

In 1967 I was engaged to warm-up an audience for the first time. A warm-up artiste is introduced to the audience in a studio or television theatre before a show commences with the job of chatting to the audience to relax them and make them feel that they are going to be an important part of the show, which of course they are.

A lot of them have probably never been inside a studio before, so you tell them about the lights, which are practically everywhere they look, the sound equipment that allows them to follow the action, together with TV monitors above their heads where they can see outside film shots that have been recorded beforehand and will be integrated into the action they will see in front of them. There will probably be about six camera crews recording the show so one has to explain that at times it will be difficult to watch the action at some points, so again they should look at their monitors. The same applies to a scene that is being shot on a small set which is completely out of their sight behind the main one.

A warm-up man also tells a few simple jokes and refers to parties that have come from a club or offices for a night out. The tickets are free of charge and have been arranged by the TV station's ticket unit on request. You have to explain that there will be some changes of costume during the show so there will be recording breaks when this happens. The 'warm-up' has to make sure the audience doesn't lose the story line if it's a situation comedy show, and encourage them to applaud and laugh in the right places. Applause is only wanted really at the end of a show or at certain parts in say a quiz programme or a chat show when a celebrity is introduced. Overall, the 'warm-up' must make friends with the audience so that they will accept him as part of the entertainment. It is very important to have some fairly lengthy joke routines up your sleeve as some breaks in the recording can be fairly long, particularly if there is a technical fault that may need time to correct.

The first show that I warmed up was *Hancock's*. It was a series of six shows starring Tony Hancock as a sort of host in a nightclub, hence *Hancock's*. It also starred June Whitfield and Australian actor Kenneth J. Warren. It was a rather sad time for Tony Hancock because he couldn't quite get things together, even though he was using a teleprompter most of the time. A teleprompter is a small screen with the actor's lines on it, sited at the performer's eye-line on the camera. News readers use them a lot as up-to-date news is fed to them. Hancock used to do only about four minutes at a time, and then call me back on again saying, 'Come on lad, there's been another technical hitch.' He just couldn't concentrate on the proceedings at all and the shows, although half an hour in length, would take ages to record. A half-hour show, even with retakes and credits, can normally be done in an hour and a bit. It wasn't a very happy experience for me having my first shot at warming-up, but it certainly gave me a chance to learn a few things in difficult circumstances. For Hancock himself it was, I think, the beginning of the end, as he went to Australia soon after and died there.

I certainly believe that much of Hancock's trouble was caused by leaving the writing partnership of Ray Galton and Alan Simpson, who had been responsible for writing for Tony throughout his radio and television career and had created marvellous scripts for him. Of course Hancock had some wonderful performers round him in his earlier days – Kenneth Williams, Sid James, Bill Kerr, Hattie Jacques and others, but he thought he could make it in other directions and that was the problem. He and the writers had found a formula and I think he should have stayed with it; perhaps if he hadn't been so revered by the public (and quite rightly so for his early work) things might have been different. Perhaps he started to believe his own publicity too much.

A little later I had a contract to warm up shows for ATV (Associated Television) at Elstree. ATV was then run by the incredible Lew Grade, later Lord Grade. He was one of three brothers, Lew, Leslie and Bernard (Delfont), later Lord Delfont. These three lads were, effectively, the business at one time. Lew and Leslie ran the Grade Agency; Bernard, having been a performer, went into production, becoming involved in West End musicals, revue and a whole lot of touring productions that introduced many unknown artistes who later became big stars. Their achievements were enormous when you think they left Russia as baby boys with their parents, the Winogradskys, with no money and settled in the East End of London with only optimism and hope, and the theory that hard work will nearly always pay off.

My job at Elstree was not too easy as I was involved with a lot of the shows ATV was selling to America. This meant there were British and American producers jointly involved. They were recording Tom Jones' shows after the boy from the Welsh valleys had become a hot property. On most occasions, Tom would record his main spot on a Sunday, and this would be inserted into the shows recorded during the week with guest artistes from both sides of the Atlantic.

I had the pleasure of introducing these guests to the audience beforehand. People like the amazing George Burns, the great timer of a silence, Jack Benny, and many others. One evening just before introducing Phil Harris, whom I had seen working with Benny at the Palladium, Harris said to me, 'My wife is in the audience tonight, I wonder if you would like to introduce her.' I said, 'Certainly,' and after I'd introduced Phil Harris I said, 'And we'd like to give a warm welcome to Mr Harris's wife who is in the audience.' Well you could have knocked me down with a feather when the lady stood up and it was the lovely film star Alice Faye whom I had seen in all sorts of movies from across the Atlantic. I apologised to Phil for my faux pas. He said, 'Think nothing of it,' and we had a drink together afterwards.

The problem with the Tom Jones' shows was that the ladies in the audience, some parties coming from as far afield as Manchester and Cardiff, were only interested in seeing their heart-throb. The shows were an hour long but took much longer to record. Meanwhile the men in the audience would get a bit restless, having travelled a long way; they were dying for a pint, apart from anything else.

I knew that the audience was not going to see Tom on some occasions, because, as I've mentioned, his spot had been recorded on a Sunday. I was generally told, after I had introduced the last act and seen everything was all right, to disappear as the Jones spot would not need an introduction. I took heed and slipped away pretty quickly before the abuse from the audience began when they realised that they would not see their Tom in person.

It was always a long evening with the actual recording lasting up to four hours after a 7.30pm start, and I would then begin the long drive back to the south coast. Opposite our house in Bognor was a small club run by a fellow I knew, and after I had taken the dog for a walk when I got home I'd pop in there and have a drink. I came out of the club about 3am one morning and found my pyjamas on the doorstep. Marion had decided she would remind me that young Jonathan needed to sleep and not be woken by his noisy father. I took the pyjamas and slept in the car that night. It was all very peaceful and when I came in next morning there was a nice breakfast waiting for me.

I also warmed up the *Norman Wisdom Kraft* (I think it was for cheese) *Music Hall Shows* which I enjoyed and which took far less time to record. One of the nicest fellows I met during my time at Elstree was Liberace. I did several of his shows and afterwards he would make sure that everyone had a drink with him, floor managers, technicians, make-up girls, dressers, scene shifters – in fact anyone involved in the production. He really was a gentleman, with impeccable manners.

In 1968, at the end of the second season of the summer show at Bognor, an impresario came up from Plymouth, Devon, saying he would like to take the whole show there for a long season the following year. They wanted to re-stage a lot of the items they had seen in the Bognor show. Would I come down to Plymouth and see a house that they had in mind for us? We decided to go, and after discussing the whole thing with the entertainment's manager, whom I had actually met sometime before, I was offered a contract.

The show was to be at the Hoe Theatre, a tented venue, but very good for a summer revue. Plymouth is one of my favourite cities anyway, and it was to be a long season at the best money I had received for a show of this kind. Marion quite rightly thought this would give us a nice little bonus which we needed with a growing young son and a mortgage. I told the folks in Plymouth I would like time to think about it and we drove home the next day with me doing a little whistling in the car. Marion said, 'You are obviously quite happy about everything.'

'No,' I replied, 'I'm happy because I just have a gut feeling about not doing it.' I didn't know why, I just wasn't going to do it. Marion really thought I'd gone off my rocker, and so did a few other people, including a long-time friend of mine Felix Bowness. I'll mention more about this very nice lad later.

So came 1969 and we were sitting in the garden in May. Although Marion has always supported me in whatever I've done, she was quite perturbed that here we were, with the summer looming and no work in the diary. Then the telephone rang and it was David Croft saying that if I was free there would be a few more appearances in *Dad's Army* for me if I liked. If I hadn't been free, it was early days for *Dad's,* so it would have been easy to bring in another actor as the Warden. Of course I jumped at the work, thinking it was just another job for a week or two. It was the second series of the show and from that time my life was to change dramatically.

When anyone asks me why I didn't go to Plymouth, I really cannot answer them, because I don't really know why – although it's easy to come up with the answer in hindsight. At the same time I started doing quite a lot of radio work in Manchester; Bognor was a long way by train or car, so we started looking for a home nearer London. We started at Wimbledon which we had got to know quite well when we had rooms there in the late 1950s. I met Bob Dorning, who had played a character in an episode of *Dad's Army*, in a pub there and he told me that there was a flat going for six months just behind the Wimbledon Village shops.

We decided to take it while we had a look around. We took Jonathan up there with us, and the dog, leaving the mums to look after the house at Bognor. Young Jonathan and the dog were quite a handful for Marion in the flat and she used to spend a lot of time walking them around Wimbledon Common to tire them both, hoping they would give her some peace in the flat. The travelling was, of course, easier for me but we couldn't find anything in Wimbledon in our price range, and our six month's stay in the flat was coming to an end. However fate was getting ready to play its hand again.

I remember going over to the Isle of Wight to do a Sunday concert and, as I was staying the night, had an opportunity to see the live television coverage of the first landing on the moon by the American astronauts. The date was July 21st, my birthday. What an extraordinary event that was; I'm sure most people didn't grasp the enormity of it at all at the time.

We went back to Bognor for a weekend to make sure everything was OK with the house and the mums, and while strolling around the shops we met up again with Stella Wills. Her family, as I've mentioned, was prominent in helping to run the summer theatre there, and she told us she was having a problem with some tenants she had living on the ground floor of an old rectory she and her husband Paul still owned in Surrey, in the village where they had lived before retirement. Marion mentioned we would have to leave the flat at Wimbledon shortly, so Stella suggested we go and have a look at the rectory as the tenants would leave soon. Marion agreed but I must admit I was against it as I didn't want to go too far away from London again, and Surrey seemed miles away to me.

Anyway one Sunday morning we drove from Wimbledon down to the village between Leatherhead and Guildford, and found a large building, in grounds that badly needed the attention of a gardener. There was something about the place we liked very much.

We looked round the area and found it was near a parade of shops which included a library and most of the things a village could provide including a garage, a pub near-by and a railway station. I sampled a half of beer in the pub and immediately got a strange greeting from the publican – if you could call it a greeting. He came over to where I was sitting and said, 'I recognise you. If you're coming in here regularly you can forget about throwing your weight about just because you've been on the box.' I ignored the comment and just thought the pub was nicely positioned, within walking distance of the rectory. As it happened, my first visit did not set the the style of my future visits. I was to spend many happy hours there, making friends with the local population, and the proprietor of the pub and his wife after that first meeting. Incidentally, it is now a super Italian restaurant with a nice lounge bar and impeccably run by Tony Orlando and his wife.

We decided to rent the rectory for a year while we looked round the area. The upper floors were occupied by two or three people who had been there for some time, one of whom was a slightly eccentric lady who had once been Winston Churchill's secretary and always hung a large Union Jack out of the window on the great man's birthday.

At the same time *Dad's Army* gathered momentum and the rectory was ideally placed for me to drive to the BBC near Shepherd's Bush for the studio recordings. The mums joined us from Bognor and life became a bit hectic but the rectory, even only the ground floor, gave us room to live happily together.

After about six months Paul Wills died and Stella said the death duties on his estate meant she would have to sell some of the properties they owned in the area, including the rectory. We thought about buying it once we had sold the house in Bognor and a price was agreed with Stella. The fates must have been with us because a husband and wife who had been fans of the summer show at Bognor wanted to buy our house having seen it advertised in the estate agent's window. A quiet couple, they used to leave a present in the bar for me at the end of each season and used to book up for every night of the summer show when they had their holidays. The sale of the house was arranged very quickly, so we were able to buy the Old Rectory.

I'm not sure that we realised what we were taking on, but with the combined optimism and enthusiasm we had for the place we set about doing some decorating and then further alterations to the lovely building. I needed money straight away for the work and approached the local bank manager. He took one look at it and said, 'Oh no, this is never going to be worth it, whatever you spend on it. I couldn't give you a penny'.

I spoke to my old friend Tony Snelling in the Isle of Wight, who had seen it, and he said, 'You can't lose; I'll have a word with a friend of mine.' Shortly afterwards a manager from Lloyds Bank contacted me and said he was coming up to see the property. He saw the rectory and asked, 'How much do you want?' I immediately changed my bank account to Lloyds, the first time in several generations that my previous bank had not served a Pertwee, and we started on the urgent work that had to be done. That Lloyds bank manager, Peter Harris, and his wife Beryl became great friends of ours, and Peter guided us through those early and sometimes difficult years at the rectory. When Peter retired he was followed by Malcolm Price, who has also become a good friend, together with his wife and two daughters who have grown up into fine young ladies.

In the later 1960s Fedge and family had moved from Ashford to a lovely house at West Wickham in Kent, where we were regular visitors. Christmas Eve was a real family affair and a particularly festive occasion, because Lizzie always celebrated Christmas on the 24th as is the custom in her native Sweden. However, the 1970s were about to take a worrying turn for them, with organisational changes and takeovers within Fedge's company which would lead to a complete change in their circumstances.

# 7 TIN HATS AND HOLLYHOCKS

Not only were we as a family starting on the adventure of living in our new property, but work-wise things were hotting up in several directions. Because of the television exposure I was getting in *Dad's Army,* I was being asked to do other types of engagements, and consequently had to find more material than I had previously had to use when I was originally doing Variety or Sunday concerts.

Marion's brothers Johnny and Norman also had career changes in the 1960s which were carried into the next decade. Johnny and his wife Ivy, the two children – Janet and Susan – and Ivy's parents moved from Yorkshire to Brighton. The two boys were about to disband the Maple Leaf Four and were in what was to be one of their last summer shows with the group at the Palace Pier Theatre, Brighton, with Tommy Trinder.

Johnny had been playing in a pub in London before that to make a few extra bob and had been writing music. He and a partner came up with the song *Baby Now That I've Found You,* which, sung by the Foundations, went into the charts and climbed to number one. Then, almost immediately, another song of theirs, *Let the Heartaches Begin* recorded by Long John Baldry, moved up the hit parade, knocking the first one off its spot two weeks later. They now had songs in both number one and two slots, being played all day, or so it seemed, by every radio station in the country. All quite incredible. Johnny was suddenly up with the pop boys, writing and producing.

A little later Norman was asked to go into the musical *Mame* in London which was to star Ginger Rogers. So now his career was about to change course as well. *Mame* was produced at the Theatre Royal Drury Lane and ran for 12 months. This was the theatre where Maudie – Norman, Johnny and Marion's mum –

had first met her husband-to-be, James Macleod, when they were in pantomime together. All the family went up to see 'Norm', as he's called, cavorting about with Ginger Rogers. 'Mum' Maudie now had to come to terms not only with Johnny's songs being played everywhere but also with seeing Norman at the 'Lane', which took her back to that first meeting with James Macleod. It was a wonderful experience for Norman and he thoroughly deserved it. Incidentally, Maudie's mum had been one of George Edward's famous Gaiety girls. What a family! If you count our son Jonathan (James) who was to later do two seasons in London, four generations had all appeared on the West End stage at one time or another.

I was playing my first London season of cabaret at the Blue Angel Club run by Max Setty in Berkeley Street. (Incidentally, his brother Stanley, the owner of a car sales business in London, had been the victim of a horrible murder when he was cut up and thrown out of an aeroplane over the marshes of the Thames Estuary.) The Blue Angel had a nice atmosphere, with the audience made up mostly of young men about town and their girlfriends. You had to do something in the region of 30 to 40 minutes, but the audience seemed to like talking acts, which was certainly not the case in a lot of late night clubs.

One night when I arrived at the venue, Max Setty said, 'You needn't go on tonight because Frankie Howerd is going to do a spot.' At that time Frank had gone rather out of fashion, and while we were talking in the lounge before he went on, he wondered whether he had lost his touch and talked about getting a 'proper job', nine-to-five. I waited to see him perform and after a slightly nervous start he was marvellous, and the audience loved him. Setty said to him afterwards, 'You haven't lost your touch, it's just that audiences go through a fickle stage with some performers.' Frank then made an appearance at the newly opened Establishment Club where he wowed his audiences. He was very quickly back on television and regained his position as one of the funniest clowns in the business.

Frankie Howerd was always an insecure person, as I was to discover personally a little later, but that was part of the reason for his unique humour and success. I remember talking to him at some length when I was writing a book about the history of Royal Command Performances and he told me that even if he'd had a success one night, he could be very nervous the next wondering whether people would like him or not. When he was doing the TV series *Up Pompeii*, produced by David Croft, I was engaged to do the warm-ups for the show. David liked to have people around him he knew, and of course I was working for him in *Dad's Army* and did the warm-ups for that series, as well as appearing as the Warden. I was happy to do *Up Pompeii*.

Frankie had a few changes of costume and while he was changing I stepped in and told a couple of jokes and chatted to the audience as I usually did. I happened to get a good laugh from a silly story one evening early on in the series and Frank rushed out with his costume half on and half off and said, 'Yes, thank you Mr Pertwee, I do the funnies, thank you, yes, you can go.' This was all done in the comic way only he could do, so I left him to it and went and sat down in the make-up room to wait for the next break in the recording, if there was going to be one. Frank apparently had a word with David Croft after the show and told him he would do the warm-ups in future, so I didn't do the rest of the series, although I got paid for them.

When we met on one occasion after that Frank said, 'There was nothing personal you know, Bill; it's just the way I am.' And, of course, there was nothing personal in his actions, he just had to keep proving himself, although it wasn't necessary. I was one of his many fans, and if I knew he was on TV or radio I always looked forward to listening to him. He had style, and could make an ordinary situation sound very funny, which in the hands of anyone else would not have raised a *titter*!

Our son Jonathan was now attending his local school, and making a lot of friends in the village. I was not spending a lot of time at home because of the continuing success of *Dad's Army*, but Marion was making new friends and re-planning the garden. She always had this thing about a cottage garden effect. Well our home wasn't a cottage by any means, but she made a start with a few hollyhocks.

Early in the 1970s we made the feature film of the series for Columbia pictures – quite an exciting project to be involved in, and one that proved at the show was going from strength to strength on the small screen. It was pretty amazing on reflection to recall that the hierarchy of the BBC had had so many misgivings about the show originally; indeed, that it nearly didn't even get as far as the first series. The comments then had been, 'Who will want to see a lot of old boys rushing about trying to play soldiers? Who will remember anything about the Home Guard?' By the end of the third year we were topping the TV ratings with audiences of millions. I remember Bill Cotton, (son of the great Billy Cotton and head of BBC1) coming up to Thetford where we used to do the exterior filming. He said, 'Boys, I just wanted to tell you personally: you've topped the comedy ratings, so I've been proved wrong.' It was really nice of him to come and tell us himself.

*Dad's Army* won the BAFTA award for best comedy series and received the accolade from Princess Anne at a wonderful evening at the Albert Hall. Everybody seemed to be there. We had a lovely dinner with plenty of wine and I said to Marion at one point, 'The chap sitting next to me seems familiar.' He was bald, so that probably confused me. Marion said, 'It's Ray Milland.' You could have bowled me over with a shuttlecock, but of course he was not wearing his toupee. On those occasions, and there have been a few similar ones since, I've always thought back to the early days: if I'd been sacked during that first summer show at Gorleston and had to leave show business, I would have missed so many wonderful events that I have been privileged to experience – like that BAFTA night.

The film for Columbia pictures was not the happiest undertaking for most of the cast. I only had a few scenes so I was not involved in it too much. The American producers had given it a time limit of eight weeks to complete, and just wanted to get as many minutes in the can each day as they could. So it was a case of keeping up the schedule of four or five minutes a day all the time. If there were a hold up because of an irregularity in costumes of the 1940 period they weren't bothered, and the

Director Norman Cohen, who was British, and Jimmy Perry, the co-writer, were always battling to get things right. There were some tricky scenes to arrange and various venues to be researched – like Chobham in Surrey and Seaford in Sussex – and the high street of Chalfont St Giles, Buckinghamshire, was transformed into Walmington-on-Sea, the little resort which was the centre of the activities of Captain Mainwaring's platoon. The interior action shots were filmed at Shepperton Studios and the exterior of the church hall in the grounds surrounding it.

One scene nearly ended in disaster: a raft, carrying not only members of the platoon but also a large white horse, was to be seen floating down a river. In fact it was being towed by ropes guided by divers but they found it impossible to keep the raft completely steady. The horse lost its balance and fell against John Laurie (Private Fraser) breaking one of John's ribs – an incident which was not seen in the finished film. A later scene where vehicles had to drive over an oil spillage involved difficult manoeuvres which had to be handled with great care.

We were all disappointed, to put it mildly, when Janet Davies, who played Mrs Pike for the television series, was replaced for the film by Liz Fraser. I've got nothing against Liz Fraser who was then, and still is, a competent actress. We just all thought it was a crazy move by the producers, who said they wanted a name artiste for the part. It was *Dad's Army* that was the draw as far as cinema audiences were concerned.

One funny little incident that happened when we were filming at Shepperton involved Arthur Lowe and Paul Dawkins, who was playing the German general in the movie. In one scene Arthur had to use a gun which was very heavy: it didn't have to be fired so Arthur asked the props department whether they had a plastic replica which would be lighter and easier when he got it out of its holster. The props man hadn't got one so Arthur got the unit car to take him to the local Woolworth store. For some reason he asked Paul Dawkins to go with him: I suppose they thought they'd have a chat about the ensuing scenes. The two soldiers appeared in Woolworth's, one dressed as a captain in the Home Guard and the other in full German general's uniform. Apparently the driver of the car said the sales assistant in Woolworth's took no notice, or appeared not to, but apologised that he had no plastic gun in the store that would 'suit sir'.

During the film I was doing some Sunday concerts at Butlin's and I decided I needed an accompanist, so I took Hugh Hastings along with me. Not heard of him? Well I'll explain how my association with him came about. He was one of the *Dad's Army* platoon for the whole of the nine years of the show and the major film. The small, but important, part in the series as a member of 'the back row of the chorus' as they called themselves was just another chapter in Hugh's colourful life.

He came over here from his native Australia and enlisted in the Royal Navy during World War 2. He'd had some success in Australia as a writer, actor and musician, but he wasn't prepared, I'm sure, for the success he was to experience as a playwright, and later musician, in this country. His first play, *Seagulls over Sorento* about life in the RN, was almost immediately a success. He was overwhelmed by the attention of West End managers and producers wanting to know when he was going to write another so they could take options on it – whatever it was. Hugh told me that there were suddenly a lot of hangers-on around him, most of them he didn't even know and were only on the fringe of the business anyway.

Once *Seagulls* settled down he adapted it into a musical, which, retitled *Scapa,* was produced in London. It didn't have the same success as the play and Hugh, having been persuaded to put some of his own money into it, found his assets disappearing fast. However, being the resilient man that he is, he turned once again to acting and playing the piano in hotel bars, and accompanying cabaret artistes. He travelled with one lady all over the Continent, enjoying the enormous success that she always generated: her name? Marlene Dietrich! He was also for quite sometime musical director for Sarah Churchill, and consequently met her parents on several occasions. And then came *Dad's Army* and, as I was looking for an accompanist, Hugh volunteered to join me. In fact he had known Jimmy Perry for some time and it was Jimmy who suggested him to me. We did quite a lot of concerts and cabaret dates together and he was always good company, with a wicked sense of humour. He did some lovely send-ups of famous pianists, particularly Liberace, and I made him put it in my concerts. It always went down well. Hugh is still going strong, despite a couple of recent operations; more importantly, he hasn't lost his sense of humour.

The film premiered in Shaftesbury Avenue; although it did well on the cinema circuit and there were some very good moments in it, we didn't think it was particularly good. The film is still played occasionally on cinema bills and gets the odd screening on television – it continues to get a good reaction from viewers.

We also started a tight schedule of radio recordings of *Dad's Army* in the early 1970s. The scripts for radio were adapted from the television versions of some 70 episodes, with one or two re-written entirely, as the originals were far too visual for radio. The radio episodes were put together by Harold Snoad, for some time David Croft's assistant on the TV series, and Michael Knowles, who had played occasional silly ass military characters in the series.

The radio programmes of *Dad's Army* were always introduced by the Daddy of all BBC commentators, John Snagge. He had gained celebrity status in broadcasting over a long period, mainly due to his commentaries on the annual Oxford and Cambridge Boat Race. John was a real gentleman, charming and brilliant at his job. I have a detailed copy of the script he used when he gave the first bulletin announcing the D-Day landings in June 1944, which is a splendid memento of the man. In each *Dad's Army* radio programme Snagge set the scene for what would ensue during the next half hour. I don't know whose idea this was, but it was certainly a masterstroke.

During one particular weekend we were recording a couple of radio episodes at the BBC Playhouse Theatre Studio on the Friday night and on the Sunday a television episode at the Wood Lane Centre. Jimmy Beck, who played Private Walker, was, as usual, with the gang for the radio recording on the Friday but the next day, when he was opening a fête near his home, he was taken ill and rushed to hospital. Unfortunately he never recovered and died a few days later. When we arrived for the Sunday TV recording we had no idea how ill he was. David Croft and Jimmy Perry made a quick adjustment to the script, as Jimmy Beck had already done the exterior filming for the episode some weeks before. If you ever watch the episode in which, half way through, Mainwaring tells the platoon he has sent Walker on an errand, this is where the rewrite came in. I am sure we, the cast, expected Jimmy to recover and carried on as if it were just a temporary loss of the character for a couple of weeks. When we heard that he had died it was hard to take in. His dear wife Kay was naturally shattered and so were we.

I was at home when one of the National newspapers rang asking if I had any comment to make about Jimmy's passing. I was still in shock, and as for 'making a comment', which is what the media always asks, I was too stunned to say anything except, 'Oh dear, I am sorry.' All very inadequate in the circumstances. It was a difficult time for the show because Private Walker had become a very popular character with viewers. The BBC had already contracted us for another series so we had to go ahead with it. The highly successful original casting of the show now had a gap in it and nobody knew how it should be filled, if, indeed, it should be filled at all.

In fact, the writers quite rightly decided that another actor should not be engaged as Walker, so they decided to bring in a different character altogether. He was to follow Mainwaring around as a local newspaper photographer doing a series of articles depicting the adventures of a Home Guard commander. The actor brought in for this role was Welshman Talfryn Thomas. He very soon settled into the part and was not at all intimidated by coming into an established series, which he could quite easily have been. He had good attack and was always saying to Mainwaring, 'That's it boyo, that's good boyo, that'll look good in the paper boyo.' Arthur Lowe played it with all the conceit the character had, with such comments as, 'I

think this is my best side, don't you?' and:'Would you like a serious pose, that lets people know I'm in charge of my platoon?'

In 1972 I was engaged to play the baron in *Cinderella* at the
Richmond Theatre. It was a lavish production under the direction of Roger Redfarn and had a really fine cast. Roy Kinnear,
who was playing Buttons, had a lovely sense of humour. Roy's
first big television success was *That Was the Week That Was* in the
1960s. It was arranged that we would share a dressing room, so
consequently we got to know one another pretty well. In the
dressing room he had a habit of eating lots of Liquorice
Allsorts, I believe because he had recently given up smoking.
On the opening night before the show I was listening to some
research tapes on my Walkman radio. Roy suddenly jumped up
and said, 'How can you do that on our opening night?' I quite
casually said to him, 'Roy, if we haven't been tumbled after 15
years [both of us had been in the business longer than that] they
won't tumble us now.' He sat down and thought about it for a
while and said, 'I hope you're right.' His dear wife Carmel told
me later that Roy thought that was the most sensible thing he'd
ever heard. I'm sure no one would call me very sensible, but it
seemed to quieten things down on that opening night.

Roy lived quite near the theatre and he would dash home in
between shows, mainly so he could give tea to his badly handicapped daughter, who was terribly important to him. I sometimes went home with him, and saw how gentle he was with
that little girl. The other two children, Rory and Kirsty, have
grown into super young people and have supported their mother, as you would expect. Roy would have been so proud of
them. The family and the theatrical world were robbed of a
lovely and compassionate man when he died in an accident
while filming in Spain. A home for the handicapped has been
named after him in nearby Teddington: a fitting tribute.

An amusing incident relating to that pantomime occurred
one night after Roy had gone home. I was just in the middle of
washing, having put our dirty clothes in the washing basket
which the wardrobe mistress collected every night, and was
bent over the basin just in my underpants. The usual knock

sounded at the door and I said, 'Come in love, the washing's in the basket.' There was a second knock, so half dry and half wet I opened the door. Standing there was not the wardrobe mistress but Princess Alexandra and her two children, with her husband bringing up the rear! The Princess said, 'I'm sorry if we're intruding, but I just wanted to say how much we've enjoyed the pantomime, and my children are such fans of *Dad's Army*, we just wanted to say thank you.' I met the Princess again at a later date, fully clothed that time. She really is the most charming person; I used to serve her mum, Princess Marina, when I worked at Burberrys. (I just thought I'd throw that in!)

The following year I was engaged to play the captain in *Dick Whittington* at the New Theatre, Coventry, a theatre that had been the home for many years of Sam Newsome's revues and pantomimes. The star of *Dick Whittington* was to be Dick Emery playing dame as Sarah the cook, and his wife, the tall elegant Josephine Blake, playing principal boy. I had worked with Dick occasionally on TV since I first did a walk on (extra) in one of his shows. That first show with him reminds me of an amusing episode from the middle 1950s.

The night before that 'extra' appearance, Marion and I had been asked to perform at a police concert at the Hammersmith Palais in West London. We arrived at the Palais and were told by the inspector in charge that the cabaret could not start until the top of the bill, Alma Cogan, had arrived. He plonked a bottle of Scotch down in front of us and told us to have a drink while we were waiting. I hadn't eaten very much recently (it was one of my financial fasting periods) and I certainly would not have had the money to drink the golden liquid in those days, so I got stuck into the police hospitality. Marion had given our band parts to the conductor (I think it was Joe Loss) and we waited.

When the cabaret started I could hardly see across the dressing room, never mind the band or audience! When we were eventually announced, Marion led me on to the stage and we started going through our routine. I must have gone through it all parrot fashion because apparently I took all the music cues, and did the quite difficult finale piece, without a hiccup. As soon as we got out in the air to go back to Victoria it really hit me, and I was sick on the steps of the Palais. We caught the Underground at Hammersmith, but had to get out at the next station for me to be sick again. When we finally reached Victoria Marion had to catch her late night train back to Brighton and I had to get back to my room in Ebury Street. Marion thought I wasn't in a fit state to find my own way there so she gave me to a passing sailor on the platform and asked him to see me home. He was apparently a bit non-plussed, but obviously did his duty because the next morning I woke up at about 6.30am lying in my fireplace still in my dinner suit. The few pictures in the room were lying on the floor so I must have been feeling for the light switch when I got in the previous night. After trying to pull myself together I set off for the BBC theatre at Shepherd's Bush. I saw the producer to tell him I'd arrived and he said, 'Are you all right? You look a bit pale.' I told him a little of the previous night's episode and he said, 'Go and see Dick Emery, he's got tablets for your sort of condition.' I knocked on Dick's dressing room door and he was lying on his couch with a green complexion. He said, 'Don't bother me now, I got rather pissed last night.' I said, 'I know how you feel,' and made a quick exit. I was quite glad that day that I didn't have any words to say in the programme we were going to do.

However, back to the pantomime at Coventry. This wasn't the happiest engagement I'd had. Dick Emery was going through one of his 'blue periods' when he could be rather erratic. He had always been keen on motorbikes and he used to have the odd one or two delivered to the theatre. He would take them into his dressing room and start them up, and you can imagine the noise that they made in a confined area.

Like quite a few others, Dick was insecure as a performer, although he had no need to be. He really was very good on both radio and television. Perhaps playing a character on stage stripped him of the security of the smaller studio environment where he had the support of those around him, producer, director and technicians. In the theatre you've got to prove yourself at every performance. On certain occasions he used to take off his wig at the end of the pantomime, an action unheard of in the theatre, as if to say, 'I'm Dick Emery.' He loved his mum, but had had no guidance from his father, a well known variety performer in his day, who in fact used to do a double act for a while with Marion's father. His father could be difficult to work with and sometimes wouldn't turn up for a performance.

I think Dick had a persecution complex. I used to go swimming with his wife and one or two other ladies from the pantomime in the Olympic-sized pool at Coventry, and Dick used to watch us from the restaurant high up over the pool. In the evening he used to say to me, 'I saw you messing about with my wife.' Now I don't know how anyone can mess about with someone in a pool, after all the whole area is very transparent. The next day he would be quite different and invite me out for a meal after the show and be very generous and chatty. He was such a mixed-up character. I remember he asked me to do the following summer season with him at Torquay. I told him it was not possible as I would be filming and recording some more episodes of *Dad's Army*. He took this as a personal affront.

I decided to have some golf lessons while I was in Coventry. I really enjoyed them and couldn't wait to get out on the course. One cold morning I wrenched my neck muscles and could hardly move my arms, while every movement of my neck was agony. We were playing on that occasion with the great football player Joe Mercer, who was then managing Coventry City, and he took me straight back to the club premises and got the physio to work on me. Although it was agony doing the twice daily panto performances for a couple of days, the physio got me right in a very short time.

Peter Elliott, whom I had first met at the Windmill Theatre when he had been the feed to Jimmy Edmundson, a lovely comic, had been with Dick Emery for several years, first as his feed and then as his personal manager. Life wasn't always easy for Peter with Dick, but they both respected one another. Peter is now the Administrator for the Entertainment Artistes' Benevolent Fund which looks after pros who are in need. He is based at the fund's retirement home, Brinsworth House in

Twickenham, and he and his wonderful staff do a remarkable and important job.

It was a long running pantomime at Coventry. We finished at the end of March, and I was quite relieved when it was over. During those months it had often been a problem to get home at weekends because the country was on a three-day week and petrol was very hard to come by. But somehow I managed it, filling up the tank during the week at Coventry and then making sure the garage in our village could give me enough to get back to the Midlands on Mondays.

After a difficult few years at West Wickham, Fedge and Lizzie moved to Canterbury. This came about after Fedge resigned his directorship with the Kellner Partington paper firm. There had been several takeovers involving the Norwegian-based parent company. He would not have taken the decision to retire lightly, and my guess is he thought the reshuffling of the companies was going to be very disruptive to the London office and his staff. I know he had the complete support of Lizzie in this move, but it must have been a difficult time with the children's education to cope with: James was then at Bristol University and Ingrid was at a teacher training college in London, so money was very tight.

Fedge and Lizzie's one good asset was the house in Kent, and when they sold it they had enough to buy the house in Canterbury and a couple of nearby flats that would give them an income. Fedge had always been fond of Canterbury and they really started this new phase in their lives with a lighter heart. James obtained his first teaching post in Birmingham in 1972 and stayed there until 1974 when he married Eileen, a domestic science teacher at the school. She is a super girl, and I remember meeting her for the first time wearing just my underpants when she and James came to visit me backstage in my dressing room. Ingrid meanwhile had got her first teaching job at Ashford in Kent.

In early summer 1974 I had a few days at Diss in Norfolk with Marion's brother Norman and my old pal Algy More. Algy was content during the day to sort out a pub or two, as he claimed he knew every good hostelry in Britain. I was about to start another filming session for *Dad's Army* at Thetford so the idea was to move on there after a few days before starting work. One morning Norman and I were on the golf course; it was idyllic, the sun shone, there was complete peace and quiet apart from a few birds singing. After a few holes a man appeared from behind some gorse bushes waving a white handkerchief. We took no notice of him and got on to the next hole where the man reappeared with the handkerchief. This time I thought I'd better sort him out with a few Warden-like words. Before I could say anything he said, 'Are you Mr Pertwee?'

'Yes,' I said.

'Can you phone your agent in London, he wants to talk to you.'

Typical, I thought, Richard Stone can find me anywhere.

When we got back to the clubhouse for some lunch I phoned him. He told me I was to get down to London to meet a Ray Cooney and John Chapman at the Savoy Theatre about a play they were going to produce. I was livid. However, after some thought I decided I'd better go. Norman drove me to Diss station and off I went in a hot train wondering what the hell I was doing. I arrived in a warm and dusty London and went to the Savoy to be welcomed by Cooney and Chapman. The play they had written, and would be producing in the autumn, was *There Goes the Bride*. They asked me to read a few lines as a grumpy Australian, which I did. The part was quite small and it took me just a few minutes to read. They both thanked me, but I thought, 'Blimey, all the way down from Norfolk to read for such a small part.' It didn't please me too much. They told me that the part was to be enlarged in a rewrite of the second act. It didn't convince me.

I got a taxi back to Liverpool Street station and caught the first train back to Diss. Luckily there was a bar on the train and I sank a tot or two which helped my annoyance at having my brief holiday interrupted. The next morning I was woken up in the hotel at 7am, bleary-eyed from the night before, by my agent Richard saying Ray Cooney had just rung him and would like me to do the part. I agreed to do it and didn't think too much more about it, as I would be moving off to the Bell Hotel at Thetford ready to start filming for *Dad*'s the next day.

On the way we called in at David Croft's house which he had bought in 1968 at Honington in Suffolk during the first year's filming of the series. We had a drink with David and his wife Ann – two of the most hospitable people I've met, as we all found out during the making of the series. We then moved on to Thetford where Norman and Algy More would be getting the train back to London. We did our usual filming sessions for a couple of weeks or more, always hard work from early morning to late in the evening, but carried out in a convivial atmosphere, with more hospitality at David and Ann's house. Then it was back to London for the studio work.

All of us connected with the series have been asked many times about the filming done in Norfolk. I don't pretend to know all the technical details, but while we were away for those two or three weeks we would film bits for all the episodes in a particular series and they would be inserted into the recordings in the studio each week. When the whole programme was put together in front of the audience they would then see those sections on the monitors above their heads so that the laughs would be recorded just as if they were taking place in front of them. *Dad's Army* never used canned laughter.

Location filming can be an advantage to a programme because the writers and artistes can experiment with ideas. You've got natural light for a start, and you are not as pressurised for time as you may be in the studio. If someone suggests an extra bit of business, or the director wants to try a certain action sequence another way, you can. If it isn't any good you forget it and use the original idea. In other words there is some freedom outside which makes each day interesting.

All the sequences were carefully written and crafted by David Croft and Jimmy Perry and the appropriate locations selected well in advance, initially by Harold Snoad in the early days of his involvement with the series. Harold really knew his job and this was borne out when he later became a director and executive producer himself. One of his productions, a big hit, is *Keeping Up Appearances*, with that awful woman Mrs Bucket and the long-suffering husband played by Clive Swift.

The Bell Hotel and the 'Anchor' were our homes for the filming sessions and there were some very amusing incidents off screen. Early in the morning there would be alarm calls ringing in all the bedrooms round about 6am summoning us to start our day. Those who needed make-up and/or wigs would probably have sorted this out before going down to breakfast, having already put on most of their uniforms. Before there were tea-making facilities in the rooms, nine times out of ten you would hear Arthur Lowe calling out, 'Where's the tea boy? He's put two tea bags in my pot again, he knows I only have one.'

Once assembled for breakfast, people would ask in what order the exterior shots would be done so that those not in the early ones could gauge how long they could take over their food. The rustling of envelopes containing the day's schedules was apparent, while others were asking the bleary-eyed waiters about the condition of the kippers or, in Arthur Lowe's case, 'Is the ham off the bone this morning? I don't want any of that plastic stuff out of a tin – and make sure the toast isn't burned!'

Someone else would probably quote a headline from the newspaper which would bring a few comments. Harold Snoad or Jimmy Perry would then walk round the tables saying, 'Don't be too long lads, the coach [which was to take us to the first location] will be here in a minute.' This remark would bring an immediate reaction from somebody of, 'I'm waiting for some more tea, the first lot was cold.' They liked to get their priorities right. Eventually the team, along with the other lads who made up the platoon from the 'Anchor', started making their way on to the coach. The make-up girls and wardrobe ladies had meantime sorted out the rooms they'd been allocated to use as storage while we were on location, and joined us too. Most of the technicians tended to use their own cars which were usually full to the brim with equipment.

During the whole of the nine years we spent in Norfolk we only had three or four days' rain, and the drive out from the hotel early on those summer mornings is something I shall never forget. The roads were almost empty, and when we turned into the long driveways up to the Stamford military training area the coach had to avoid pheasants running out of the woods and dashing hither and thither across its path. I suppose it was the anticipation of what we were going to do during the day, but it was also the whole atmosphere of the lovely scenery, and the banter in the coach from those awake enough to want to listen or comment. The journey would probably only take half an hour or less, but in that time it seemed reminiscent of naughty schoolboys going on an outing. It was the start of a day out for the *Dad's Army* Club.

By about 10.30 the first shot or two had been taken care of and the morning break would be ready from the food van: tea, coffee, orange juice, bacon or sausage rolls. Those who hadn't fancied an early breakfast would tuck in and some who had partaken at the hotel also used to fill their boots. By that time Althea Ridley, Arnold's wife, would have joined us along with Joan Lowe, Arthur's wife, and the next priority would be to see who could complete *The Times* crossword first. The race between Joan Lowe, Ian Lavender and John Laurie would then get interrupted by a call to action, invariably leaving Joan the winner with groans from John, 'Why can't the director give us a few more minutes, the crossword is important!'

After a long day a coachload of tired and grubby actors and actresses would be deposited back at the hotel ready for a comforting bath, sometimes a pint at the bar first, in preparation for a jovial evening over a protracted dinner and drinks in the lounge afterwards. We were never very early to bed, even though we knew we'd have another long session in front of us the next day. It was fun to relax with a few drinks swap silly stories or just to comment on what we'd filmed that day.

In the very early days of the series we used to go up to the local cinema after they had finished their film programme, as arrangements had been made for the rushes (rough cut sequences) to be shown on the big screen. These were generally two or three days old and had come up from London after processing. You can imagine the comments that were made; invariably there would be one about me overplaying a scene: 'How many more faces is he going to pull.' It must have been a funny sight to see the bunch of us strolling down the road near midnight back to the hotel.

I have covered in some detail the particular experiences we had during the nine years of the show in my book *Dad's Army – The Making of a Television Legend* which is due once again for reissue as I write these lines.

During summer 1974 there was a strike at the BBC in some of the technical departments so the studio work had to be postponed. Meantime I started rehearsals for *There Goes the Bride*. My part had indeed been enlarged, and I was on for almost the entire second act. It had a marvellous cast: I was really delighted to be working with Peggy Mount, Bernard Cribbins, whom I'd always admired, Jeffrey Sumner, who was a really nice bloke, Marguerite Hardiman, who played 'the bride' and a lovely girl, Trudi van Dorn, who played the ethereal character that only Cribbins could see in the play, a condition that had been brought on by a bang on the head. This situation was the basis for the fun of the play with everyone getting mad at Cribbins who talked to someone who, as far as the rest of the cast was concerned, wasn't there.

I was told by my agent not to mention the fact that I had never done a play before. I was, however, pretty sure that Peggy knew the secret and she was very encouraging. She said on the last days of rehearsals, 'You're going to be very good in this.' Bernard Cribbins is such an inventive comic actor, and a joy to watch during rehearsals. I had the pleasure of working with him again in the early 1980s in another successful Cooney play.

We opened in *There Goes the Bride* at the King's Theatre, Southsea, at the beginning of a short tour which everyone hoped would lead to the West End. That first night at Southsea was quite nerve racking as I had to wait for the whole of the first act and the interval before making my entrance in the second. My first few lines were shouted off stage, 'Mr Westerby, Mr Westerby, where the bloody hell are you?' before I burst on to the stage in a rage. Everything passed off well and the play was well received. I remember when we were taking our bows at the end Jeffrey Sumner, who was standing next to me, whispered in my ear, 'You were marvellous.' So I had got over my first night in a play without the audience throwing anything. We all had a lovely meal with Ray Cooney and John Chapman and their respective wives, Linda and Betty. The tour went well, playing Leeds, Norwich, Nottingham and one or two others before we moved into the Criterion Theatre in Piccadilly. There was I with my name up in lights in the West End in my first play. That man with the white handkerchief on the golf course at Diss had a lot to answer for, in the nicest possible way.

We hadn't been at the Criterion very long before a spate of bombings started in London. This certainly had an effect on potential audiences coming into the West End. I remember arriving at the stage door one night and hearing an almighty bang. A bomb had gone off in a letterbox outside Swan and Edgar. Ray Cooney kept the play afloat, and in February it started to pick up and we once again played to good houses.

During one afternoon matinée Bernard and I were on stage having our usual toe-to-toe argument, which had developed into a sort of double act during the run, when there was a scream from a lady in the audience. Two more joined in shouting, 'A mouse, a mouse.' Bernard and I looked down and there was a mouse staggering about round our feet. It had obviously been through one of the little poison cartons that are put down to get rid of vermin. Most buildings have them. Bernard, without saying a word, went over to a drinks trolley on stage, picked up a glass and put it over the mouse and carried on where we'd left off. Now I am a terrible giggler on stage in certain situations and the sight of Cribbins just looking me in the eye set me off. He also started to laugh but managed to control himself. Not me, I could not say a word, and with tears pouring down my cheeks, I left the stage. Peggy Mount was due on and took an early cue. When she came on she said to Bernard 'What's the matter with him?' before carrying on with the prescribed dialogue. Several years later, meeting Su Pollard for the first time when we did pantomime together at Bournemouth, the first thing she said to me was, 'I saw you in *There Goes the Bride* and I screamed when I saw a mouse on stage.' So she had started the crazy sequence of events at that matinée.

During the early weeks of the run in London the strike at the BBC had been resolved so we started on the studio work of *Dad's Army*. It was quite tiring for me as I was rehearsing the series during the day and then going on to the theatre for the nightly performances and twice weekly matinées. We recorded the television shows on a Sunday so I was busy seven days a week without a break for nearly two months. I certainly wasn't seeing much of the family during this period except to say 'good morning' and 'goodnight'. However, we were getting to know a lot of folk round about in the village. Jonathan had left his first kindergarten school and was now at a comprehensive near at hand and was making a lot of new young friends.

My mother was spending quite a bit of time with Fedge and Liz, which helped the situation a bit at the Rectory because Marion's mother was with us almost permanently. Folks passing our house used to stop for a chat if we were in the front garden and always mentioned how lovely our hollyhocks looked. They practically covered the whole of the front area adjoining the road, and all from one small packet of seeds. My nephew James was now teaching at a school in Slough so we saw quite a lot of him and Eileen. They stayed there until 1976 before going to Germany for a year teaching English.

As far as *Dad's Army* was concerned, it was proposed that Bernard Delfont, in association with two other impresarios, Louis Michaels and Duncan Weldon, should present a stage version in London in 1975. Jimmy Perry and David Croft got down to writing it, and we looked forward to another period in the life of the Home Guard. We rehearsed in London and then went to Billingham in Cleveland to produce the show before coming back to the Shaftesbury Theatre. It was a mad time for all of us, as taking a TV production and adapting it for the stage was not going to be an easy task

The rehearsal period at Billingham was very hard work for

everyone, most of all perhaps for the production staff at the theatre. There were some complicated sets to be made, including electrically operated trucks; all the costumes to be made and fitted, and a host of dressers to be engaged for a lot of quick changes. Apart from the television cast we had a large chorus of singers and dancers, some of whom would be understudying the principals who were all taking part, except John Laurie. He thought nightly performances might be too much for him; after all he was no spring chicken when the television series started, but what great value he was in the TV shows. The late Jimmy Beck would also be missed, but their characters were brought into the production in a minor capacity played by John Bardon and Hamish Roughead. It wasn't an easy task for them trying to follow in the footsteps of Jimmy Beck and John Laurie, but they made a good job of it nevertheless.

While certain numbers were being rehearsed those who were not involved had the odd day or two off. We were able to visit some of the beautiful coastal villages and towns in Yorkshire, including Staithes, with its delightful harbour, and Whitby with its great fishing traditions and atmosphere. There was a super pub right up on the moors in the middle of nowhere with a great selection of ales and good food. At weekends session musicians used to come up from London and make music just for the hell of it. John Le Mesurier, a real jazz enthusiast and no mean pianist, got to know the pub and would go up there on Sundays to join in the jam sessions.

We eventually produced the whole show at Billingham, and the opening night seemed to go pretty well. It was not an easy production to stage but director Roger Redfarn did the job well with the help of Jimmy Perry and David Croft and our American musical director, Ed Coleman, and choreographer, Sheila O'Neill. It was rather too long, but this was sorted out when we got back to London for a few more rehearsals before opening at the Shaftesbury Theatre in September. The opening night in London was wonderful. We had friends and family in the audience, together with the first night critics, and also obvious fans of *Dad's Army*. A packed house made it swing along.

You'll have to excuse me if I mention a little bit of personal magic. First of all, here I was treading the same stage that some of the greats had trod – including one of the world's greatest stars, Fred Astaire with his sister Adele in the days when the theatre was called the Princes. Then I was included in a sort of wartime radio interlude where I had the privilege of re-creating probably the finest front cloth comedian of all time, Max Miller. The sequence included Arthur Lowe as Robb Wilton, Pamela Cundell and Joan Lowe as Elsie and Doris Waters, and Arthur Lowe, Ian Lavender and Michael Bevis as 'We three in Happidrome', a popular wartime radio trio. I remember standing in the wings, dressed in the outrageous Miller costume that was his trademark, waiting for his opening music *Mary from the Dairy* to start, and wondering how it was going to be received by the audience. It had gone reasonably well at Billingham but London might be a different kettle of fish where Max was still remembered by his many fans. As I walked on I looked down and saw in the front row Bernard Delfont, who had known Max well and had presented some of his shows. As I looked at Bernard he winked at me, and I thought that might be a good sign. My contribution was pretty well received, and to hear the applause from that packed audience was really something.

That opening night had one lovely surprise for the audience. The actual finale was the whole cast coming on stage at intervals singing *Hometown*, a huge hit for Bud Flanagan and Chesney Allen way back in their early 'Crazy Gang' shows. In our finale Arthur Lowe and John Le Mesurier, dressed as the two great entertainers, walked across the stage à la Flanagan and Allen. They were followed by two more of the cast similarly attired entering with them on the walk back. They would then pick up another two, and so on until the whole stage was filled with Flanagan and Allen lookalikes, some of them coming on solo carrying a life size cut-out of one or other of them. By this time the whole audience were joining in with the song. On the opening night at the Shaftesbury Arthur Lowe led on dressed as Bud Flanagan, but the Chesney Allen part was actually played by Ches himself. He had been invited out of the retirement he had been enjoying for several years on the Sussex coast, just for that one night. It took a few seconds for the audience to realise it really was Ches, but when they did there was a huge burst of applause and cheering that seemed to continue for ages. It was one of those unforgettable moments in the theatre.

One funny incident happened when my brother and family brought my mother up to see the show. I had got them a box, and my mother seemed to be enjoying herself. I was not only playing the Warden, who started off rushing in through the audience at the beginning of the performance shouting, as usual, at the Vicar and Verger who were on stage. I also played the German general in sequences that represented the German High Command planning the invasion in the 1940s and, as I've mentioned, Max Miller. So I was on quite a lot throughout the show. When I met my mother afterwards we took her for a drink before she went back to Canterbury with Fedge and Liz.

'Did you enjoy the show, Mum,' I asked.

'Oh very much dear. What part did you play?' That brought me down to earth in no uncertain manner.

We later heard we would be taking part in the Royal Command Variety performance at the London Palladium that year. This was certainly another excitement to come. The occasion of this great annual theatrical event is difficult to comprehend unless you are involved in it. Basically there are four days' actual rehearsal at the theatre where it is to take place, but the planning beforehand is enormous. Picking the artistes and current show excerpts, and presenting the suggestions to the Royal Family is one thing. Artistes from abroad who have agreed to come have to be accommodated in hotels along with their managers, and in some cases their musical director, plus occasionally a full band of musicians. Some shows have to close for the night so that their artistes can take part. Accommodation for the night of the show has to be arranged very near the theatre as there are only a certain number of dressing rooms available.

In the show we had various companies such as the Ross Male Voice Choir, the Kwa Zulu African Dancers, the Count Basie Orchestra, ourselves and the 'Billy Liar' company from Drury

Lane, and all of us had to be found accommodation for that one night. The Palladium itself was able to cope with Telly Savalas (Kojak of TV fame) and his cabaret company, Bruce Forsyth, Vera Lynn, Charles Aznavour and some others.

A complication that year was that there had been a few bomb incidents in London so security was very tight. The evening was to be in the presence of Her Majesty the Queen and His Royal Highness Prince Philip so the organisers could not take any chances. Harry Secombe, appearing at the Prince of Wales Theatre decided not to cancel his show but to come on afterwards as he was only involved at the end of the Royal Performance with Vera Lynn and the Ross Male Voice Choir.

In all there were 378 people involved in the show and everything went off like clockwork under the brilliant direction of Robert Nesbitt. Bob never raised his voice, but was very firm and sorted out any distractions pretty quickly. I have often thought that the short rehearsal period of four days at the theatre would make a wonderful video or programme in itself. I think the viewers would be absolutely amazed, and wonder just how the finished product all comes good on the night.

An amusing moment just before the finale of the performance occurred in the wings where we were waiting to take our places on stage, standing in lines four or five abreast, with all the other artistes lined up behind us, eventually stretching out through the stage door, waiting their respective calls. I was standing next to Arthur Lowe and next to him were members of the Kwa Zulu African Dance Company. Arthur and I were suddenly aware of a slight noise nearby, and when we looked around one of the dancers was feeding her baby at her breast. Arthur was not a very tall man and the lady's breast was level with his eye line. Arthur did one of his double takes and said to the lady, 'Enjoys a drink does he?' Then after a slight pause, 'I could do with one right now.' I'm not sure she was amused, but it made me laugh! Perhaps Arthur was slightly embarrassed to have noticed the incident, but of course there was no need for this. It was just a lovely natural thing for mum to think of her hungry baby amidst all the excitement.

*Dad's Army* stayed at the Shaftesbury for five months and then went out on tour with the show in 1976 for a further six months all round the UK. Apart from the opening date at the Opera House Manchester, where there had been some hold up in pre-publicity, and the next week at Blackpool out of season and raining practically every day, we had a wonderful tour with sell out business at Newcastle, Brighton, Birmingham, Bradford, Bath, etc. We also enjoyed some marvellous social occasions. We played a cricket match in Arthur Lowe's home village of Hayfield in Derbyshire to raise money for repairs to the pavilion of the cricket club, of which Arthur was president. It was such a big success, with people coming from miles around, enough money was raised to rebuild the pavilion completely. Over the years, because of the popularity of *Dad's Army*, we have had the opportunity to help raise quite a lot of money for various charitable causes and lend our weight to some good causes that might otherwise have sunk without trace.

There was another great day when we were in Bath. We were invited to lunch by Prime Minister Neville Chamberlain's daughter-in-law. We had a wonderful meal and had the privilege of seeing some of Chamberlain's private letters to his son written from Germany during the Munich crisis in 1938. Quite revealing, I can tell you. Another guest at the lunch was President Roosevelt's son, General Roosevelt.

At the end of the tour in September 1976 I realised that not only was I a bit tired but I hadn't seen much of my family since 1974. In fact during that time I had only about three weeks off. There were some newly written radio shows to record on Sundays, apart from theatre and television commitments, and I remember travelling down from Blackpool one Sunday to do a recording, having done a matinée and evening performance in the theatre the night before. I caught the 5am train from Blackpool. changing at Preston, to get me down to Paris Studios in London by lunchtime. Arriving at the studio a little early, I decided to have a shower before we started. I was obviously tired because I fell asleep in the shower. Anyhow, after the recording I dashed back to Surrey to see the family before setting off early on Monday for Newcastle where we had a first night to cope with.

I took a nice rest after the stage show finished, just doing the odd few concerts in early spring 1977. Then it was off to Thetford again to film for the last series of *Dad's Army*. On arrival we were told not to be too surprised when we met up with John Le Mesurier, as he hadn't been well. He had certainly lost a lot of weight, although John was never fat. He was on the mend though, and his timing and good humour continued to make us laugh. We finished recording the studio sequences later in the summer and then it was all over: nine wonderful years, having the opportunity to work with a marvellous cast and make long standing friendships. I don't think any of us thought that 25 years later the general public would still be watching the repeats and, judging by their reactions, enjoying them, in some instances, even more than when they were orig-inated. Perhaps distance lends some enchantment. Maybe peo-ple think they are still better than a lot of programmes produced nowadays. They could be right! As one critic recently observed, 'There's a lot to look at on television but not much to see'!

The BBC rather forgot to give us a send off as it were, but the *Daily Mirror* newspaper found out about this slight error and they gave us a wonderful dinner in London. They had some 'long service' medals struck and an accompanying picture over the whole front page of the next day's edition. One very sad note at the end of that last series was the death of Edward Sinclair, who played the Verger. Teddy was one of life's gentle-men, he had been tremendous value in the show. He only had to look round a door or appear at the side of the Vicar when he was chastising Mainwaring, and that wonderful face of his was worth a hundred words.

My working partnership with Arthur Lowe and his wife was to be extended after the run of the series as we went out on tour in a play together for a few months in 1978. I was very fond of them both, and we had a wonderful time with laughs on and off stage in the very funny play *Caught Napping*, written by Geoffrey Lumsden who played Captain Square in several episodes of *Dad's Army*, and he wasn't half good in the part.

The tour of the play had one or two very funny moments. When we were playing Bath, Arthur decided to see his doctor as he was not sleeping properly, and was given some tablets for this. Arthur would forget to take them at night, and so would, on occasions, take them during the day to make sure he wouldn't forget before going to bed. I was in my dressing room one night when Arthur's dresser came to me and said Mr Lowe had changed into his opening costume for the play – white T-shirt, shorts and tennis shoes – but was asleep in his chair and she couldn't wake him. I went into his room but I couldn't wake him from his slumber, so I called Joan, his wife, and she couldn't either. The sleeping pills had really done the trick, but at the wrong time of the day. As there were only about ten minutes to curtain up, Joan and I got Arthur out of his chair and put his head out of the window, with him still gently snoring.

'There's only one thing for it,' Joan said and she took the soda siphon off his table and squirted it on the back of Arthur's neck. This did the trick to a certain extent, but he was still a bit dopey. His first entrance was down a long flight of stairs, so he had to climb up a rather rickety sort of wooden staircase from the stage level to get to the top of the staircase quite high up in the wings. Somehow we got him to the top and then the curtain went up and Arthur started his descent of the staircase. It took a bit longer than usual for him to descend, but the amount of comedic business he got out of it, most of which must have been instinct, was wonderful to watch, and the audience applauded his entrance even more than usual on that occasion.

We had a great cast, including Fiona Fullerton (what a lovely girl she is, and I'm delighted to say is now happily married and blessed with a gorgeous baby girl), Sheila Keith, a very funny lady and good company, and the suave Timothy Carlton, who is married to a lovely actress, Wanda Ventham, with whom I have also worked in subsequent plays.

Marion and son Jonathan came to stay with us for a few days during the tour and Arthur and Joan made a great fuss of him. When they had their lovely steam yacht moored at Teddington

Arthur and Joan would ring us up and invite us down for the day. Marion and Joan used to sit and paint while Arthur and I just sat on deck chatting and having a glass or two of wine. One day when Arthur and I went into Teddington village to buy a couple of bottles a group of snotty nosed kids shouted out, 'Go on, give him one Napoleon.' This was the nickname I had addressed Arthur by in some episodes of the series. Arthur put his hands up as if he was going to give me a punch and all the kids shouted, 'Go on, we're behind you Napoleon.' All good fun, and after we'd signed a few autographs for them they went off quite happily.

I was quite busy again for the latter part of the 1970s with pantomime, one of which caused a problem or two. Ian Lavender and I were playing the robbers in *Babes in the Wood*. Half way through the performance one night, large pieces of plaster and cement started falling from the ceiling. Melvyn Hayes, the dame, started rushing about shouting, 'Evacuate the building, get on to Equity, bring in the Fire Brigade.' We started the second half in front of the front tabs and carried on like this without any scenery until the end. On my first entrance after the interval I came out wearing my Warden's hat which I always kept handy in the car, and I must say my appearance got quite a laugh and some applause. After the plaster incident we had a couple of nights off while repairs were carried out.

I also went on the road with a couple of plays written by my cousin Michael Pertwee. The first one was based on a true murder mystery and called *Find the Lady*. It was a very good vehicle for a friend of ours, actress Mollie Sugden, but not quite right for me. I was playing the murder suspect and although very serious, complete with sinister moustache, audiences still thought of me as the Warden from *Dad's Army*, and in a few instances started chuckling when I made my entrance. I didn't mind about this, because for one thing the Warden had done quite a lot for me over the years, but chuckles weren't right in this play. A few years later I had no problems playing a variety of different parts, once the initial impact of *Dad's Army* had evaporated a little, but 1979 was just a bit too early.

However we did have some fun on the tour of *Find the Lady*. At Norwich we hired a boat to spend the day on the Norfolk Broads and among our party was our stage manager who had a teddy bear that was really like a child to her. It used to sit in the prompt corner of the stage during performances and the SM would talk to it about the show. It was driving us all potty, so we kept thinking of schemes to punish the bear. On the Broads we got hold of it, blindfolded it, and made it walk the plank. This brought a few laughs and cheers and Mollie Sugden was hysterical with laughter. However the SM was in tears and very upset with us, so we had to abandon that punishment.

Michael's second play, *Don't Just Lie There, Say Something*, was out on tour for quite a long time, and repeated the success of previous outings of the play. I think it was one of Michael's very best, and would easily stand up today. It was about a government minister who got embroiled in a scandal concerning his junior minister and a few flighty girls. I played an investigating police officer, Inspector Ruff. We were taking over from a cast who had been doing it for the season at Plymouth. It was really nice working with Michael, who was directing it, and we all got on with him well. He had a lovely sense of humour and was able to cope with a couple of difficult situations during the two weeks rehearsal at Plymouth. One of the actors became a bit difficult, but Michael quietly dealt with the situation without raising his voice.

Another problem came up towards the end of the two weeks' rehearsal, when one of the actresses became ill and had to go into hospital for an operation. It was too late to start rehearsing anyone else so it was decided that the stage manager, who had been with the company at Plymouth and would be coming with us, should take over the part; she was very good in it. A new stage manager had to be found, and Michael talked to a young lady who had been involved in the Fringe Theatre at Plymouth. Although she had never stage managed a major tour before, she agreed to have a go. Michael asked us to give her as much support as possible in the early stages, which we naturally all agreed to do: that is nearly everyone. Certainly one of the cast, realising that the girl, Wendy, would be a bit vulnerable, played on it for ego purposes. However, when we opened in Eastbourne and Wendy did very well on the book, we took her out for a meal afterwards and told her not to take any notice of the egocentric who had tried to upset her. The tour went well round the country and finished just before pantomime rehearsals started for Bournemouth. I really got to know Michael quite well during that time and I wish I'd had the pleasure of his company before that period. I have mentioned to his lovely wife Maya that we ought to do *Don't Just Lie There, Say Something* again, I know it would go well.

The pantomime at Bournemouth was to be presented by the same management involved in *Find the Lady* and *Don't Just Lie There, Say Something*. Wendy was engaged again as stage manager, a big production to handle, including Curries' Dancing Waterfalls and several other big effects. Accommodation was quite hard to find in the resort even at Christmas time, but I managed to get a large and delightful flat near the East Cliff area. Wendy and her friend, who was in charge of the wardrobe – not an easy job in pantomime with all the costumes and cleaning to deal with and dressers to organise – could not find a flat, so I suggested they came and shared mine. I said I'd pay the rent if they bought the food and did the cooking. This all worked out very well.

Eventually the wardrobe girl left to find a flat on her own, as her boyfriend was going to join her. This gave enough room for Marion and Jonathan and Marion's brother Norman and his wife Bunty to come down for a few days at New Year. As for the pantomime itself, we had Liz Esterson and Polly James playing the babes, and jolly good they were too. Bob Todd, well known from his appearances in the Benny Hill television shows, was playing the nurse, and Matthew Kelly and Michael Robbins the robbers. Su Pollard was the fairy and Sheila Mathews the principal boy. Su Pollard had just recorded the trial TV show of *Hi-De-Hi* and we watched it on the television I had in the dressing room. We all wished Su well with it and were delighted to hear eventually that the BBC was to do a series. It turned out to be another big success for our friends, writers Perry and Croft.

We got on well as a company, going out together on various social occasions, quite often to one particular club in the town. It was decided that the club should stage a fancy dress night. We all went as something or other and we kept asking Su Pollard what she was coming as but she wouldn't tell us. When we duely arrived at the club there was still no clue. When it came to the judging, Su said she'd come as a blue tit, and with that she took out her left breast which she had completely covered with a blue pen. She naturally won first prize. This was only the start of my experiencing the eccentricities of this clever actress. More was to come in subsequent meetings.

Bob Todd used to like a drink or two occasionally which brought a few unexpected moments on stage. He made his first entrance in the pantomime in a comedy car driven by a character dressed as a dog. Bob had to press a button when he arrived centre stage to let himself out of the back. At one matinée performance he pushed the button too early and fell out. He then approached the audience and said, 'Nanny isn't too well tonight, it's the rheumatics again, I'll have to go and get some medicine.' Luckily I was prepared for all eventualities with Bob, and as I came on through the house I met him and caught him taking a nip out of a bottle he'd hidden. I got really cross with him, and told him he was upsetting Liz and Polly and he'd got to behave professionally. He started to cry and said 'Don't be cross with me Billy.' He had so much charm about him, but I had to try and sort him out. Before the evening show he brought me in a large bottle of whisky and said, 'Am I forgiven?' What could I say. As he left my dressing room he said, 'Can I have a nip before I go?' When Bob was on form he was very funny. But after so much television he got bored with the routine of twice daily performances.

Michael Robbins and I became great friends and when he became ill a few years ago I visited him in hospital and found he hadn't lost his sense of humour. I was pleased to say a few words about him at his funeral. He was a man with a great sense of charity and would travel miles to support good causes. Who will forget his performances in that long running series *On the Buses* and his super cameo roles in films such as *The Pink Panther*? His lovely wife, actress Hal Dyer, has picked up the pieces and is working again in various theatre productions, including doing a brilliant one-woman show based on the life of theatre-legend Ellen Terry.

After the pantomime Mathew Kelly went on to great things on television, introducing game shows and quizzes. A lady I greatly admired in the pantomime was Sheila Mathews. She had appeared in many a West End production and had great presence on stage with a lovely and appealing voice. At Bournemouth one of her songs always drew me to the side of the stage to listen – *All the Things You Are*. This song had been a great favourite with my cousin Rosemary back in the late 1930s. She was always singing it, and apart from the pleasure of listening to Sheila interpreting the song, it also transported me back to those earlier years spent with my cousins, the Tobins. Stage manager Wendy eventually went on to direct in fringe theatre, and I'm sure the experience she gained with the play and pantomime would have helped her.

The 1970s had been such an eventful period, with an immense variety of work, that one tended to forget domestic life. Marion had been keeping it all together, which hadn't been easy on her own, sometimes having to make decisions after phone conversations with me from various parts of the country. Jonathan was growing up into a teenager, and the Mums had to be looked after in their latter years, so it wasn't easy.

We did have some wonderful social gatherings with friends and relatives at the Rectory when I was home. I remember one party when the whole of the *Dad's Army* crew came down, which was a real fun day. At one point Arthur Lowe went to visit the loo. Apparently one of the bolts holding the seat in place had come loose and Arthur finished up in the bath. Arthur came out and said, 'Don't use that toilet, the Warden's up to his tricks with the plumbing.' He was always able to top a funny situation with his dry sense of humour.

One wonderful occasion during the early days of *Dad's Army* was the opening of a fête on the Isle of Wight. This had been arranged with our old friends the Snellings. The fête was at Bembridge and David Croft had agreed to let us off rehearsals at midday, so we could get a mini-bus down to Fairoaks aerodrome in Surrey where Tony Snelling and a Norman Brittain Islander aircraft would fly us down to Bembridge airport on the island. We had a few drinks on the mini-bus and took-off in good heart. The plane circled over the fête before landing and there appeared to be thousands of people waving at us from the ground. The weather was very hot and we spent a long time sitting at tables signing autographs. Afterwards it was back to the Snellings for more drinks and food before returning home. Marion and Jonathan had gone over earlier in the day by ferry but came back with us on the plane. For Jonathan flying really was a new adventure.

We had a similar trip to the island later on in aid of the RNLI open day at Bembridge. We were taken over by the Bembridge lifeboat from Portsmouth and again there seemed to be thousands of people waiting to greet us when we got there. After spending the usual period signing autographs, for what seemed a never ending queue of people, we again spent the evening at the Snellings for refreshment and the odd glass of liquid.

Many afternoons were spent at Clive Dunn's house at Barnes after we'd finished rehearsals for the day. His wife Cilla would always have a bottle of wine open for us and we would sit and listen to their two daughters, Jessica and Polly, playing the piano and talking about their next painting project. Clive and his daughters are extremely good artists. Right through our association with the show Clive always managed to make me laugh in any situation we happened to be in. We still talk regularly on the telephone now he has retired to Portugal, and meet up with the members of our *Dad's Army* club when he visits this country. Just in case anyone should think that stars in the series were purely comedic, you only have to look at the number of Shakespearean roles and fine film performances that John Laurie had featured in over the years. Arthur Lowe also put in some wonderful performances in the TV series *Pasteur*, based on the life of the great medical scientist. His portrayal of Herbert Morrison, the Labour Home Secretary, in the television play *Philby* was uncanny, and his hilarious butler with Peter O'Toole in the film *The Ruling Class* was brilliant. Incidentally John Le Mesurier won a Best Actor Award for his performance in the the TV play *The Traitor*.

One amusing incident, or it seemed so at the time, was early in the 1970s when I had been asked to go to the Mermaid Theatre to audition for Bernard Miles, who had several years before realised an ambition to build this theatre in the heart of the city. Bernard was a distinguished actor and had also been a very good solo performer on the 'halls' recalling anecdotes from the countryside. However on the day of my audition I missed the train I meant to catch and decided to go into the nearby pub to have a pint. When I caught the next train it became evident I should have spent a penny before leaving, although I thought I could last out until arriving in London. We then had problems on the line, and a couple of quite lengthy unscheduled stops. My predicament became quite desperate. There were no loos on board, and the train was packed with people and so I had to wait until everybody got off. I was wearing a very light coloured suit so you can imagine my lot was not a happy one. I went straight down to the hairdressers on the station and asked the assistant if I could borrow a hairdryer. I took my trousers off and while he dried them I sat on a seat just in my pants. And do you know, the customers who were there, and those coming in, didn't bat an eyelid at this strange sight!

I got to the Mermaid a little late and apologised to Bernard. The play I was reading for was a slightly obscure Bernard Shaw piece and my character was an Australian. I read a few lines and Bernard thanked me. My then agent rang me and said I had got the part but there was a problem because I had several cabaret dates booked which would be impossible to postpone. The play was eventually produced but only lasted a very short time, so perhaps it was just as well I was unavailable for it.

Two significant events happened at the end of the 1970s, one of them sad for our family. My first book *Promenades and Pierrots* was published, a history of seaside entertainment over a 100-year period from the 1850s. The idea for the book came about when my friend Algy More gave me some pictures of summer Pierrot and concert parties playing *al fresco* around our coastal resorts. He had been a part of these in the early 1900s. I had great fun researching the subject, and I'm pleased to say it has been used in schools and colleges ever since as part of our social history. The media were very nice about it and several radio and television companies have used it as a guide on the subject.

The other significant but sad time was the death of our dear mother, Dulce. I had been speaking at a cricket dinner in Leicester the night before when Fedge rang me at 6am telling me that she had passed away. She had been in a retirement home run by nuns at Folkestone in Kent for a few months. I got the first train out of Leicester and went straight on to Folkestone. I went to see her and she looked so peaceful and serene. One had to think that she was now at peace after her many years of sadness and problems from a young age.

A few weeks earlier I had been filming a sequence for the television series *Worzel Gummidge* and I bought a raffle ticket in Marion's name. Would you believe it, the ticket won first prize, a holiday in Greece! As we hadn't had a break of any consequence for many years this was wonderful. We arranged that we could take young Jonathan with us as well. Our departure date had been fixed several weeks before, and it was on the actual day of my mother's funeral. I phoned Fedge and asked him what we should do. He said, 'You must go, you haven't had a break for a long time,' besides which, knowing our Mum, she would have said that we should go. We left Gatwick in pouring rain which apparently covered most of the country. There was just a handful of people at Mum's funeral: Bunty, Norman, Fedge, Liz and two others. But she was buried in the same grave as my father, so she was back with her dear Jimmy, the great love of her life.

One slightly amusing incident took place not long before she died. I had brought her up from the retirement home to see young Jonathan in his first play in a youth group, *Toad of Toad*

*Hall.* She was really thrilled to see her grandson, whom she adored anyway. When I drove her back to Folkestone after the weekend we stopped half way to eat our sandwiches and have a cup of coffee. She suddenly said to me, 'Is your father doing pantomime this year.' I had to think pretty quickly because I realised she was confused in her mind about our relationship, and believed she was talking to Jonathan. So I said, 'Oh I expect so.' She replied, 'I hope he's not working too hard,' and then carried on in the same vein, 'And how are you getting on at school, dear?' Remembering what a bad scholar I'd been I said, 'Oh you know, same as usual, but I'm enjoying myself.' She then said, 'Well that's the main thing.' She had always only wanted us to be happy.

She was 89 when she died and it seemed amazing, looking back, that she had survived all the ups and downs of her long life, including two bad falls in her senior years, one of which ended in her fracturing her hip which she coped with remarkably well. She had arrived in this country from Rio at the age of 12 to start her schooling in the company of nuns at the convent in South London and ended it in the environs of another order of nuns at Folkestone.

During our holiday in Greece we teamed up with a lovely family, a Judge Chevasse, his wife and two daughters. On various outings the Judge and I used to sit in the back of the coach having a crafty cigarette together and at the end of the day drinking a glass or two of brandy in the roof top bar of the hotel after our respective wives and children had gone to bed.

The 1960s and 1970s had been a most amazing period in our lives, and certainly in my case the family as well. However the early 1980s were to take me in another direction, at least for a time.

# 8 RUN FOR YOUR COONEY!

After the pantomime at Bournemouth spring 1980 started off for me with a play that should never have been let loose on the public. It was an adaptation of a saucy film — although adaptation is not quite the right word, because it had been cobbled together with just a hint of the film. When negotiations started, I only had the first act to read, but it was a good part — that of a Scottish retainer who over-indulged in the amber liquid. He hid bottles of it all over the set in flower vases, under the furniture and in the piano, etc. I agreed to do it. The director, who had done some very good work with the National Theatre and the RSC, was engaged and rehearsals started, still with only the first act. The young leading lady would be appearing mostly in her underwear, and the owner of the house, another leading part, would be wearing her dressing gown most of the time. The two other significant parts were taken by comedy actors from a well known TV series. We eventually got the second act, which was no improvement on the first, but I was getting into my stride as the drunken character. The management was not known to Equity so a guarantor had to be found. He was someone I knew who had made his mark presenting pantomimes and summer shows.

We opened at the King's Theatre, Southsea, and the first thing that went wrong was a sequence that required a piano to explode on stage, for what reason I cannot remember. The piano exploded at the wrong moment, frightening the life out of me. It gave me an excuse to fly to the bottle. After that the exploding piano never did explode again, thank goodness. During that first week at Southsea I got a telephone call from the Entertainment's Manager at Plymouth asking whether I would like to go down there for the summer in a play called *A*

*Bedfull of Foreigners,* in which Terry Scott had appeared in London. I rang my agent and told him, he said, 'What if the play runs during the summer?' I told him I didn't have any confidence in that happening. He immediately got on to Plymouth and, with his expertise in getting a package together, he had cast the rest of the play for Plymouth, including the director, actor and writer Jimmy Thompson.

After Southsea we moved to Coventry and that's where the fun really started. By the middle of the week it was apparent that we were not going to do much business and the management said we had to spice it up a bit and told our leading lady that from then on she would be doing the play in the nude. She refused and was sacked. She took them to court as there was nothing in her contract about appearing nude and the case was settled out of court in her favour. The night she left the play I thought, as others did, that we would now have a break, perhaps permanently, from the piece. The director resigned and was never seen again, lucky fellow, and one of the comedy actors took over the reins.

When would we re-start? After all we had to re-rehearse the girl's part with someone else. Not a bit of it! The Antipodean wardrobe mistress was asked to take over the following night holding the script. I began to have my doubts that I was in a play at all. Anyway, the girl went on and apart from having to use her own underwear, which was not really suitable for the stage, she was given no help from two of the actors who took the mickey out of her with lines which had nothing to do with the play, spoken direct to the audience: 'She should have come on five minutes ago'; 'Now you go off through that door dear'; 'She'll improve with age.' The girl was in tears at the end of the performance and refused to go on again.

Were we now to get a break? Not a bit of it! The next day I walked about Coventry with pains literally all over my body – I suppose it was the stress. I got to the theatre in the evening and wondered what would happen next, I daren't ask. I certainly was not prepared for the next saga of events. The stage was suddenly occupied by two nude girls throwing a large beach ball to one another. Neither of them spoke a word. I once again flew to one of my whisky hiding places, thinking I was in a funny farm, or a nightmare. When I came off stage I asked what was going on and was told it was the management's idea to spice the play up a bit. Spice it up! A train load of curry couldn't have spiced it up! We already had a lad who came on at intervals playing the accordion, again for what reason I could not comprehend.

We continued for the rest of the week with the girls throwing the beach ball about and the lad playing violently on the accordion. The girls were apparently models from Manchester and, apart from their strange introduction into the proceedings, were extremely nice. One night the beach ball took on a life of its own and bounced into the footlights, one of the girls dashed to the front of the stage in case it went into the audience. She bent down indiscreetly to pick it up, exposing her lack of stagecraft and a few other things. She obviously hadn't heard of the old stage maxim, never turn your back on the audience. This brought whistles from the sparse two front rows of the macintosh brigade which now made up our audiences, the word having got round that there was a 'naughty' play on at the theatre!

Our next date was at the Theatre Royal, Norwich, by which time I had told my agent to get me out of it. He was told I would be sued if I left. When we arrived in Norwich we were told that the transport company carrying the scenery would not unload unless it was paid for the cartage not only from Coventry to Norwich but also from Southsea to Coventry, still outstanding. Dick Condon, the manager at Norwich, decided to pay the bill as we had advance bookings and he wanted to keep faith with his audiences.

The one redeeming factor at Norwich was that the accordionist in the play had decided to live on a boat on the Norfolk Broads for the week. It was quite a big boat and the weather was fine so I, along with other members of the cast, spent nearly every day on the water. We all sunbathed and stopped at various pubs for our lunch, so at least we could forget about the nightly performances for a while.

The next week was at the Queen's Hall, Burslem in the Potteries. Come the Tuesday and the young company manager came to me in tears saying that no more cheques could be cashed on the company's account. The young fellow said the stage management hadn't been paid at Norwich, and now they would get nothing at Burslem. I told him to phone the management, which he did. He was told the advance booking at our next date, Hull, would easily take care of everything. I decided to phone Hull and ask how much there was in advance bookings. Absolutely nothing! I immediately phoned Equity who arranged for a representative to come up.

It was decided there and then to bring the play off after that night's performance. I arrived at the theatre next morning to collect my things and saw scenery being thrown out into the road. Some cast members called me a Judas for putting people out of work. I told them that I wasn't prepared to work for nothing, even if they were. It was then obvious that we would not be paid for that week, at least until something was sorted out. I left for home, whistling to myself with the sheer relief of coming out of a bad experience. I had been lucky that this was only the second time this financially, and almost more importantly, physically bruising sort of thing had happened to me.

Just as the 1970s seemed to have been dominated by *Dad's Army* and a lot of good things, so the 1980s were to prove to be slightly different. During early 1980 I had been getting an idea together for another book, this time about the theatre's connection with royalty, a history of the Royal Command Performances which went back as far as Queen Elizabeth I's time and not – as I had always imagined – to 1912 and the reign of George V. I had done some research and would do some more work on it while I was at Plymouth. Meantime son Jonathan had been invited to go to America with a young theatre group from Twickenham to tour a play. Marion was also invited as one of the minders for the group. They had a great time there, and it was a first for both of them.

I went off to Plymouth to do *Bedfull of Foreigners* and what fun we had down there. The cast included Norman Vaughan whom I knew, Jack Smethurst, Peter Bland, Kirsten Cook, who would soon break into television with *Allo, Allo* ('I will say this only once') and singer Ruth Madoc, with whom I had worked many years earlier in pantomime. Ruth, too, was on the threshold of becoming a household name in *Hi-De-Hi* ('Hello campers').

Plymouth is a delightful place to be for a season and I had rented a cottage a few miles out at Yealmpton. Frankie Howerd had recommended it, having stayed there when he was in pantomime. The cottage was near a lovely pub and a disused railway line which provided sylvan walks. We used to have parties at the cottage at weekends and super trips to the surrounding area. I also got to know Marion's cousin Kenneth Macleod again; he was a very popular presenter for TV South West. Marion and Jonathan came down for a few days when they got back from America, but Marion was not keen on the place because the cottage was a converted barn and still had rather a lot of spiders, which she just cannot stand.

We did wonderful business at the revamped Hoe Theatre, apparently 98 percent capacity for the whole season. The Council was so pleased it presented us all with some lovely glassware. But the new Theatre Royal was nearing completion in the city, and the chap who was to take over when it opened was introduced to us and the assembled company on our last night. He told us, 'When we open the new theatre we shall not be putting on the rather nondescript sort of entertainment you've had here for the season.' What an almighty clanger to drop after the business we had done! The subsequent artistic director at the Theatre Royal, Roger Redfarn, who many of us knew, was instrumental in putting the new theatre well and truly on the map.

Family life all round was gathering pace in the early 1980s. Fedge and Lizzie's children James and Ingrid were spreading their wings: James had changed his teaching job for one of accountancy at Reading and then he and his wife Eileen moved to Nonington, half way between Canterbury and Dover. James got a job with a music business in Canterbury, and this at least seemed to fulfil his working life. He and two friends eventually bought the company from the original owners just a few years ago and I'm glad to say the business goes from strength to strength. James and Eileen also had their first child, Edward, in 1983. He has turned out to be academic and very fond of music. Their second boy Richard was born in 1986. He's a bit of a lad, and he and his brother are happily continuing their education at King's School, Canterbury. Eileen has now resumed her teaching career.

Fedge and Liz gave a lot of time in support of Oxfam in the city and Fedge was also involved in other charities, as well as becoming a tour guide at Canterbury Cathedral. Their daughter Ingrid, after college, went to Sweden for four years to teach English and then went up to Aberdeen to train as a probation officer. It was in the granite city that she met and married Bob Pringle (when I heard, I thought that we'd be all right for sweaters, but Bob is no relation to that family; actually, he is an agricultural engineer). They now have two lovely sons, Andrew and Martin.

During the rest of that year I spent time researching for the Royal Command book which was to be published in 1981. I had very pleasant dealings with the royal libraries at Windsor and Balmoral, the Victoria & Albert Museum in London, and many individuals from all sections of the theatre.

Christmas 1980 and I was back again with pals Ian Lavender and Norman Vaughan in *Mother Goose* at Bromley. The book seemed to be progressing well, and I was beginning to enjoy putting pen to paper. Other work was drying up for me apart from some concert and cabaret engagements, for which I had teamed up with Marion's brother Norman to do a double act. It was quite successful and certainly enjoyable to do. We played the Butlin Camps, one or two-night spots, and also a Scottish theatre managed by my old friend Stewart Pearce. I don't think that the Scottish audiences were quite ready for our comedy, but the impressions and songs went down quite well. Anyway we had a lovely week, full of laughs and visiting some of the wonderful Scottish countryside, particularly around Crieff.

Back in London I began to realise that some of the glamour (if that's the right word) surrounding *Dad's Army* was beginning to evaporate as I was offered one or two plays for less money than I had been getting, and suggestions that my billing would be demoted to the wines and spirits (as we call it) on posters etc. Not wanting to finish up below the printer's name, I decided to retire from the theatre and concentrate on writing. It was risky, a turnabout in my career, but I was prepared to give it a go. My agent Richard thought I was barmy, but realised I was serious. Money was becoming a real problem but Marion was behind me in the decision.

The book *By Royal Command* was eventually published and the first television promotion was at BBC TV's Pebble Mill in Birmingham. It could not have been a better showcase for, as it happened, the Queen was visiting the studios on that day. Some of us met her after the show finished, and she naturally mentioned the book. I am sorry to say that although I went all over the place doing newspaper and radio interviews for the book, it didn't sell as well as we had all hoped. It wasn't helped by shops not having it in stock in towns where I was promoting it – even in Birmingham on the day it was launched. I was very proud of the book and it was very well presented. One thing I did realise was that my lack of any real education had in some way been remedied not only with the royal book but also with my Pierrot publication a couple of years earlier. Furthermore I had learned a lot of history from the research for both of them.

The publishers did three leather-bound copies for me, one of which was sent to the Queen, another to the Queen Mother and a third we auctioned for a charity I've always been interested in – SPARKS (Sportsmen Aid into Research of Crippling Diseases). As we wouldn't be able to get the auction copy signed by the royal family I asked the six living Prime Ministers to sign it: Margaret Thatcher, Edward Heath, Sir Alec Douglas Home, Harold Macmillan, Harold Wilson and James Callaghan. All very willingly obliged and the book raised £2,000 at the auction.

In the summer I had a call from Richard Stone saying that the stage version of *Worzel Gummidge* was going to be presented in

London after its try-out at Birmingham the previous year, and Cousin Jon thought it would be a good idea for me to play Sergeant Beetroot, the Crowman's assistant. The character had been played in Birmingham by my old friend Bill Maynard. I said the thought of playing with Jon appealed to me; and, as Richard said, 'You can go back into retirement afterwards' – his crafty way of saying he didn't believe in this retirement business. I had to audition for the part, which included doing a song, as they were writing a new number for the production that involved me. I wasn't too keen on testing my lack of musical prowess in London; still, in for a penny, in for a pound! The new song was called, *We'll Be There* and turned out to be a winner.

The season at the Cambridge Theatre was very enjoyable, apart from the fact that I had to be covered in deep red make-up twice daily to take on the beetroot hue. I made some new friends – Una Stubbs playing her original part of Aunt Sally, Norman Mitchell and Geoffrey Bayldon who played the Crowman. What a nice chap Geoffrey is. We used to have long chats at the beginning of the second act awaiting our entrance at the back of the barn. As for Cousin Jon, I think *Worzel* was his finest hour. The project on television had been partly his idea, and its transfer to the stage lost none of its great appeal to the public. I had, of course, seen Jon in *Dr Who* and thought he was one of the best doctors. He was also very good in an early play in which Marion and I saw him called *Touch it Light*, a military piece, and also *A Funny Thing Happened on the Way to the Forum*, both during their runs in London.

Jon had always been a successful broadcaster since the late 1940s, and in variety on the halls, but I have always thought that Worzel was just about the best thing he ever did. It ran the whole gamut of emotions: pathos, naughtiness and great humour, which both children and adults enjoyed. Norman Mitchell told me a lovely story. During the Birmingham season, when Jon was in the middle of one of his songs – *It's Me Birthday* – a little boy in the front row jumped up and said, 'I'm just going to the toilet Worzel'. Without interrupting the song Jon said, 'Save a seat for me.' He would always try an ad lib if he was in a happy mood, and I think he was always happy as Worzel. After Christmas the box office started to take a dip because the weather became so bad. Snow was playing havoc with the whole country. We, the actors, being out of town, had our fair share of problems going backwards and forwards to London. *Worzel* came off in February but was to be repeated the following year.

Early in 1982 I did a try-out of a new play called *Sting in the Tail* written by Brian Clemens and Dennis Spooner, who had created *The Avengers* for television. I was offered a nice part as a policeman, and the two main characters were played by Pete Murray and Jack Douglas. It was to be produced at Guildford, which was not too far from my home. A London impresario had taken an option on the play for transfer but it didn't really have enough 'sting in its tail' for his liking, so there was no London season, which I don't think I would have done anyway as I was determined to try and stick with the writing idea.

I pottered about during the rest of that summer doing an odd concert or two, but nothing else was happening. Had it not been for a friendly bank manager that period could have been disastrous. But in late summer came one of those extraordinary turns of fate that make this business of ours so amazing.

I attended a charity race meeting at Sandown Park and decided to have a very small bet at the tote window. Who should be standing standing next to me but my agent Richard. He said, 'I'm glad I've seen you. Ray Cooney is going to try out a new play of his at Guildford for a couple of weeks in the autumn. As you live nearby it would be nice for you to renew your friendship with him. It won't interfere with your retirement, but I'm sure Ray would like to see you some time.' I said, 'OK,' and rather forgot about the conversation. A few days later Ray rang and asked if he could he send me a script of his new play *Run For Your Wife* as he'd like me to read the part of the policeman, Sergeant Troughton. I told him I'd retired from acting, but agreed he should send it on for me to look at. I read it and rang him to say that I thought it was funny but I didn't fancy the part, which seemed to me to be a straightforward investigative policeman. I told him I quite liked the other policeman Sergeant Porterhouse, who was a bit of a PC Plod type – very friendly and happy to accept the twists and turns of the play. Ray had already offered that part to another actor, and that was the end of the conversation.

A couple of days later Ray rang me, said the other actor would not be available and offered me the role of Porterhouse – which I accepted. We eventually gathered together in London for rehearsals which immediately ran into problems. The lead, playing a taxi driver, didn't seem to be able to get hold of it, although he had been involved in a successful television series. The rest of us got on with putting the piece together, and we all thought it was very funny. Friendships were cemented which are still active today: Carol Hawkins, Helen Gill, Royce Mills, Jimmy Thompson from the Plymouth season and our assistant stage manager Boris (Miss Wilkinson). For Ray Cooney this was a mad period in the theatre, but I somehow think Ray thrives on excitement and a little bit of danger. His enthusiasm and drive is equal to none. Having been an actor he also thinks from an actor's point of view, which is good. He never stops thinking, and getting the performers involved. I have never met anyone quite like him.

Four days from our opening at Guildford the leading actor in the play decided he could not come to terms with the role and left. It was too late to get another actor lined up to learn the part, so Ray decided to take it over himself. The opening night at Guildford was on us but Ray, who had a terrible cold and had practically lost his voice, was as enthusiastic as ever. It really was an opening night that I and the rest of the cast will never forget. Ray was directing the play while off and on stage, whispering in one's ear to 'get nearer the door' or 'move behind the sofa a bit more', and all the time keeping his part going. Jimmy Thompson had put the whole play down on tape and rushed about with earphones glued to his head listening for cues. By the time he'd got to his entrance his cue would probably have been changed, so at times there was a lot of breathless acting going on. Poor Helen Gill had very bad tummy trouble and each time she came off she had to lie flat on the floor. Carol Hawkins was certain her voice would go at any moment so she was throwing everything down, port, lozenges, ice cream. I was really having a ball, the part of Sergeant Porterhouse was doing fine. I remember at one point Helen Gill had to burst into the room carrying a suitcase, trip over it and fall on the floor. The rest of the cast on stage were supposed to bend down and try to pick her up, ad-libbing such things as 'Have your hurt yourself?', 'You poor thing', 'What's the matter?' On that opening night the cast got down on the floor but didn't say anything and Ray in a loud voice said, 'Make a noise'. At this point of drama I, Sgt Porterhouse, having made tea for the families and friends, should have come through the door saying, 'Anyone not take sugar?' The sight of Ray shouting this line right out of the blue just paralysed me with laughter and I went straight off again without saying my line. But there was no doubt about it, the audience was obviously enjoying the play. Marion, who was watching, said afterwards that the atmosphere was absolutely wonderful.

Before the end of the play I think we all realised it was a success. During the two-week run Ray rewrote bits of it every day, giving us the new lines when we arrived in the late afternoon. At one point we had a nun who appeared to deliver the final line of the play and another day two nuns appeared. Word had got around, and during this period people were coming down from London − managements, actors and actresses − to see it. After we had finished at Guildford Ray took the play to Australia with Bernard Cribbins playing one of the leads. This was really done to cement in the rewrites.

I was due to do a second Christmas season with *Worzel Gummidge* with a couple of weeks at Wimbledon followed by a short season at Southampton. Wimbledon went very well, but when we moved on to Southampton the situation was slightly different. The TV station based at Southampton, Southern Television, had made the TV series of *Worzel* so it was expected that it would obviously have a great following down there. When we arrived in the city the publicity for the show was practically non-existent. There were no pictures outside the theatre, and only a large handwritten hoarding in the theatre foyer announcing that *Worzel* was coming soon. Jon Pertwee was stunned but, to give him his due, he didn't lose his temper and we all went out spreading the word around the town. The show never really recovered from this, and on several nights we played to small audiences when the theatre had seating for three and a half thousand.

I stayed the first night at a small hotel but couldn't stand the early morning racket of commercial travellers running baths, pulling loo chains and Hoovers being rushed up and down corridors, so I checked out and enquired at the theatre about other places. Some of the girls and boys in the show learned of my predicament and said they would speak to the lady running the guest house where they were staying. After some rearrangement of rooms I was able to move in there. The lady of the house was an ex-nurse, and she already had about seven or eight of our company staying with her. She was very sociable and threw a few parties for us and some of the rest of the cast.

During that time England were playing Australia in a test match series in Australia. I listened to the commentaries from Down Under on my transistor radio under the bed clothes as I didn't want to wake up the other guests. Two of the young ladies in the show heard about this and, as they were also cricket fans, they started coming into my room to listen, bringing cups of cocoa and biscuits with them. One night our landlady knocked on the door about two in the morning asking whether I had a radio on. We asked her in, and the sight of me in pyjamas and two girls in night clothes brought her to a stop. 'What's going on?' she enquired. We told her we were listening to the cricket from Australia and she said, 'Well I've heard it all now.' She too was a bit of a cricket fan, and after that she also joined us, accompanied by a bottle of whiskey.

After *Worzel* finished Ray Cooney rang to say things had gone well in Australia and that *Run For Your Wife* would be opening at the Shaftesbury Theatre in the spring. Ray had taken a long lease on the theatre with another large group of actors and actresses. It was being refurbished as it had been closed for some time, and it would be titled 'The Theatre of Comedy'. It sounded marvellous; Ray was once more embarking on an adventure. He asked me to play my original part in the production which would have Richard Briers and Bernard Cribbins in the two lead parts, plus some of the other folk from Guildford, Carol, Helen, Peter Blake, Royce Mills and a fellow called Sam Cox playing the small part of the newspaper reporter, originally played by Arthur Bostram. When we heard that Arthur would not be coming with us I suggested he write to David Croft who was interviewing people for a new TV series he was writing with Jeremy Lloyd called *Allo Allo*. David saw Arthur and cast him in the part of the policeman who never quite grasped the language. I am sure we all know of the success of that character and all the others in that show.

I felt I couldn't miss out on being part of the London opening of *Run For Your Wife*. On that first night at the Shaftesbury it had been raining like mad before we started, and water was dripping through the roof of the theatre at various points, including the stage. The whole cast and stage management spent most of the day rushing about with buckets, Richard Briers saying, 'Where shall I go next?'

'Follow the drips,' replied Bernard Cribbins.

The opening performance repeated the success at Guildford, and it appeared we were set for a long run. Cooney and Cribbins had obviously worked hard in Australia, and some little gems had been introduced into the play. We spent six months with that cast at the Shaftesbury. Because of the advertising, our names on buses and photos outside the theatre, and with good reports in the national press, our names were being bandied about the business. I was asked to do a rather good commercial and a radio series in Manchester: all this meant that the writing career had to be postponed, maybe even forgotten altogether.

Two of the cast were changed in autumn 1983. Terry Scott came in for Richard Briers and Eric Sykes for Bernard Cribbins. After Christmas we moved to the Criterion Theatre in Piccadilly as Ray was going to direct a well known wartime comedy thriller *See How They Run* at the Shaftesbury. I didn't go with *Run For Your Wife* to its new home as I had already done ten months in the play, and Ray had asked me to play Army Sergeant Towers in *See How They Run*. I was going to have a rest for a few weeks before starting on that.

Then my agent and Ray had an idea that I could do both plays at once, going back into *Run For Your Wife* as well. As I was only in the last act of *See How They Run,* they said they could start a little later at the Shaftesbury; I could change into my uniform at the Criterion after the curtain came down and then hop on to a motor scooter which they would hire and scoot up for the third act at the Shaftesbury. They were convinced it was possible. I must have been mad even to think about it, but quite quickly said no. Richard and Ray asked me where my spirit of adventure had gone. The cast of both theatres had a good laugh about it and the jokes went round about an army sergeant tearing up Shaftesbury Avenue every night shouting, 'Get out of my way, I'm on in two minutes' and being done for jumping the lights and arrested for impersonating an army officer.

*See How They Run* brought me into contact with some players with whom I had not worked before. Lisa Goddard, a lovely, jolly person, when she wasn't learning her lines amused us with tales of her family and menagerie of animals – one of which, her dog Gertie – was in the play and proved to be a very competent actress, even paying attention to director Ray Cooney's session notes. Maureen Lipman invented some wonderful comic business as the inebriated Miss Skillern. Then there was Michael Denison, Christopher Timothy, Derek Nimmo all of whom I enjoyed meeting and working with. We had one memorable day with the Denisons – Michael and wife Dulcie Gray – at their home along with a veritable who's who of the entertainment industry.

After the first production of *See How They Run* had finished the original cast of *Run For Your Wife* was asked if they would like to go to Australia for three months. I had to decline as Marion wasn't in the best of spirits following the recent death of her mother, dear old Maudie. Her Mum had certainly had an active life, and in her later years she had been a bingo addict, always winning something or other. Up to the last she never lost her enthusiasm for show business. I really didn't think I could be away for such a long time playing several cities Down Under.

Later in the year we did a second production of *See How They Run* with several changes of cast, and a filmed version of the play with the original team for Southern TV Films.

Christmas of 1984 was one of those periods where you say to yourself, 'well this job is going to be a mixture of fun and drama' and you have no idea at all of its outcome. I was contracted to do a pantomime season at the Chichester Festival Theatre. This venue (in the round) was in itself going to be completely new to me. Not knowing who some of my fellow artistes were to be was an even greater surprise. The subject was *Babes in the Wood* and I was to play the bad robber. Spike Milligan, in his first pantomime, was to play the good robber. Perhaps the biggest surprise, and I'm sure to everyone's delight, was that legendary actress Evelyn Laye was to play the Fairy. She had worked with practically everyone in the business one way or another, even with Flanagan and Allen, the Crazy Gang of Nervo and Knox, and Naughton and Gold. She had conquered the Americans on Broadway with Noel Coward, and here we were going to work with someone you really could call a star.

The pantomime was directed by Dennis (Slim) Ramsden. Slim had much experience of film, stage comedy and farce. He endears himself to the actors straight away by asking if you have any ideas of your own. If you have, he marries them up with his thoughts, and never asks you to do anything you are uncomfortable about. A quick discussion with Slim seems to solve all problems. He has a lovely sense of humour, is not at all dictatorial and you just feel you want to do your best for him.

In the initial rehearsals he noticed that Spike was holding my hand rather a lot on entrances and in certain scenes. As Spike knew I had done a pantomime or two, he was obviously going to go wherever I went. Slim caught on to this. 'That looks funny' he said, 'why not do it on stage? If you think of a funny line or bit of business Spike, just do it and we'll go along with it and see how it works out.' Spike began to relax and put bits and pieces in when the opportunity arose. Slim took me on one side and said, 'You'll soon get to know when he wants to ad lib, let him go ahead but keep him on an invisible rope. If the gag doesn't come off, pull him in and get on with the plot, but if the gag is leading somewhere let him go until he has delivered it and then get him back on track.'

All this worked out pretty well and Spike came out with some wonderful ad libs. I used to take notes of them because he couldn't always remember what he had done. Eventually the ad libs became part of the script. I had worked with him before in television so I knew the look in his eye when he suddenly thought of something. After the opening night at Chichester we were booked for the following year to repeat our partnership at Richmond. As far as Evelyn Laye was concerned, she looked wonderful as the fairy and was a joy to work with. She even coped with Spike's ad libs like the seasoned pro she was. The dame was played by an old mate, the versatile Bernie Gosney. He always turns in a good performance in whatever he does.

We had some delightful social evenings at Chichester. Spike and his dear wife Sheila used to like to have a convivial meal after the show where the banter would start all over again. Spike's response to children was quite amazing. Of course he used to do some ridiculous things, like suddenly going to sit in the audience amongst a group of kids saying, 'It's better from down here,' and giving them sweets. I made sure he always had an abundance of them in his pocket. This would cause a bit of an uproar in the audience but, as we all said, if you buy Spike Milligan give him his freedom and you'll get your money's worth. Unfortunately, the following year's repeat performance didn't quite work out as well. However Richmond meant I would be spending the festive season at home – well at least Christmas Day anyway. From that time on I was involved in various short seasons at the Criterion Theatre in *Run For Your Wife* with a variety of new casts, and some of the original ones like myself. The play was still pulling in the audiences and had become a West End legend as far as comedy was concerned.

For Christmas 1987 I was back in pantomime with Roy Hudd at Bromley in Kent, the first we had done together since our debut at Leeds in 1959, and again Christmas 1988 at Guildford in Surrey. We had Lyn Paul of the New Seekers playing principal boy in the Bromley production of *Dick Whittington* and on one occasion we really had to stifle our giggles. The gentleman who was playing the cat used to like the occasional drink, and sometimes got into the wrong position on stage. One evening he had got right behind Lyn and as she stepped backwards she fell over him. She got up, brushed herself down and said to the audience, 'Has Dick Whittington ever shot his cat?' There were few straight faces on stage after that remark. Lyn is great fun to be with and has a lovely sense of humour as well as a lot of charisma on stage.

The following year, at Guildford, we had a reunion with Jack Tripp and Allen Christie, Jack playing dame, and Roy and I the robbers in *Babes in the Wood*. This really was a super version, the book written by Roy. After the Guildford season I was engaged to play in a tour of Alan Bennett's *Habeas Corpus*. This was a slightly strange piece for me, but we had a good time running round the country, after producing it at Nottingham Playhouse. In the cast was Julian Glover, known for his film and theatre performances with the Royal Shakespeare, Jane Freeman from TV's *Last of the Summer Wine* and Duncan Preston, with whom I became great mates, going to a race meeting or two and trying to play golf together. Adam Robertson was also in the play; a very fine young actor – he died tragically in a motorcycle accident just after we finished the tour.

Alan Bennett came to see our first night in Nottingham and was very complimentary. He came into my dressing room and said, 'You are much taller off stage.' I was playing a Dr Shorter who had nearly always been played by a slighter actor. Actually all I did was to play the part with sagging shoulders, which obviously gave the impression of a smaller man. Alan is a really charming fellow to meet.

After *Habeas Corpus* I left for Canada to do *Run for your Wife* on Vancouver Island. I knew most of the cast. Jeffrey Holland,

Judy Graham, Brian Godfrey and Ron Aldridge I had worked with before, but not Jan Hunt and Brian Murphy, although I'd met them both. Murphy was a real rascal, and knew exactly what would make me giggle on stage. He also makes me laugh a lot off stage as well. Ron Aldridge and I are two dangerous people to put together in a production. As soon as we meet in a scene we have to try very hard to control the twinkle in our eyes, and the slightest thing can set us off. Neither of us knows the reason for this. Ron incidentally has become a very good playwright and two of his plays have already been produced. He is also a very competent director.

The Canadian trip was a great experience. The scenery was magnificent from our first glimpse of it as we landed at Calgary. The short journey from Vancouver to Vancouver Island above all the lakes and forests on our way to Victoria, where we were to appear, was breathtaking. The local hospitality was wonderful, and the city itself must be about the cleanest in the world. You could eat off the pavements.

The play itself was a big success and the theatre very comfortable to work in. During the day, for a bit of fun, I used to arrange 'Pertwee Tours' all over the island. Some of these trips landed us in a few strange places, and I would get a lot of stick from the cast whom I instructed to meet in the hotel lobby every morning at 11am. Brian Murphy was always a few minutes late because his second boiled egg hadn't gone quite right. There were grumblings of 'Where's he taking us today this early?' However once I'd got everyone organised and fallen-in in an orderly fashion and marched them up to the nearest coach station, they began to enjoy themselves, or at least I told them they were enjoying themselves!

One day instead of the coach we were supposed to catch we got on a bus by mistake. It went on a circular tour, going round and round the same areas for several hours. As we were the only passengers, I think the driver enjoyed our company. When we arrived back in the city he said, 'I've enjoyed having you with me, perhaps I'll see you tomorrow.' In chorus, my charges said, 'Not if we see you first!'

In one big store in Victoria a couple came up to me and said, 'We've seen you shopping in Guildford, we used to live quite near there. Apparently after taking a holiday on the island they decided to stay on. They didn't even return to Surrey, just sent for their furniture and that was that. I must say they had certainly chosen a lovely place to enjoy their retirement.

After the season there I flew back alone as Bernard Bresslaw, who couldn't do the first leg of the tour, came out to take over from Vancouver City. A lovely person Bernie, warm, generous and a fine classical actor, which perhaps not a lot of people realised as he was best known for his silly parts in *The Army Game* and the 'Carry On' films in which he was always very good. It was a sad loss to the business when he died.

Towards the end of that year a pilot programme was being made of a new writing collaboration by Jimmy Perry and David Croft called *You Rang M'Lord*. It was a rather chaotic recording on the night as some of the sets were not quite completed, and with such a big production and large cast, all in period costume, everything was rather hectic. A few cues were missed, including my first entrance which I was to take from someone on another set, but what with the noise and hustle and bustle it wasn't easy for anyone. It was also a 50-minute show instead of the usual half hour Perry and Croft production. However we got through it and afterwards we all had a very nice letter from David thanking us for coping with the difficult conditions in the studio. It was decided to make a first series of six, and it eventually ran for 26 episodes, from 1988 to 1992.

During the early planning stages of *You Rang M'Lord* I had said to Jimmy and David that I thought a book about the making of *Dad's Army* should be written because repeats of the show were well received by a whole new generation of viewers and interest seemed to be gathering apace. I was sure the whole background of the actors and film location venues etc. would be of interest. David and Jimmy said they just hadn't got the time, but suggested I do it.

I set about the task with enthusiasm. David and Jimmy were very helpful when I needed their input and although I was back

again for another session at the Criterion in *Run For Your Wife,*
I worked hard on the book in whatever time I had, including
periods in my dressing room when I wasn't actually involved in
scenes on stage. Eventually it was finished, my horrid scrawl and
bad punctuation being brilliantly deciphered by my new typing
partner Geraldine. This autobiography will be the fourth book
we have worked on together. I would find it very hard now to
write anything without her help, but don't ever tell her that if
you should meet her; she'll want more money!

My literary agent, Tony Mulliken, thought the obvious pub-
lisher to do the *Dad's Army* book would be BBC Enterprises.
They had it for six weeks but eventually said no. Another pub-
lisher, David & Charles, was waiting in the wings and contracts
were quickly signed in the Great Western Hotel at Paddington
station over breakfast. We had a marvellous launch of the book
at the Imperial War Museum in 1989. Many friends were there,
including most of the cast of *You Rang M'Lord* and from other
shows I had been involved in, including *Dad's Army.* We were
particularly happy to have with us the wives of some of the cast
who had sadly passed on. We still keep in touch with them, and
they always have cheery words to say. Joan Le Mesurier does
wonderful work looking after stray horses, most of which she
has named after the characters from the show. One of them,
who always causes a bit of trouble, is called Hodges. He would
be, wouldn't he! Gladys Sinclair is still her bubbly self, in spite
of going through some health problems in recent years. Althea
Ridley's infectious enthusiasm has not diminished even though
she suffered a bad accident a few years ago. Kay Beck is a
remarkable lady, and is always a joy to meet again.

The book quite quickly went to number four in *The Times*
bestseller list, and everyone seemed happy except for someone
quite high up at the BBC, who said, 'Why didn't we get a
chance to publish the book.' I said, 'You did, you had it for six
weeks and turned it down.'

# 9 WHERE WILL IT ALL END?

Not yet, there's more for you to endure before I've finished.

Actually the chapter heading was a line repeated many times by Perry Benson (the boot boy) in the TV series *You Rang M'Lord* and he always timed it beautifully and got a resulting laugh. The series marched on into the 1990s and was a delightful experience for all of us involved with it. There were laughs galore in the rehearsal rooms in London, and some great filming sessions in dear old Norfolk. We were based at the George Hotel in Swaffham on those occasions, with different locations all over north Norfolk. The characters had all been well thought out, and we once again had wonderful words from the pens of Croft and Perry. We all enjoyed the casual evenings spent in the bar of the hotel discussing the day's work, and what we would be doing the next day, over leisurely meals.

We worked long hours and got involved in various scenes that included driving vintage vehicles of the 1920s, the era in which the series was set. I actually spent two days driving an old coach round the countryside, with much grinding of gears. Paul Shane always seemed to be driving a motorbike complete with suit and overcoat, at one stage during one of the hottest summer periods. I can remember Paul had to keep having his wing collar changed as it was soaking wet with sweat.

We spent quite a lot of time at a stately home near Holt where the family joined in collaborating with the film schedules. It was a beautiful setting with lovely grounds by a river which was just the place to relax in during our coffee and tea breaks. We also had another house and gardens not far from Swaffham which we used quite a lot. The owner had a fascinating collection of vintage radio sets and radiograms. We had a marvellous crew, a lot of whom we had worked with before. The make-up girls worked ceaselessly to keep our faces from looking shiny from the heat and Mary Husband, who has been friend, sweetheart and mother to all in most of Perry and Croft shows, and her team of dressers rushed about making sure all the costumes were in order. Cameramen, lighting and sound crews played their part in making the series look wonderful when it got on to the screen.

One quite amusing incident happened during the making of the last series. Su Pollard and I overslept one morning and missed the coach out to the location. Neither of us were in the very first shot of the day so we got left behind. A car was sent to pick us up about an hour later. By that time Su and I had missed the location breakfast and were starving. As we arrived near the spot we would be working, Su spotted a gentleman trimming his hedge round his bungalow, and asked him, 'Have you got any bread and butter handy, as we've missed our breakfast.' The gentleman looked a bit nonplussed but said he would see what he could do. We went into his garden and the gent brought us out a couple of chairs and some warm bread that he said his wife had baked, plus some marmalade, and we sat in the early morning sun eating the delicious repast. The gent told us he was a retired car salesman from south-east London and just loved living in Norfolk. He had good taste, as it is a delightful and peaceful county to live in.

Su told him why we were hungry and how we had missed breakfast because the bastard coach driver was a ***** together with other expletives about the situation. The gentleman took all this in with a smile, and I can just imagine him telling his friends that he'd had two lunatics for breakfast, one dressed as a maid, the other as a policeman in 1920s attire, carrying on about oversleeping and a coach driver. Actually of course Su was just exaggerating about the coach driver to make it all a bit more dramatic. In fact the coach drivers we had at Swaffham were super and became our friends, as did a lot of other folk in that charming market town, especially those with whom we drank in the hotel bar.

I have to say that people who write to me or meet me nowadays ask why the programme has never been repeated. I cannot answer this question, but can only imagine that someone on high within the corporation just doesn't like it. It has been repeated, so I'm told, on Sky so maybe mainstream TV will put it out again one of these days. I honestly think that *You Rang M'Lord* was the best thing Jimmy Perry and David Croft had conceived. It had class. It showed the great divide in community living in the 1920s very accurately, although the character of Lord Meldrum, played beautifully by Donald Hewlett, encouraged loyalty in his staff by the occasional gestures of goodwill towards them. Paul Shane's performance told you exactly what type of person he was, always having to fight his corner in his previous occupation as a not very good music hall entertainer.

All the kitchen staff were beautifully drawn in great depth, and certainly Su Pollard's performance was lovely as the poor housemaid, with the little touch of pathos when she told her dolly about the day's happenings every night before she went to sleep. Jeff Holland played a completely different character to that in *Hi-De-Hi*. The cook and scullery maid, Brenda Cowling and Barbara New, were very believable, and the ladies of the house, Catherine Rabbet, Susie Brand and Mavis Pugh, and silly arse Michael Knowles, made up the team. Guest appearances by some fine actors and actresses like John Horsley, Yvonne Marsh and Angela Scoular added to its success.

One of the other fairly regular characters was Felix Bowness, who has been a friend of us all for many, many years. He's been a variety act, summer show and radio performer, and his face has cropped up in various TV shows. A featured role came his way for the whole series of *Hi-De-Hi* playing the disgraced jockey. He has appeared in Croft and Perry productions one way or another for over 20 years, and that brings me to one little problem he has. He gets a little excited before delivering his first line in a scene and the word 'action' from the director can often paralyse him. David Croft got over this by saying 'in your own time Felix', and it's worked like a charm ever since. In *You Rang M'Lord* he played the local grocer who served the family. Incidentally Felix has done something like 5,000 warm-ups for nearly every audience show you can think of.

Because of the profile some actors and actresses are lucky enough to attain through their appearances on the 'box' they are invited to some really nice social functions, sometimes to be part of a fund raising effort for a charity. In my case, if the function should include the company of cricketers I am really delighted; there were several events around that time I was privileged to attend. One of them a 'Saints and Sinners' luncheon included a host of cricketing greats. I was able to renew my acquaintance with Bill Edrich. What a fun, enthusiastic and marvellous sportsman he'd been in his time! I also met the legendary Kent and England wicketkeeper/batsman Les Ames.

Another event was when Fred Trueman invited me to a wonderful evening paying tribute to his old friend and Test Match bowling partner Brian Statham. There was I sitting at the top table with some of the legends of the cricketing world. What a thrill. I was asked to speak at a couple of dinners in Sheffield by the Cricket Lovers' Society. The first was to honour commentator, poet and writer John Arlott. It turned out to be a magical evening. John was to speak about his cricket memories and I had to follow and propose the toast to 'cricket'. Being a great admirer of the man, it was wonderful to be in his company that night. After hearing him speak I debated how to follow that, so I changed the opening at the last minute and started with an impression of him that I had always included in my stage act. It involved Arlott commentating on a ladies' cricket match. It got me away to a good start, but I still can't remember what I said after that, probably a lot of rubbish. John had his own supply of red wine under the table which he shared with some of us.

At the end of the event he said to me, 'The Snooker Boys are playing at the Crucible,' we were staying in the hotel there, 'so let's go and see them. They'll probably buy us a drink.' We did just that, and in the course of the conversation John said, 'What are you doing tomorrow?' I said 'Going back home'. He said 'Why don't you come over to Headingley with me, I'm having lunch with Bill Bowes the Yorkshire and England cricketer at Brett's fish and chip shop.' I jumped at the idea and next day accompanied John and his driver on the short journey to

Headingley. Apparently Brett's fish and chips were very popular with the commentary team during the Test Matches up there.

When we arrived at the fish shop we were shown into a very small dining room and the owner said, 'I'll shut up shop now, so we won't be disturbed'. The driver brought out some bottles of red wine and the cricket talk started. Bill Bowes regaled us with stories about the Bodyline Series of 1932/33 from his first-hand knowledge, having taken part in it in Australia. At about three o'clock we ran out of wine so John sent his driver out to buy some more. Not only was Brett's fish and chips some of the best I've tasted, but the wine was going down well too, and by five o'clock I didn't know whether I was on foot or horseback. John asked his driver to take me to Leeds and put me on the train to London. I don't remember much about that journey, but I have the photos to prove it happened. I've already mentioned the other wonderful occasion at Sheffield with Sir Len Hutton.

I have been made welcome in the commentary box of radio's *Test Match Special* by Producer Peter Baxter on more than one occasion, and I was thrilled to be included in dear Brian Johnston's *View From The Boundary* lunchtime interludes. The Test Match on that occasion was against the West Indians. There were only 24 overs bowled all day due to rain, so our lunchtime chat extended to about an hour and a half. Brian and I talked about everything, including the theatre in general, particularly his love of seaside shows. I proceeded to do a few impressions of people I had worked with and Brian seemed to enjoy that, and we had a lot of laughs.

Neither of us had had lunch, and at one point a very large plate of sandwiches arrived, organised by his wife Pauline. The plate was put in front of me and I finished the lot. Brian said, 'That was supposed to be for both of us you know.' I just started to laugh hysterically, and Brian joined in, seeing the funny side of it. No doubt he had one of his listener's customary cakes hidden away somewhere. When we met after that he never let me forget the sandwich episode. It is occasions like those when the entertainment business gives you the chance to indulge in your interests away from the footlights.

During 1990 and 1991 I had two more books published, both of them quite different to the other. *The Station Now Standing* was very well received, and dealt mainly with the rather small band of people who still look after our railway stations, keeping them tidy, planting flowers and generally keeping some of our historical and architecturally lovely buildings in some order of preservation. I travelled an awful lot in pursuance of stations I had heard about that were still being cared for. I met all sorts of people, some of them locals who used their spare moments to maintain the stations, and also quite a lot of British Rail staff who in their off duty hours were determined to bring some joy to the travelling public. Wymondham (pronounced Wyndham), Aberdour in Scotland and St Austell in Cornwall gave me particular joy to visit. Many of the preserved railways up and down the country are also doing a wonderful job. Some of these delightful little railways have restored in a small way the massive Beeching cuts of the 1960s. They have large groups of volunteer helpers, who enjoy putting back some of their energy into systems that were once the life blood of many communities.

The second book *Stars in Battledress* was completely different. It concerned service personnel during World War 2 who had been seconded into entertainment units worldwide, but were still on call as trained soldiers, sailors or airmen. Most of them learned their trade, having started in a small way, during their service career and went on to fame and some fortune when they joined the professional ranks of entertainers after they were demobbed. I also made friends with a lot of POWs who had, under very primitive conditions, provided their fellow prisoners with some wonderful entertainment. Even those who were prisoners of the Japanese managed to produce concerts. How, it is difficult to understand. I talked with many of the survivors of those dreadful camps in the Far East, and they are wonderful people. My interest in their experiences went a little further because, as you may remember, my cousin Pat Tobin was one who didn't come back from the Kwai.

During the last few years Marion's arthritis has really proved a problem, and certainly one operation that should have been done at an earlier stage was now imminent. One of our regular visitors, at least once a week during that time, was Bernard Cribbins. He would call in after having done some early morning shooting or fishing and he always caught Marion either in her night-dress or dressing gown. Bernard's awareness of Marion's increasingly difficult arthritic problems has always been a comfort to her. A dear fellow Bernard, and he and his wife Gill have always been involved in raising money for charity. He is a super person to work with on stage, and I hope we may be able to join up again one of these days. There is one particular play I would very much like to do with him.

Our lad Jonathan was building on his early experiences as a Butlin Redcoat with some Fringe Theatre and various stage management jobs. One quite difficult engagement for him was touring the Middle and Far East with Derek Nimmo's theatre company. You have to be aware on those trips of the actors' and actresses' well being, and also make sure the props and costumes are safe and sound travelling from one date to another, plus airline departure and landing times etc. But the actual trip was a wonderful experience for him. He has since played in various summer productions and two seasons in the West End in *Italian Straw Hat* at the Shaftesbury and *Travels With My Aunt* at the Whitehall Theatre. In 1995 he was featured in three films in Germany and Russia alongside Oliver Reed, David Warner and American actress Barbara Carreras. A wonderful experience for a young actor. He even coped in his very early days with a few difficult experiences as a Butlin Redcoat. We both feel very lucky to have a son like him. He works, by the way, under the name of James Pertwee.

I had been pantomiming again with old mates Roy Hudd, Jack Tripp, Allen Christie and someone I hadn't worked with before, June Whitfield, although of course I had known June and her husband Tim for sometime. This was once again a season of hard work with plenty of coloured splosh being poured over one another in the kitchen scene. But in the 1991–92 pantomime season I had a bad experience with another company.

The production was *Cinderella* and the young man playing

Buttons didn't have much idea of the medium. He had mainly been a children's TV programme presenter where at least you would have thought he might have learned the basic disciplines, but I'm afraid he was not only sadly lacking in that aspect but he was also rather coarse in his solo bits with an audience which was, quite naturally, mainly children. The sad part was we were doing very good business at the box office and neither management nor theatre staff seemed to mind as long as the tills kept clicking away. After this I thought I should be careful for whom I worked in pantomime in future as some people cared very little so long as the money was coming in. I am not sure I will ever do another pantomime, unless it's for people I know well. I have been in some wonderful productions in the past but I rather think the recent introduction into Christmas seasons of performers who have no experience of this wonderful children's entertainment and are only given major roles because they happen to be from certain TV programmes, or local radio personalities, is giving the business a bad name.

For Christmas 1992-93 I was back with my old friend Ray Cooney in London at the Playhouse Theatre which he had recently purchased. The play was *It Runs In The Family*, a mad situation set in a hospital with all the usual Cooney twists and turns. I was in company with some old mates like Slim Ramsden and Jackie Clark, who I had worked with on radio quite a lot. We had tried the play out sometime beforehand at Guildford, so this was yet another successful transfer to London from that Surrey theatre.

Later in the year I was asked whether I would like to play the father in a tour of Bernard Shaw's *Candida*, starting off yet again at Guildford. I was to be reunited with Director Val May and two actresses I had worked with before, Lisa Goddard and Su Douglas. It was to be a countrywide tour including dates in Scotland, a country of which I'm very fond. Having got the rehearsal and tour dates sorted out, Marion was called into hospital for her first operation, a hip replacement. This decision was quite sudden and coincided with the first week's rehearsal at Guildford. James Barber, the General Manager, whom I had known for a long time was, and still is, doing a marvellous job at the Guildford Theatre, and Val May and the cast were most co-operative, so I was able to have the odd hour or two off to visit Marion in hospital.

The operation went well and then started the business of the organising of people to stay with her while I was away on tour. It was a lovely cast, apart from one person who made a great nuisance of himself, and in one case was quite vile to Lisa Goddard's understudy, who had to go on for Lisa for a couple of days when she lost her voice. She did terribly well but got no co-operation from the 'gentleman' in question. However we had some super social occasions, particularly in Scotland, taking in all the beautiful scenery north of the border. I also met Lisa's husband, film director David Cobham, for whom I subsequently worked in an episode of the children's series *Woof*. He really knows how to handle people in a friendly and quiet way, and I really enjoyed 'playing trains' in that episode on the preserved Great Central Railway in the Midlands. David is a great wildlife supporter, with a particular interest in owls. I'm sure there's plenty of scope for that at their farmhouse in Norfolk.

I also had the added pleasure of spending some time with my niece Ingrid and her family in Aberdeen. A few problems were cropping up at home with Marion's post-op care, and I used to fly home from Scotland on a Sunday and go back again on Monday morning, having taken stock of the situation. Everything was under control thanks to some kind people in the village who were always on tap in an emergency. We were very lucky in that Bunty and Norman, Marion's brother and sister-in-law, who had always spent the odd few days with us decided to take overall charge. Bunty and Marion had always been very close so to have her around gave Marion peace of mind. Bunty was a real live wire, and her cries of 'Norman!', to which Norman always replied, 'What have I done now?' became family catch phrases, with much laughter.

The last week of our tour was at the Alexandra Theatre in Birmingham, and early in the week there I had a phone call telling me that Bunty, back in Brighton for a few days to collect a change of clothes, had died quite suddenly. What a blow this was. Marion kept saying she hoped it wasn't as a result of looking after her. Actually Bunty had not been in the best of health for the previous three years or so, and had had two major operations herself. She never let this get in the way of her lively enthusiasm and continued living of a normal life. Bunty had always been very proud of her two children, Gordon and Fiona, and she had seen them grow up into their chosen professions, Gordon now the Production Manager at the King's Theatre in Edinburgh and Fiona in an important position with a finance company.

Norman asked me to say a few words at her funeral, which, of course, I said I would. However, towards the end of the week at Birmingham I caught a dreadful cold and just had to have at least the mid-week and Saturday matinées off. The cold, or whatever it was, seemed to get worse, and driving home on the Sunday I felt delirious and went straight to bed, and was not in any fit state to attend the funeral. Marion was determined to attend, even though it must have been very traumatic so soon after the op.

For a while after Bunty's death our good friends Doug and Audrey took over some of the responsibility at the house, with the help of Jonathan who was not working at that time. In fact at times like those you really do find out who your friends are, and it seemed all our acquaintances in the village, particularly those members of the local dramatic society, rallied round.

A great night organised by BBC radio a couple of years ago was a concert to say farewell to the famous Paris Studios in Lower Regent Street in London. These studios had been the home of some huge radio successes for 50 years. The lease was now up, and the BBC had decided that, to save money, all future shows should be produced at the revamped Concert Hall in Broadcasting House. I was delighted to be included in this tribute to the Paris Studios that had really put me on the ladder to any success I might have had since then. Although sad for many people like myself, who had become fond of the place over a very long period, it was a joyous occasion of meeting old friends we hadn't seen for some time. There were musical memories, a ton of laughs and all held together in a delightful and relaxed way by Bob Holness.

I had also been spending quite a lot of time in Manchester recording radio series with an old friend, producer Mike Craig. We did four series with *Jimmy's Cricket Team*. This programme was headed by the delightful funny man Jimmy Cricket and included myself, Peter Goodright and Noreen Kershaw, a talented actress who was well known from TV's *Brookside*. We used to record several programmes in the space of about three days. They were jolly experiences, saying some of the lovely words from our old friend writer Eddie Braben. Eddie had written for Morecombe and Wise for many years, and also for Ken Dodd in his earlier days. He is a very inventive writer, and you never knew what he was going to produce out of his comic hat.

While I was in Manchester I used to stay with Mike Craig and his lovely wife Susan and children, not forgetting Susan's mum. We had some super parties with the most generous Craigs. We eventually took the radio show on to a cruise in the P&O liner *Canberra*. We also did a lot of other things on that cruise, chat shows, variety nights, etc, and the passengers seemed to be pleased to see us whatever we did. I had a couple of days at stop-over points, and one particular place, Portofino, seemed the most idyllic spot you could wish for, with a lovely harbour where the sea lapped up to the large square surrounded by cafes and bars. It was in fact the home of the late Rex Harrison. He certainly chose a wonderful spot.

In 1993 Jonathan decided to flee the nest permanently and bought himself a flat nearer London. This was a good move for him as he was now nearer the 'action' as he called it. His life-long friend David Bryant accompanied him as he was now firmly settled in his job in London as a high flyer in the travel business. They appear to be known to their friends as the 'Odd Couple'. The first scene of that wonderful Neil Simon play is rather reminiscent of the boys' flat in town. It also appears to be a stopping off point for their various girlfriends. After Jonathan left home we thought it was about time we relinquished our rather large property for something more manageable. This decided, the move coincided with Marion's second operation on her knee. Actually the move from a large property into a small residence should have been a complete nightmare, but as we had time to organise it, it didn't seem quite so bad.

The only problem was space. The morning after our move I had an early engagement in London and I couldn't find my clothes. I realised that at least a quarter of a van load had to be left in the front garden under a tarpaulin. There was I, rushing about in underwear at 8am searching for a suit that was obviously somewhere on the front lawn. I thought afterwards about the neighbours who may have witnessed this saying 'We've got a madman on the estate, he keeps his clothes on the front lawn.' Actually they are lovely neighbours, very friendly and a joy to know. I hope they forgive me for my sometimes eccentric behaviour. We do, because of my profession (if you can call acting and writing a profession), tend to keep odd hours and peculiar meal times. Toast and marmalade for supper and a nice chicken sandwich for breakfast have been known to be on the Pertwee menu.

This year, 1996, has included a short season, once again at the Playhouse Theatre, in Ray Cooney's latest farce *Funny Money*. teaming up with some old friends, and one I'd never met before, the arm waving Rodney Bewes, he of the very excellent TV series *The Likely Lads*. Carol Hawkins, Anita Graham, Henry McGee, Ron Aldridge and Ray Cooney himself, I had worked with several times. Although I had never worked with Trevor Bannister, who made up the cast, I did know him. Ray's back-up staff were very good as usual, headed by the irreplaceable Angela Graham-Jones. The DSM – deputy stage manager, as the person on the book relaying all the cues and artistes calls is now called – was a young girl called Sarah, the daughter of one of my earliest contacts in a Cooney play, Jeanne Cook, who was Peggy Mount's understudy in *There Goes The Bride*. Sarah is a really good DSM with a nice sense of humour, which you have to have in a Ray Cooney company.

I began writing this book while I was in *Funny Money* but

only got as far as part of Chapter 1 as it is difficult to concentrate on your cues for different scenes in the play and write in a reasonably coherent manner. During the run we got news that cousin Jon Pertwee had died in America during a holiday there with his wife Ingeborg. As someone said to me shortly afterwards, one always thought of Jon as being indestructible. He had done almost everything there was to do in the entertainment business: radio, films, television and stage work from the time he was in repertory before the last war up to his recent appearances in the West End. Jon had always played hard all his life and both his friends and colleagues in the business were enriched by his company. Ingeborg has the support of her lovely children, son Sean, already established as a fine film and TV actor, and daughter Dariell, who immediately gave up her season with Alan Ayckbourn's company in Scarborough to come back and stay with her mum.

However, back to the notes I have been jotting down through the past three months, on the backs of envelopes, soggy note pads in the bath, and even on my hand when I've woken up in the night remembering something I should have written the previous day. It has been quite a task, but a most pleasant one, particularly finding out about my family's early life and whereabouts. I have been able to throw some light on my mother's first marriage but not all.

She was definitely not married in this country, as exhaustive searches have proved. So we can presume that she went back to Brazil after her schooling here and was married there. I am still trying to find out if this was the case from the Brazilian Embassy in London, and whether her husband and little child died there or came back here before that. The reason for her going to Wales to get over her loss may have been because her brother Tommy was married at some time around then to a Welsh girl and my mother may have stayed with her family. If I don't find out the final solution, maybe the mystery is better left unsolved as my mother was obviously reluctant to talk about it in any depth while she was alive.

By the time one or two people have bought this book I will

be getting ready to embark on yet another 'silly' phase in this mad business. I am almost certainly going into opera at the end of the year. I can already hear some of my friends saying, 'Could it be that he's finally gone potty – who does he think he is? He barely survived the sack from a small seaside concert party, spends a few years rushing about wearing a white helmet, doing funny voices on radio and cavorting about on stage with nude ladies and a beach ball, and now he's setting himself up in competition with Pavarotti!' Some friends can be very hurtful you know, but just wait until they want free tickets to see me!

Actually I will be playing the gaoler in *Die Fledermaus*. Not knowing anything about opera, unlike my wife and son who are fans of it, I agreed to do it as I thought Flaid-er-mouse was a sort of send-up of a Tom and Jerry cartoon. Well the world would be a poorer place if we were all know-alls wouldn't it!

I believe the gaoler is a non-singing part, but as I'm told there are several moments for ad-libbing I may very well join in with the better known songs. Pavarotti's agent has already taken out an injunction stopping me performing the part in Italy, as he is worried that it might be the finish of opera as they know it in that country. But there is no ban on my doing it in Mozambique or Skegness and Clacton, out of season. Covent Garden has not yet decided whether to include me in next year's season, but they'll have to be quick as I know Mozambique is getting quite excited and they may want me for a second season if I pull in the tourists.

You may think this is all far fetched, but you don't know the entertainment business! I mean, BBC television for instance is taking over BBC radio, and the World Service will then probably only be transmitted to the Isle of Wight. When that little island gets its independence under its President-in-waiting, Sybil Snelling MBE, even that will be different, because the BBC will have probably moved there by then and be broadcasting to the rest of the British Isles. The Isle of Wight will have to rely on smoke signals from Portsmouth: it doesn't bear thinking about!

# REFLECTIONS

Writing this book has given me an insight into my own character. A lot of it was probably formed when I was quite young, which I'm sure is the case for most people. One or two things have become apparent to me as I proceeded with this book. One of them is realising that all my lady friends, and I count my wife as a best friend, appear to have been intelligent people, certainly more so than I am. It seems from what I have heard that men generally don't really like intelligent female mates: well it's never bothered me, I've always been happy to receive information on historical or worldly subjects that had previously been beyond my train of thought. I expect a psychiatrist could sort this out, but I'd rather leave the situation as it is, it's more fun! Mind you, certain ladies I think lack basic common sense (I'll bet that will bring howls of derision from lady readers of this book) but you're all lovely anyway! I do have my serious moments, although I can assure you I'm no sad clown, but I am passionate about certain things in life.

I was a compulsive child, apparently, and just didn't think about the consequences of doing something until after I'd done it. There has been a suspicion of danger in me for as long as I personally can remember. This, I suspect, had a great bearing on my taking the chance to go into show business, a business I really knew nothing about. I know I was a trial to my mother and it was her complete security as a mother in sometimes very difficult circumstances, that gave me the urge to take chances knowing Mum would be at home whenever I needed steadying. I am quite sure that a lot of problems with family life have been created by both parents working at the expense of securing a sound base for their children during the important years of growing into teenagers, which is always a difficult time for young people. We all tend to say 'they won't listen'; well, perhaps we're not always around to listen to them at the important moments. This has led to a lot of the problems that some parents have experienced when their kids have gone off the rails.

During the last 30 years or so it has been a great temptation for parents to see earning as much money as possible as their most important function. Only by doing this can they go to sunny Majorca, just as their friends do, on a package holiday, or have a second or third family car, or get a 100 percent mortgage to buy the house of their dreams. The day that families got caught up in these material things without being able to afford them was very sad. One parent or other should be around in the nest; after all, one of you can always work from home until the children are old enough and then if you want to go out to business again, why not?

I always admire actresses who try to take care of their young families when they are working in theatre or television. I have been with them when they have arrived at rehearsals having organised their home for the day, and in some cases taken their children to school. At the end of the day these ladies want to get home as soon as possible so they can share tea with them, and then spend the rest of the evening learning lines for the next day. My admiration extends to amateur dramatic societies when members of these societies work all day, and sometimes travel long journeys in the course of their work. The ladies in these societies who also work or run their homes for their families are probably very tired after all this when it comes to evening rehearsals that might go on until late in many cases, but are still enthusiastic at the end of it.

I personally have been very lucky, particularly when I've been working hard, in having a wife like Marion who was on hand while our lad Jonathan was growing up. She also looked after our two Mums for the best part of 20 years in spite of her progressive arthritic condition. However the Mums, in their turn, were very good with Jonathan. When Marion was going through the post-operative periods during the last three years or so, I hope I've been of some help on the domestic front. I'm a reasonable cook now, which is an improvement on my early experiments which included setting fire to the kitchen curtains when Marion's brother Johnny and I forgot we had a pound of sausages cooking on the stove. So thank God for microwave ovens! I've learned to cope with the washing machine and that awful event of putting a new cover on the duvet. I'd rather do anything than that! Me and a duvet is like six puppies fighting in a sack. My hands are still quite soft in spite of twice daily, or more, sessions of washing up, because I use that 'washing up liquid that keeps them soft and mild'! I haven't got a mob-cap and apron yet but I'm sure they would suit me if I did.

I do find shopping trips a bit of a bore, but I've made a lot of friends in the supermarkets and local shops, in front and behind the tills. It's rather like a club outing in some way: 'Oh hello dear, what are you after today, a bit of streaky to go on the roast chicken?' and 'I see baked beans are down again this week, and there's a free model with the tea bags' etc. I am not relating all this to gain any sympathy for the situation, it doesn't really bother me at all. I do have to organise myself a little better now when I'm away working or making time to learn a few lines, or keep to the discipline one needs for writing.

I have realised how important it is that we should all be very aware of the full time carers in our society. It is not an easy job when it is required 24 hours a day which is not the position in our case, but since I've been on the committee of the Entertainment Artistes' Benevolent Fund this problem has come home to me more and more; you realise just how important it is for those people who have given their life to entertaining the public – and, indeed, working for theatrical charities themselves – and now need that extra care which has finally proved impossible in their own homes because of declining health. The fund is, and has been since 1912, supported by succeeding generations of the Royal Family, and really it could not exist without them. The Royal Variety Performance, which has been attended by the Royal Family year after year, is our main source of income. Other supporters are the Water Rats who, as a group and individually, are very good to us, and theatre producers and individuals are most generous in their support.

Folk ask me whether I have any other ambitions. Well quite honestly I can't really say I have ever had any real ambitions, I've just tried to cope with whatever has been on offer. However I would like to do a chat show, either on radio or TV, a sort of after dinner table talk, with a glass of wine thrown in to keep my guests company, and maybe a small but serious part in a good film or TV series. So you never know. I have already been involved in a pilot TV programme regarding the architecture and history of some of our fine railway stations which one of these days may become a series.

In the meantime, however, there are the important things to see to, like the garden always needs attention. I think my compost should win a prize this year, and I've just seen a hollyhock crouching behind some roses. The cheeky devil must have followed us from our old house. I expect by next year it will have a lot of brothers and sisters to keep it company. Our gardens in the past have always been Marion's province; not only did she have green fingers but she also talked to the flowers, and occasionally sang to them too which was a bit worrying! I have now taken over trying to sort out plants from weeds and generally potter about, under 'Madam's' instructions of course.

For the past 20 years Marion has derived much pleasure and satisfaction from her involvement with our local dramatic society, and has written and produced pantomimes and revues and directed plays including an open air production of *A Midsummer Night's Dream* which she had always wanted to do. Her involvement with the society started with the young members, some of whom have gone on to careers in the theatre themselves. Although the arthritis has curtailed her physically, her enthusiasm is as strong as ever. Marion and the WH Dramatic Society have given much happiness to each other, and her enthusiasm for the stage is still very much part of her life which goes back to her young days in a family of theatre folk. The society is very much a part of the village community life and each production it does generates a substantial contribution to a local charity, over the years amounting to thousands of pounds.

Our son Jonathan was a young member of this drama group, and I know benefited from his experiences. We are both thankful that he was able to grow up in nice surroundings, which is not the case for many children living in inner city areas. He coped very well living for much of the time with three ladies in the house when I was away working, but he obviously derived a lot of pleasure from his grandmothers too, because he gets on very well with older folk, like his 'wrinkly' old dad!

Communities have always been the lifeblood of any country, and particularly ours. People are at the core of all our lives and unfortunately this has sometimes been forgotten in the last few years. For instance, communities were smashed to pieces in the 1960s with the wholesale closure of country railway systems. We don't know yet whether rail privatisation is going to work. I suppose it will depend on what order of importance is given to shareholders of the private companies and the travelling public.

Railways are of particular interest to me, and I hope those in charge are honest with us when they say they want to get us off the roads and on to the railways. Which brings me to a very important clause, or non-existence of it, in the Franchise Contracts. All companies should be made to re-man railway stations. I know families who will not let their women travel after dark because it is a very threatening situation for ladies (and gentlemen) to alight or get on at a station that is boarded up and completely empty of any staff. I have met elderly travellers who feel threatened sitting on their own on a railway station during the day. Why should anyone feel like this, even if it's a short journey to visit their family for a few hours, let alone in the course of business? Any incident they say is recorded on camera in stations nowadays, but supposing you just get the back of a villain's head: that's not much use to anyone, and certainly not the victim in a dangerous situation. At least if you have staff on the station you prevent anything happening in the first place. I know of two stations leased from British Rail where there has never been a problem because people are on site all day, and in one of them at night as well, sleeping on the premises. What about the disabled with no help at hand, how can they possibly travel? And that goes for the really elderly senior citizens, or a lady with children and a pram trying to cope with getting over a footbridge! The answer to lack of staffing is supposed to be a ticket machine outside the station which invariably throws back your notes on to the pavement, or has broken down completely; and just watch the confusion they cause amongst the elderly and foreign visitors.

Even schoolchildren in our area now travel a few miles to school with a minder, because there is no one in charge on the train. Why should we put up with this on our railway system? It is now almost the norm to arrive at a London terminus and find as many as six barriers unmanned. Until somebody is prepared to take the whole situation by the scruff of the neck we shall meander on in this way. However I'm optimistic, and am sure one of these days the people will rise and condemn those in charge until something is done to restore safety to our railways. Not that long ago I was talking to a group of MPs from all parties about the problem and they all, without exception, agreed with me, but have they come out in public about these ongoing problems? Only one of them, Paddy Ashdown. If I were 20 years younger I'd stand for MP of railway stations. I know there is not a bottomless financial pit and that soon half the working population will have to look after the other half of us who are getting old (actually I feel about 30, and I wasn't half having a good time then) but it would not take much for local councils and the railway bosses to come together to look after some of our dear old and architecturally fine railway stations. The money saved on cameras and ticket machines, and putting right the damage done by naughty juveniles, all of which runs into millions each year, could well be spent on staff.

We're told 'We want you to travel on our trains for an enjoyable day out! Who do you think you are kidding Mr Transport! I said I was passionate about some things; railway stations is one of them!

Finally, I have never tried to give advice to aspiring actors and actresses, it is much too complex a business for that, but I will pass on a couple of the comments that were made to me. Kenneth Horne said, 'Know your capabilities and your limitations, combine them with some common sense, and you can't go far wrong.' David Croft said, 'If you're afraid of failure, you have little chance of being a success'.

If I have any advice to suggest regarding entertainment in

general, I'd say learn your lines, some before you start rehearsing to give yourself a good idea of the piece, but usually I find they come more easily once you have the moves under your belt. Don't take too much notice of applause: you only learn from mistakes and not from flattery. 'I thought you were wonderful darling,' – you'll know in your heart when you've turned in a good performance. As far as performances are concerned, watch people like George Formby, yes Formby, in some of his old films, probably made on a shoestring budget. He communicates with the cameras like few others have and creates tremendous pace; and don't forget he started in musical comedy.

The early films of John Mills are always worth watching for his complete command in his scenes, and if you want to see actors giving everything a bit of 'Wellie', look no further than Robert Newton and Wilfred Lawson, they held nothing back, which perhaps confirms my theory that you can never overact, something about which many actors seem to be worried. If you've got confidence in your director he or she will tell you when to tone it down. Even the throw away lines delivered by Arthur Lowe and John Le Mesurier had a stamp of authority about them. For economy of acting just watch Humphrey Bogart and, more recently, Clint Eastwood; also David Jason, too, is well worth watching whatever he's doing.

One other thing that seems to have been forgotten in our business, as far as comedy is concerned, is that four-letter words are no substitute for wit.

A little personal tip: when I am on stage with an actor or actress I always know whether or not they have had 40 winks before a show. If you possibly can, have half an hour's sleep before you go on. Your voice production will be sharp, as will your senses, and that will give you an extra edge. If you are tired it's your voice that suffers most. I always have a sleep in the afternoons and this should be the rule for young and old alike.

I have always been very conscious of the good unsung artistes who just haven't been in the right place at the right time, or had that little bit of luck that we all need. This includes actors, actresses and some very entertaining music hall and cabaret artistes who have been quite happy to earn a living, but might have progressed even further given the right opportunity. I feel I must mention a double act very definitely climbing the comedy ladder during the past few years. The Simmons Brothers – Keith and Alan – are, I think, the obvious successors to Morecombe and Wise, writing their own, clean material.

I have had the good fortune to enjoy a close relationship with my agent, the Richard Stone Partnership, for many years, apart from a short break in the late 1960s. Richard Stone's enthusiasm for the business, and his efforts to keep his artistes working, was never in doubt. He has now retired but keeps in touch. Lynda Ronan now looks after me in that office, and her understanding during the last few years when I have been unable to take on long tours so that I can keep an eye on Marion at home has been much appreciated. She has informed management and producers of the situation who in turn have been very understanding, which helps because, of course, I still enjoy theatre work, but in small doses now.

There are many stories about agents who used to be in abundance around the Charing Cross Road area. One operated from a coal cellar just off Shaftesbury Avenue. There was a telephone box on the pavement outside and everyone knew its number. When the agent heard it ringing he would dash up and do his business that way. Another agent, Sid Royce, had the smallest office you've ever seen with a little hatch in the door. You'd knock on it and he'd either say, 'I can fix you Newcastle next week, but you'll have to take a cut,' when you were on a low fee anyway, or 'nothing this week,' and quickly slam the hatch down. One particular act had received this sort of reply for several months but still carried on his weekly visits. On one occasion he put his hand down on the hatch and said to Sid 'I just wanted to let you know I'll be on holiday next week'. I know that is very much a story for the pros, but it's quite true!

# THANKS

Whatever you say in the way of thanks it always seems inadequate, but I hope these few words go some way to recording that I am sincerely grateful to everyone for the help I have received in getting this book together.

I have a special thank you for the help of three or four people particularly. The first is tinged with some sadness, and I have to recall the weekend of 20-21 July 1996 to explain it. On the evening of the 20th Marion and I were invited by friends Jo and Tony to their lovely house to celebrate Jo's birthday, in the company of some of our good mates. It was a wonderful evening and at midnight we drank Jo's health, and then she surprised me by bringing on a lovely cake and drank a toast to my 70th birthday on the 21st. We had decided to just have a quiet tea on the Sunday as I had to get on with this book. At 8.30am I was rung up by my nephew informing me that his dad, my dear brother Fedge, had died rather suddenly in the night.

I will not even try to explain how we and Fedge's wife Lizzie, her children and grandchildren, felt at that immediate moment. Stunned and shocked of course, as other folk in similar circumstances feel at a time like that. I was about half way through this book, about which Fedge had been so enthusiastic and had helped with so much of the early family history as I have already mentioned in earlier chapters. There was no way that I could continue for a while, and I am very grateful to the publishers for their understanding, and giving me more time to complete it.

But when I had pulled myself together I realised that with the book I now had the chance to record my thoughts in print of a generous, kind and good brother. The huge amount of letters that Lizzie has received from people who knew him, and from people who only knew of him and his charitable works in Canterbury, their home for many years, has been quite amazing. He was a guide at Canterbury Cathedral for a long time, and his charity work included the local Oxfam organisation to which he gave a lot of time. But it was his kindness and help he gave to individuals that really amazed me when I heard about them after he died. He helped to sort out young people's financial problems and one of them remarked, 'I wish he'd been my father.' He took a blind and deaf lady under his wing and every Christmas went to visit a senior citizen who was on her own. It was, however, his love for his wife, children and grandchildren that we will all remember him by, and his sense of humour, sometimes almost childlike.

On one occasion when we visited the family he opened the door wearing a ridiculous false moustache, false nose and glasses. No one took any notice, least of all him, and without batting an eyelid offered us his usual welcoming glass of sherry. Without smiling he said, 'I went to the joke shop this week.' Well of course he had; where else did we think he'd got the ridiculous face pieces from? I remember when I was quite small he used to love putting on some silly disguises at Christmas and asking people to guess who he looked like and laughing with excitement when they guessed right. And I'll not forget his impression of London matinée idol Jack Buchanan singing *Goodnight Vienna* – he loved doing that. Aren't we as a family lucky to have had someone like him as our kith and kin!

Geraldine Guthrie deserves a medal for her hard work in helping to get this into print. I really mean it when I say it would have been practically impossible without her. She has corrected bad phrasing, and even moved some sentences to make more sense of them, which is quite easy (so she says) with her word processor, a wonderful machine I cannot, and don't intend to try, to understand. Her final copies have brought congratulations from the publishers and I thank her for her encouragement and patience. I know her husband John and son Robert have been trying to find their way through the dust that has accumulated while she has been concentrating on typing this book.

The publishers themselves have been enthusiastic from the word go, and the Governor, Suneel and his very friendly and helpful associates Jo, Alison, Keith and Simon have given of their time and help to ensure the publication will be presented in the very best way possible. This is always a great boost to one's confidence after spending so much time, well actually three and a half months, in putting it together. I am informed that this sort of book normally would take a year to finish so I feel I have done reasonably well in the time.

Tony Mulliken who set the whole deal up has always sounded cheery on the phone when perhaps I have been tired or depressed with what I had written the previous day. He does, of course, still make me mad when he keeps disappearing from his office to have yet another lunch, leaving his secretary Alison to sort things out, which she does with great charm. But I forgive him, as I have known Tony as a friend for a very long time now.

Marion, my wife, deserves a special mention. Not only has she advised me on certain chapters that she thought might not be quite right in the first draft, but she has also looked at the whole thing in an objective way, including helping me to sort out photos, etc. from the many I seem to have in boxes and carrier bags all over our home. This has all been a tremendous help. She has never worried when the floor has been strewn with paper, pens and other paraphernalia for a day or two, or when I have decided to carry on writing late into the night.

As in my other books, Dawson Strange of Cobham have done a wonderful job in copying precious family photos!

I mentioned earlier that the first chapter of this book was written mainly in the theatre, but the rest of it has nearly all been written in what you might think is an unusual place to write a book, a pub not half an hour's drive from my house. The 'King William IV' has been my morning home now for about three months. During this time the 'King Billy' has been refurbished without losing any of its charm. It must now be one of the most successful pubs and restaurants in Surrey.

It is entirely due to Val and Dennis, mine hosts, who took up residence two years ago. They are backed up by their supporting cast of Brian the Don, Alison the Koala Bear (well she's just as cuddly) who makes a lovely cup of tea, mad Jess (who would also be at home singing in a Western Saloon with a six shooter at her hip), Karen the chippie (the best in town) and Nick the Joint.

The 'Billy' is a real community pub, and on my various dashes into it for a last 30 minutes of relaxation at night it is always a pleasure to see the familiar faces of Fred the Weld, Robert the Plastic, Chris the Pyke, Monocle Chris, Chris the Gas, Graham the Music, and Fred the Finance. Brian and his shiny new (well almost new) Penny, John the Post and Tony the Waterfall.

A gentleman, Mike the Pipe, and I have spent many sessions, more than I care to remember, trying to put the world to rights and sorting out England's cricketing problems. I'm sure our teams would beat the world if we had our way, but of course Compton, Bedser, Underwood, Snow, Trueman, Statham, Bailey and others are not available now! All these 'Billyites', and more, are the cornerstone of community living which is the most important thing we have and should be preserved and cherished.

One last thing before I finish:

Does anyone know where the moths go when we '*put that light out*'?!